D1221670

THE WORLD'S CLASSICS

418

FIVE PRE-SHAKESPEAREAN COMEDIES

[*EARLY TUDOR PERIOD*]

Oxford University Press, Amen House, London E.C.4

GLASGOW NEW YORK TORONTO MELBOURNE WELLINGTON
BOMBAY CALCUTTA MADRAS KARACHI KUALA LUMPUR
CAPE TOWN IBADAN NAIROBI ACCRA

FIVE PRE-SHAKESPEAREAN COMEDIES

[*EARLY TUDOR PERIOD*]

Edited
with an Introduction by
FREDERICK S. BOAS

LONDON
OXFORD UNIVERSITY PRESS

This volume of Pre-Shakespearean Comedies (Early Tudor) *was first published in* The World's Classics *in 1934 and reprinted in 1950, 1952, 1958, and 1961*

PRINTED IN GREAT BRITAIN

CONTENTS

INTRODUCTION

THE five plays included in this volume range over a period of rather more than sixty years, from about the close of the fifteenth century to the opening decade of the reign of Elizabeth. They represent distinctive dramatic types in the formative earlier Tudor period which preceded and led up to the unparalleled achievement of Shakespeare and his fellows. This achievement needed the combination of professional playwrights and public theatres. The authors of the five plays here collected were highly gifted amateurs catering for the entertainment of special circles. Henry Medwall was chaplain to Cardinal Morton, who died in 1500, and wrote the play for performance in his patron's hall, presumably that of the palace at Lambeth. John Heywood is mentioned in the accounts of the Royal Household as a 'singer' in 1520, and a 'player of the virginals' in 1525, and was afterwards in high favour with Princess Mary. His *Four PP* was probably a production at Court or under royal patronage. Nicholas Udall was a schoolmaster and wrote *Ralph Roister Doister* for performance by his boys. The author of *Gammer Gurton's Needle*, though his identity is uncertain, was a Cambridge don, who had an academic audience in view. And George Gascoigne, when he adapted *Supposes* from an Italian original, was contributing to the 1566 revels of Gray's Inn. Thus the five playwrights with whom we have here to do were connected with different elements in Tudor social life, and each helped in his own way to further the advance of English drama.

Henry Medwall is a link between the old world of the theatre and the new. In his interesting two-part morality, *Nature*, he carries on the medieval allegorical type of play, which had an intermittent vogue till the end of the sixteenth century, but whose real day was over in the epoch of the Reformation and the Renaissance. The influence of the latter movement is seen in Medwall's choice of the subject for his other extant play, *Fulgens and Lucrece*, of which a single copy survives. The plot is derived from a Latin treatise, *De Vera Nobilitate*, by an Italian humanist, Bonaccorso, which had been translated into French by Jean Mielot, and afterwards into English by a Yorkist nobleman, John Tiptoft, Earl of Worcester. His version was printed by William Caxton, and it was this that Medwall used. It relates how the Roman Senator, Fulgens (as Medwall spells the name), had a daughter, Lucrece, who was wooed by Publius Cornelius, a rich pleasure-loving patrician, and by Gaius Flaminius, a virtuous man of humble birth. Lucrece refers them to her father, who appeals to the Senate for a decision which, in the treatise, is not pronounced. Medwall gives the issue a much more dramatic turn by making Lucrece, after hearing the pleadings of the two rivals, bestow her hand upon the worthy Flaminius.

The story is entirely fictitious, but the characters are the first, so far as we know, to appear in an English play within a framework that is neither Biblical nor allegorical but purely secular. Cornelius and Flaminius are little more than types, used to point a moral. But Fulgens, the father, anxious for his daughter's welfare yet leaving her choice of a husband unfettered, and Lucrece, with her clear insight and her eloquent tongue, move us to genuine interest.

If Medwall had done no more, it would have been much. But where he proves himself a born playwright is in his addition of a comic underplot of his own invention, in which the servants of Cornelius and Flaminius are rivals for the affections of Lucrece's handmaid. In this humorous variation on his serious theme he even crudely anticipates a feature of Shakespeare's technique. And the burlesque duel between A and B, to win the favour of the 'flower of the frying-pan', is still effective as a piece of 'knock-about' farce, as was shown in a recent production of *Fulgens and Lucrece* in a London college hall.

It is to be noted that when the play opens A and B, though doubtless acted by members of the performing company, are mingling among the crowd of spectators. It is only when Cornelius (l. 354) addresses 'So many good fellows as been in this hall' that B comes forward to serve him, while A later follows suit with Flaminius.

The arrangements were thus evidently of the primitive kind when a space was cleared for the performance in the great chamber and the audience stood or sat around. The intimacy between the actors and the spectators is brought vividly home by speeches like that of Cornelius and others similarly addressed to the guests in the hall. Indeed the play was only part of the general entertainment under the direction of 'the marshal' or *major-domo*, and Part I at any rate appears to have been an interlude between two banquets. Everything suggests that the Cardinal was honouring important guests, and we know that at Christmastide 1497 there were special festivities for the Ambassadors of Spain and of Flanders. If it was in their presence that *Fulgens and Lucrece* was acted there would be a reason of courtesy in the performance before Lucrece of 'a base dance after the guise of Spain' (II. 380–1) and in the otherwise strange introduction of a line in Flemish (II. 389). But whatever the occasion may have been, the production of Medwall's secular play must count as a memorable 'first night' (or, more strictly speaking, *matinée*) in English stage history.

The Four PP, named after the quartet of characters in this 'merry interlude', was first published in 1544, almost half a century later than the production of *Fulgens and Lucrece*. Yet it belongs to a simpler dramatic type. It is without action, and the speakers are merely representatives of their different vocations. John

Heywood in his earlier interludes, of which *The Play of the Wether* is the most notable, had set forth conflicting views on some debatable topic. In *The Four PP* three typical figures from the medieval religious and social order, the Palmer, the Pardoner, and the Pothecary, display their skill respectively as liars, and another stock figure, the Pedlar, acts as judge. It is an artless enough framework, but within it Heywood, though he has less sense of stagecraft than Medwall, shows far higher verbal artistry.

Like William Langland two centuries before, Heywood combined steadfast religious orthodoxy, for which in his later years he was to suffer exile with heroic constancy, with a remarkably keen sense of the practical abuses in the Church. No Lutheran could have exposed more scathingly the vices and tricks of those who turned religion to personal profit. The Palmer, self-righteous and concerned solely with his own salvation, thinks that he has secured it by tramping from one shrine to another. He is a spiritual 'hiker'. The Pardoner upbraids him with wasting his time (ll. 101–2):

> Nor, since ye might have sped at home,
> What have ye won by running at Rome?

But he himself is turned to mockery as he displays his relics, including 'the great toe of the Trinity' and 'a buttock-bone of Pentecost'. The Pothecary seeks to outdo him with his high-sounding remedies (ll. 617–19):

> Diagalanga, and sticados,
> Blanka manna, diospoliticon,
> Mercury sublime, and metridaticon.

In the lying contest his contribution is a coarse tale, in Munchausen vein, of a cure that he effected on a woman who had the falling-sickness. The Pardoner caps this with the tale of an even more marvellous feat, his rescue of a deceased friend, Margery Corson, from hell. His story, told in some two hundred lines (ll. 771–976), is a masterpiece of narrative which could be detached with little loss to itself from its setting in the interlude. For if Heywood recalls Langland in his religious attitude, so here in the easy flow of his verse and the gay sparkle of his wit he has no less an exemplar than Chaucer. And he shows a fine tact worthy of his great forerunner in his management of the denouement. After the Pardoner's tale any other narrative would have been an anti-climax. But this account of the harrowing of Hell gives the Palmer his cue. Lucifer had gladly set Margery free (ll. 937–9):

> For all we devils within this den
> Have more to do with two women
> Than with all the charge we have beside.

The Palmer professes to be astounded (ll. 1001–4):

> . . . in all places where I have been,
> Of all the women that I have seen
> I never saw, nor knew, in my conscience,
> Any one woman out of patience.

Without more ado, and with the approval of the other competitors, the Pedlar proclaims the Palmer to be the winner of the contest. And then, somewhat abruptly giving a serious turn to the dialogue, the Pedlar, speaking evidently for Heywood himself, discourses on the right use of pilgrimages and pardons and on good works generally, and takes us back with his final adjuration into the medieval sphere:

> Beseeching our Lord to prosper you all
> In the faith of his Church Universal!

Thus both as churchmen and as dramatists Medwall and Heywood belonged to the old order. For though the former wrote a secular play on a humanist theme, and the latter, if *The Pardoner and the Frere* and *Johan Johan* are his, may have added a polish to his wit from French models, yet neither of them was affected in his plot-construction and technique by the classical influences which in the second half of the sixteenth century were to revolutionize English drama. It was in the grammar schools, in the colleges of Oxford and Cambridge, and in the Inns of Court that these influences were particularly felt, and each of the three groups is represented by a play in this volume.

Nicholas Udall, the author of *Ralph Roister Doister*, belonged to the opposite religious camp from Heywood, but he seems to have been able to accommodate himself more easily to changing conditions. Though there were vicissitudes in his life he managed to keep in favour alike with sovereigns who professed the old faith and the new. Born in 1505 and educated at Winchester and at Corpus Christi College, Oxford, he had a remarkable association with famous schools, for he became Head Master of Eton in 1534, and though he left under a cloud in 1541 he was appointed in December 1555, about a year before his death, Head Master of Westminster. For a time during the interval he had been schoolmaster in the household of Stephen Gardiner, Bishop of Winchester.

Udall was deeply interested both in the humanist Renaissance and in the religious Reformation, which were complementary aspects of one movement, though sundered by later Puritanism. Hence, after gathering *Flowers for Latin Speaking* (phrases from three plays of Terence with their English equivalents), he later took part in producing a version of the *Paraphrase* of the New Testament by Erasmus. It was characteristic of his adaptability that he contributed to a pageant in honour of Anne Boleyn's coronation in May 1533 and that he was so much in favour with the daughter of Katharine of Aragon, Queen Mary, that in December 1554 she directed the Office of the Revels to supply him with the apparel needed for the Christmas entertainments.

With his wide scholastic experience and his versatile talents, Udall was marked out as a leader in the

Renaissance Movement that turned the drama to educational use. On the Continent this had resulted in schoolboys performing classical or neo-Latin plays. English schools had to some extent done likewise. But the native dramatic instinct was too powerful to be content with the revival of the comedies of Plautus and Terence or with the production of new Latin plays closely following their model. It was of capital importance for the future of English drama when Udall began the fashion, so far as we know, in *Ralph Roister Doister* of writing for his pupils in the vernacular tongue, but adopting the classical division into Acts and Scenes, and presenting in a Tudor setting some of the typical figures which the Roman stage had borrowed from the Greek 'new comedy' of Menander.

Ralph Roister Doister survives in only one copy, which lacks its title-page, but which probably belongs to the edition entered to Thomas Hacket in 1566. The play must, however, have been written before 1553, when Thomas Wilson in the third edition of his *Arte of Logique* quotes as an example of 'ambiguitie' the mis-punctuated letter in Act III. iv. 32–70, and states that it comes from an interlude by Nicholas Udall. It is only in this indirect way that we know that Udall wrote the play. Though the surviving copy is now in the library at Eton, it was probably written long after Udall had ceased to be Head Master. Otherwise Thomas Wilson, himself an Etonian, would presumably have mentioned it in the first or second edition of his *Arte of Logique* (1551 and 1552). In 1553 Udall appears to have been in Gardiner's service, and the boys in the Bishop's school at Southwark may have created the parts of Roister Doister and Matthew Merrygreek.

In any case nothing could have appealed more to any set of schoolboys than Udall's plea in his prologue to the play for 'mirth which is used in an honest fashion'.

For mirth prolongeth life, and causeth health,
 Mirth recreates our spirits, and voideth pensiveness,
Mirth increaseth amity, not hindering our wealth;
 Mirth is to be used both of more or less,
 Being mixed with virtue in decent comeliness.

And there could have been no pleasanter form of scholastic merry-making than impersonating home-grown varieties of the classical *miles gloriosus* and parasite. Roister Doister, vainglorious of his exploits in love and in war, is the braggart soldier of Roman comedy. But when his wooing of the wealthy widow, Dame Custance, who is plighted to the merchant Goodluck, does not prosper, and he collapses on the stage, the burlesque requiem in Act III, scene iii, strikes a note unknown to Plautus or Terence. And the battle in Act IV, scene viii, between his retainers and the widow's household armed with kitchen implements, is in the same mock-heroic vein as the duel between the servants in *Fulgens and Lucrece*. And Dame Custance's maids with their gay back-chat and their songs are manifestly of English birth. Matthew Merrygreek himself has the greed and adhesiveness of the traditional parasite. But his boon companions with their alliterative double names are of true Tudor stock (I. i. 17–20):

Sometime Lewis Loiterer biddeth me come near;
Somewhiles Watkin Waster maketh us good cheer;
Sometime Davy Diceplayer, when he hath well cast,
Keepeth revel-rout as long as it will last.

There is no real malice in his mischief-making, though it not only turns Roister Doister to ridicule but brings Dame Custance's loyalty into suspicion. But in the end she is united to Goodluck, and the comedy closes, in the spirit of honest mirth forecast in the prologue, with an all-round reconciliation and a resolve to 'let all quarrels pass'.

One is almost tempted to wish that the extant

copies of *Gammer Gurton's Needle* had, like the Eton copy of *Ralph Roister Doister*, lost the title-page. It is true that we learn from it—and for this we are grateful—that the play was acted at Christ's College, Cambridge. But the veiled indication of authorship 'Made by Mr. S. Mr of Art' has provided a singularly baffling enigma. Isaac Reed in his *Biographica Dramatica* (1782) attributed it on totally mistaken grounds to John Still, afterwards Bishop of Bath and Wells, whose name even yet crops up in text-books from time to time as the author. When Henry Bradley edited the comedy in 1903 he assigned it to William Stevenson, who was a Fellow of Christ's College from 1551 to Christmas 1554, and who during this period took a leading part in its dramatic activities. The evidence is in the College account-books, and the payments were made to Stevenson as a producer, not as an author, though he may, of course, have set forth his own plays. It would be easier to accept Bradley's attribution were there not contemporary evidence pointing to John Bridges, of Pembroke Hall, Cambridge, afterwards Bishop of Oxford, as the author. In two of the *Martin Marprelate* pamphlets, *The Epistle* and *The Epitome* (1588), Bridges is credited with *Gammer Gurton's Needle*, and it will be found that there are numerous verbal similarities between the play and his other publications. But, if he wrote it, Thomas Colwell, the publisher of the 1575 quarto, must either have been mistaken or have used 'Mr. S.' as a 'blind'.[1]

The date of the composition of the play is almost as difficult a problem as its authorship. The only extant edition was published by Thomas Colwell in 1575, but in the year ending 22 July 1563 he had paid the Stationers' Company 4*d*. for licence to print a play called *Dyccon of Bedlam*. As Diccon is a leading character in the Christ's College comedy it is highly pro-

[1] A detailed discussion of the problem can be found in chapter iv of my *University Drama in the Tudor Age*.

bable that the reference is to *Gammer Gurton's Needle*. But if the play was written early in Elizabeth's reign or during that of Mary, why is there a reference in Act v. ii. 236 to 'arrest in the king's name'? The atmosphere throughout is so orthodox that the king is not likely to have been Edward VI, and it has even been claimed that the play dates back to the reign of Henry VIII. We must be content at present to state the problem without solving it.

And there is yet another difficulty. But for the statement on the title-page no one would have guessed at first sight that *Gammer Gurton's Needle* was of academic origin. Nothing could be more remote from the collegiate sphere than the life in a rural township where so trivial an incident as the loss of an old woman's beloved needle sets up a train of complications and quarrels that need the intervention of the law in the person of the chief magistrate, Master Bayly. The author, whoever he was, had a keen insight into every grade of the rural community, from the free-spoken crones, the Gammer and her neighbour Dame Chat, with their hard-driven servants, to the lazy, tippling parish priest, Doctor Rat, and the shrewd, tolerant Bayly. Diccon, who stirs up so much of the trouble, is really an alien, roving from place to place, and living by his wits, one of those Bedlam beggars of whom Edgar in *King Lear* was to give a gruesome impersonation. Diccon is akin to Merrygreek in his love of mischief, but owes nothing, as he does, to classical ancestry. Indeed throughout the play the characterization is completely English. The fruits of the dramatist's study of classical models are to be found elsewhere. He shows himself even more skilful than Udall in adapting the plot-construction of Roman comedy, with its division into Acts and Scenes, to his particular purpose. There is true artistry in the ironic use of this elaborate machinery for such insignificant episodes, and in the economy of dialogue by which every line helps forward the action, till the paradoxical close when the needle is found sticking in the breeches of the Gammer's farm-labourer.

Thus Tudor comedy had been enriched in different ways from the archiepiscopal palace and the Court, from grammar school and college. But in every case, though with different metrical forms, it had used the traditional instrument of rhymed verse which dates back to the earliest Miracle plays. It was the privilege of Gray's Inn, by a happy accident, to supply the new and infinitely adaptable vehicle of prose for dramatic dialogue in English. In 1566 George Gascoigne, a member of the Inn, who was afterwards to become distinguished as a poet, novelist, and satirist, presented before the Society a version of Ariosto's comedy *Gli Suppositi*, performed at Ferrara in 1509. Ariosto's play is a very skilful adaptation of the types of Roman comedy to Renaissance Italian conditions. The 'supposes', from which it takes its name, the misunderstandings and equivocations, have their chief source in the interchange of names and offices between a young master and his servant in order that the former may carry on an amorous intrigue. Hence arise a number of other complications which in the end are deftly unravelled. Such 'supposes' had an extraordinary fascination for the Elizabethans, and Gascoigne's version of his Italian original is spirited and adroit. But what gives it importance in dramatic history is its flexible prose dialogue. Ariosto himself, after writing *Gli Suppositi* in prose, had refashioned it in verse. It would have been natural enough, therefore, for Gascoigne to have translated from the later draft, but a happy instinct led him to choose the earlier. He thus led the way for the use of prose by Lyly in his Court-comedies, by Shakespeare himself and Ben Jonson, and by a long line of brilliant successors till the present day.

A few words may be added on the form in which the plays appear in this volume. In accordance with the purpose of 'The World's Classics' series, which has in view the 'general reader' rather than the specialist, the five comedies are here presented in modern spelling and punctuation. In the somewhat exacting labour that this has involved I am greatly indebted to the skilled help of Mr. R. D. Binfield, of the Oxford University Press. But I am responsible for any doubtful interpretations, and for an important group of exceptions to the general rule of modernization. Where this would have interfered with the rhyme the original spelling has nearly always been retained.

Stage-directions in the original texts have been kept, though where they are in Latin, as in *Fulgens and Lucrece*, they have been translated. Some others have been sparingly added, where they seemed to be required. In the three last plays there has been some deviation, for the sake of clearness and of uniformity, from the methods in the early texts of indicating at the head of a scene the entrances of the *dramatis personae*.

The use of annotation in 'The World's Classics' has always been restricted, and, so far as is possible, I have sought to follow the tradition of the series. But there is much in the language of early Tudor plays that is unintelligible without some explanation. Hence, though my notes are mainly glossarial in character, they are inevitably to be found on almost every page. Their sole aim is to facilitate the understanding and enjoyment of the plays.

F. S. B.

1934

Here is cõteyned a godely interlude of Fulgens Cenatoure of Rome. Lucres his doughter. Gayus flaminius. & Publi⁹. Corneli⁹. of the disputacyon of noblenes. & is deuyded in two ptyes / to be played at ii. tymes. Cõpyled by mayster Henry medwall. late chapelayne to ẏ ryght reuerent fader in god Johan Morton cardynall & Archebysshop of Caũterbury.

PD

Characters in the Play

Fulgens, *a Roman Senator*.

Publius Cornelius, *a Patrician.*

Gaius Flaminius, *a Plebeian.*

A, *a youth, afterwards servant to* Gaius Flaminius.

B, *a youth, afterwards servant to* Publius Cornelius.

Lucrece, *daughter to* Fulgens.

Joan, *handmaid* (*ancilla*) *to* Lucrece.

FULGENS AND LUCRECE

PART ONE

A *enters and speaks*

A. Ah! for God's will,
What mean ye, sirs, to stand so still?
Have not ye eaten and your fill,
And paid nothing therefore?
I wis, sirs, thus dare I say,
He that shall for the shot pay
Vouchsafeth that ye largely assay
Such meat as he hath in store.
I trow your dishes be not bare,
Nor yet ye do the wine spare; 10
Therefore be merry as ye fare,
Ye are welcome each one
Unto this house without faining.
But I marvel much of one thing,
That after this merry drinking
And good recreation
There are no words among this press,
Non sunt loquelae neque sermones,
But as it were men in sadness
Here ye stand musing 20
Whereabout I cannot tell:
Or some else pretty damsel
For to dance and spring.
Tell me, what cal't, is it not so?
I am sure here shall be somewhat ado,
And I wis I will know it ere I go
Without I be driven hence.

6 the shot] the reckoning. 17 press] crowd.
18 Non . . . sermones] There are no words nor talk.
21 Whereabout] About what. 24 what cal't] whatever you call it, whatever your name may be.

Enter B

B. Nay nay, hardily, man, I undertake
No man will such mastries make,
An it were but for the manner sake; 30
Thou mayest tarry by licence
Among other men and see the play,
I warrant no man will say thee nay.
A. I think it well, even as ye say,
That no man will me grieve.
But I pray you tell me that again,
Shall here be a play?
B. Yea, for certain.
A. By my troth thereof am I glad and fain,
An ye will me believe;
Of all the world I love such sport, 40
It doth me so much pleasure and comfort,
And that causeth me ever to resort
Where such thing is to do.
I trow your own self be one
Of them that shall play.
B. Nay, I am none;
I trow thou speakest in derision
To liken me thereto.
A. Nay, I mock not, wot ye well,
For I thought verily by your apparel
That ye had been a player.
B. Nay, never a dell. 50
A. Then I cry you mercy,
I was to blame, lo therefore I say.
There is so much nice array
Amongst these gallants nowaday,
That a man shall not lightly
Know a player from another man.
But now to the purpose where I began,
I see well here shall be a play than.

28 hardily] assuredly. 29 such mastries make] put such constraint upon you. 50 never a dell] not in any way. 53 nice] elegant. 58 than] then.

B. Yea, that there shall, doubtless,
And I trow ye shall like it well. 60
A. It seemeth then that ye can tell
Somewhat of the matter.
B. Yea, I am of counsel,
One told me all the process.
A. And I pray you what shall it be?
B. By my faith, as it was told me
More than once or twice,
As far as I can bear it away,
All the substance of their play
Shall proceed this wise.

When th'empire of Rome was in such flower 70
That all the world was subject to the same,
Then was there an noble senator,
And as I remember, Fulgens was his name,
Which had a daughter of noble fame;
And yet, as th'author saith in very deed,
Her noble virtue did her fame exceed.

Albeit there was not one almost
Throughout all the city, young nor old,
That of her beauty did not boast;
And over that her virtues manifold 80
In such manner wise were praised and told,
That it was thought she lacked nothing
To a noble woman that was according.

Great labour was made her favour to attain
In the way of marriage, and among all
That made such labour were specially twain
Which more than others did busily on her call,
On the which twain she set her mind especial,
So that she utterly determined in her heart
The one of them to have, all other set apart. 90

62 of counsel] 'in the know'. 63 process] plot.
70 th'empire] the dominion. 83 according] suitable.

One of them was called Publius Cornelius,
Born of noble blood, it is no nay:
That other was one Gaius Flaminius
Born of a poor stock, as men doth say;
But, for all that, many a fair day
Through his great wisdom and virtuous behaviour,
He ruled the common weal to his great honour.

And how so be it that the vulgar opinion
Had both these men in like favour and reverence,
Supposing they had been of like condition, 100
Yet this said woman of inestimable prudence
Saw that there was some manner of difference,
For the which her answer she deferred and spared
Till both their conditions were openly declared.

And yet to them both this comfort she gave,
He that could be found more noble of them twain
In all godly manner her heart should he have.
Of the which answer they both were glad and fain
For either of them trusted thereby to attain
Th'effect of his desire; yet, when they had do, 110
One of them must needs his appetite forgo.

Hereupon was araised a great doubt and question:
Every man all after as he was affectionate
Unto the parties said his opinion;
But at the last in eschewing of debate,
This matter was brought before the Senate,
They to give therein an utter sentence
Which of these ye two men should have pre-eminence.

And finally they gave sentence and award
That Gaius Flaminius was to be commend 120
For the more noble man, having no regard
To his low birth of the which he did descend;
But only to his virtue they did therein attend,

92 it is no nay] it cannot be denied.
113 affectionate] affected, disposed.
117 utter] final.

Which was so great that of convenience
All the city of Rome did him honour and reverence.

A. And shall this be the process of the play?
B. Yea, so I understand by credible information.
A. By my faith, but if it be even as ye say,
I will advise them to change that conclusion.
What, will they affirm that a churl's son 130
Should be more noble than a gentleman born?
Nay, beware! for men will have thereof great scorn,
It may not be spoken in no manner of case.
B. Yes, such considerations may be laid
That every reasonable man in this place
Will hold him therein right well apaid,
The matter may be so well conveyed.
A. Let them convey and carry clean than,
Or else he will repent that this play began.
Howbeit the matter toucheth me never a dell, 140
For I am neither of virtue excellent
Nor yet of gentle blood, this I know well,
But I speak it only for this intent,
I would not that any man should be shent;
And yet there can no man blame us two,
For why in this matter we have nought to do.
B. We! no, God wot, nothing at all,
Save that we come to see this play,
As far as we may by the leave of the marshal.
I love to behold such mirths alway; 150
For I have seen before this day
Of such manner things in many a good place
Both good examples and right honest solace.
This play, in like wise, I am sure
Is made for the same intent and purpose
To do every man both mirth and pleasure;
Wherefore I cannot think or suppose

124 of convenience] accordingly. 136 apaid] satisfied. 144 shent] blamed. 149 the marshal] the marshal of the hall in which the play was acted.

That they will any word therein disclose
But such as shall stand with truth and reason
In godly manner according to the season. 160
A. Yea, but truth may not be said alway,
For sometime it causeth grudge and despite.
B. Yea, goeth the world so nowaday
That a man must say the crow is white?
A. Yea, that he must, by God Almight,
He must both lie and flatter now and then
That casteth him to dwell among worldly men;
In some courts such men shall most win.
B. Yea, but as for the parish where I abide
Such flattery is abhorrèd as deadly sin, 170
And specially liars be set aside
As soon as they may with the fault be spied;
For every man that favoureth and loveth virtue
Will such manner of folk utterly eschew.
Wherefore I can think these folk will not spare
After plain truth this matter to proceed,
As the story saith; why should they care?
I trow here is no man of the kin or seed
Of either party, for why they were bore
In the city of Rome as I said before. 180
Therefore leave all this doubtful question
And praise at the parting even as ye find.
A. Yes, be ye sure when they have all done
I will not spare to show you my mind,
Praise who will or dispraise I will not be behind;
I will jest thereon whatsoever shall befall
If I can find any man to jest withall.
B. Peace, no more words, for now they come,
The players been even here at hand.
A. So they be, so help me God and halidom! 190
I pray you tell me where I shall stand.
B. Marry, stand even here by me, I warand.

167 casteth him] sets himself. 179 bore] born.
190 halidom] holy relics, upon which oaths were sworn.
192 warand] warrant.

Give room there, sirs, for God avow!
They would come in if they might for you.
A. Yea, but I pray thee, what cal't tell me this,
Who is he that now cometh in?
B. Marry, it is Fulgens the senator.
A. Yea, is? What, the father of the foresaid virgin?
B. Yea, forsooth, he shall this matter begin.
A. And where is fair daughter Lucrece? 200
B. She cometh anon; I say, hold thy peace!

Enter Fulgens

Ful. Everlasting joy with honour and praise
Be unto our most dread Lord and Saviour,
Which doth us help and comfort many ways,
Not leaving us destitute of his aid and succour,
But letteth his sun shine on the rich and poor,
And of his grace is ever indifferent,
Albeit he diversely committeth his talent.

To some he lendeth the spirit of prophecy,
To some the plenty of tongues' eloquence, 210
To some great wisdom and worldly policy,
To some literature and speculative science,
To some he giveth the grace of pre-eminence
In honour and degree, and to some abundance
Of treasure, riches and great inheritance.

Every man oweth to take good heed
Of this distribution, for whoso doth take
The larger benefit he hath the more need
The larger recompense and thank therefore to make.
I speed these words only for mine own sake 220
And for none other person, for I know well
That I am therein charged, as I shall you tell.

193 God avow] I vow to God. 195 what cal't] *See* l. 24. 207 indifferent] impartial. 212 literature . . . science] learning and philosophical knowledge. 214 degree] rank.

When I consider and call to my remembrance
The prosperous life that I have alway
Hitherto endured without any grievance
Of worldly adversity, well may I say
And think that I am bound to yield and pay
Great praise and thanks to the high King
Of whom proceedeth and groweth every good thing.

And certes, if I would not praise or boast 230
The benefits that he hath done unto me,
Yet is it well known of least and most
Throughout all Rome, th'imperial city,
What place in the Senate and honourable degree
I occupy and how I demean me in the same;
All this can they tell that knoweth but my name.

To speak of plenty and great abundance,
Of worldly riches thereunto belonging,
Houses of pleasure and great inheritance,
With rich apparel and every other thing 240
That to a worthy man should be according,
I am and ever have been in meetly good case,
For the which I thank Almighty God of his grace.

Then have I a wife of good condition
And right comformable to mine intent
In every thing that is to be done,
And howbeit that God hath me not sent
An heir male which were convenient
My name to continue and it to repair,
Yet am I not utterly destitute of an heir. 250

For I have a daughter in whom I delight
As for the chief comfort of mine old age,
And surely my said daughter Lucrece doth hight.
Men saith she is as like me in visage
As though she were even mine own image,
For the which cause nature doth me force and bind
The more to favour and love her in my mind.

249 repair] restore. 253 doth hight] is called.

But yet to the principal and greatest occasion
That maketh me to love her as I do,
Is this which I speak not of affection, 260
But even as the truth moveth me thereto:
Nature hath wrought in my Lucrece so
That to speak of beauty and clear understanding
I cannot think in her what should be lacking.

And besides all that, yet a greater thing
Which is not oft seen in so young a damsel,
She is so discreet and sad in all demeaning
And thereto full of honest and virtuous counsel
Of her own mind, that wonder is to tell
The gifts of nature and of especial grace. 270
Am not I greatly bound in this case
To God, as I rehearsèd you before?
I were too void of all reason and grace
If I would not serve and praise him therefore
With due love and dread, he asketh no more.
As far as he will me grace thereto send
The rest of my life therein will I spend;

Albeit that I must partly intend
To the promotion of my daughter Lucrece
To some meetly marriage, else God defend! 280
She is my chief jewel and riches,
My comfort against all care and heaviness,
And also she is now of good and ripe age
To be a man's fere by way of marriage.

Wherefore if I might see ere I die
That she were bestowèd somewhat according,
Then were my mind dischargèd utterly
Of every great cure to me belonging;
It was the chief cause of my hither coming
To have a communication in this same matter 290
With one Cornelius; came there none such here?

267 sad] serious. 278 intend] devote myself. 280 meetly] suitable. 284 fere] mate. 286 somewhat according] in a suitable fashion.

Enter Publius Cornelius

Cor. Yes, now am I come here at the last,
I have tarried long, I cry you mercy.
Ful. Nay, no offence; there is no waste
Nor loss of time yet hardily,
For this is the hour that ye and I
Appointed here to meet this other day.
Now show me your mind, let me hear what ye say.
Cor. Then will I leave superfluity away,
For why ye know already my mind in substance. 300
Ful. I wot not whether I do, yea or nay.
Cor. Why is it now out of your remembrance
That my desire is to honour and advance
Your daughter Lucrece, if she will agree
That I, so poor a man, her husband should be?
Ful. Ye need not, sir, to use these words to me,
For none in this city knoweth better than I
Of what great birth or substance ye be.
My daughter Lucrece is full unworthy
Of birth and goods to look so high, 310
Saving that happily her good condition
May her enable to such a promotion.
But if this be your mind and such intent
Why do ye not labour to her therefore?
For meseemeth it were right expedient
That we know therein her mind before
Or ever we should commune thereof any more,
For if she would to your mind apply,
No man shall be so glad thereof as I.
Cor. Suppose ye that I did not so begin 320
To get first her favour? Yes, trust me well.
Ful. And what comfort would she give you therein?
Cor. By my faith, no great comfort to tell
Save that she abideth to have your counsel,
For as she saith she will nothing
In such matter to do without your counselling,

318 to your mind apply] consent to your desire.

Nor otherwise than ye shall be content.
And thereupon it was my mind and desire
To speak with you of her for the same intent
Your good will in this behalf to require, 330
For I am so brent in love's fire
That nothing may my pain aslake
Without that ye will my cure undertake.

Ful. Sir, I shall do you the comfort that I can,
As far as she will be advised by me;
Howbeit certainly I am not the man
That will take from her the liberty
Of her own choice, that may not be;
But when I speak with her I shall her advise
To love you before other in all godly wise. 340

Cor. I thank you, sir, with all mine heart,
And I pray you do it without delay.

Ful. As soon as I shall from you depart
I will her mind therein essay.

Cor. For I shall think that every hour is twain
Till I may speak with you again.

[*Exit* Fulgens.

Now a wise fellow that had somewhat a brain
And of such things had experience,
Such one would I with me retain
To give me counsel and assistance, 350
For I will spare no cost or expense
Nor yet refuse any labour or pain
The love of fair Lucrece thereby to attain.
So many good fellows as been in this hall,
And is there none, sirs, among you all
That will enterprise this gear?
Some of you can do it if ye lust;
But if ye will not, then I must
Go seek a man elsewhere.

[*Exit.*

B. Now have I spied a meet office for me 360
For I will be of counsel, an I may,

332 aslake] alleviate. 356 gear] business.

With yonder man—
A. Peace, let be!
By God, thou wilt destroy all the play.
B. Destroy the play, quotha? nay, nay,
The play began never till now.
I will be doing, I make God avow,
For there is not in this hundred mile
A feater bawd than I am one.
A. And what shall I do in the meanwhile?
B. Marry, thou shalt come in anon 370
With another pageant.
A. Who? I?
B. Yea, by Saint John.
A. What, I never used such thing before.
B. But follow my counsel and do no more.
Look that thou abide here still,
And I shall undertake for to fulfil
All his mind without delay;
And whether I do so, yea or nay,
At the least well dare I undertake
The marriage utterly to mar or to make.
If he and I make any bargain 380
So that I must give him attendance,
When thou seest me come in again,
Stand even still and keep thy countenance,
For when Gaius Flaminius cometh in,
Then must thou thy pageant begin.
A. Shall any profit grow thereby?
B. Hold thy peace, speak not so high!
Lest any man of this company
Know our purpose openly
And break all our dance, 390
For I assure thee faithfully,
If thou quit thee as well as I,
This gear shall us both advance. [*Exit.*

368 feater bawd] cleverer handy-man. 371 pageant] show, scene. 390 break all our dance] spoil our whole game.

A. Nay then, let me alone hardily!
If any advantage hang thereby,
I can myself thereto apply
By help of good counsel.
This fellow and I be masterless,
And live most part in idleness,
Therefore some manner of business 400
Would become us both well.
At the least wise it is merry being
With men in time of wooing,
For all that while they do nothing
But dance and make revel,
Sing and laugh with great shouting,
Fill in wine with revel routing.
I trow it be a joyful thing
Among such folk to dwell.

Enter Fulgens *with* Lucrece *and Maid*

Ful. Daughter Lucrece, ye know well enough 410
What study and care I have for your promotion,
And what fatherly love I bear to you,
So that I think, in mine opinion,
It were time lost and wasteful occupation
This matter to rehearse or tell you any more
Sith ye it best know, as I said before.

But the special cause that I speak for
Is touching your marriage; as ye know well,
Many folk there be that desireth sore
And laboureth in that behalf with you to mell: 420
Ye know what is for you, ye need no counsel.
Howsobeit, if ye list my counsel to require,
I shall be glad to satisfy therein your desire.

Lu. Truth it is, father, that I am bound
As much unto you as any child may be
Unto the father living on the ground;

407 revel routing] uproarious merriment.
420 mell] deal. 422 require] ask for.

And where it pleaseth you to give unto me
Mine own free choice and my liberty,
It is the thing that pleaseth me well,
Sith I shall have therein your counsel. 430

And now according to this same purpose,
What think ye best for me to do?
Ye know right well, as I suppose,
That many folk doth me greatly woo.
Among the which there be specially two
In whom, as I trow and so do ye,
The choice of this matter must finally be.

In that point your mind and mine doth agree.
But yet right now ere I came here,
For Publius Cornelius ye advised me 440
As touching ye would have me only rest there.
If that be your mind, I shall gladly forbear
All other and only to him assent
To have me in wedlock at his commandment.

Ful. Nay, daughter Lucrece, not so I meant,
For though I did somewhat to him incline,
Yet for all that it is not mine intent
That ye should so thereupon utterly define,
But look whom ye will, on God's blessing and mine;
For trust ye me verily, it is all one to me 450
Whether Gaius Flaminius wed you or else he.

Lu. Then, sith I have so great liberty
And so good choice, I were unfortunable
And also too unwise if I would not see
That I had him which is most honourable.
Wherefore may it like you to be agreeable
That I may have respite to make inquisition
Which of these two men is better of condition.

448 define] decide. 449 look] look at, regard.

Ful. I hold me content, that shall be well done,
It may be respited for a day or twain; 460
But in the meantime use this provision,
See that ye indifferently them both entertain,
Till that your mind be set at a certain
Where ye shall rest: now, can ye do so?
Lu. At the least my good will shall I put thereto.
Ful. Then sith I have business at home for to do
I will go thitherwards as fast as I may.
Lu. Is it your pleasure that I shall with you go?
Ful. Nay, I had liefer that ye went your way
About this matter. [*Exit.*
Lu. Well, God be with you than! 470
I shall do therein the best that I can.
[*After a pause.*
I will not disslander nor blame no man,
But nevertheless, by that I hear say,
Poor maidens be deceived now and than;
So great dissembling nowaday
There is conveyed under words gay
That if—
Maid. Peace, lady! Ye must forbear,
See ye not who cometh here?
Lu. Who is it, wot ye e'er?
Maid. It is Gaius Flaminius, perdie, 480
He that would your husband be.
Lu. Eh, good lord! how wist he
For to find me here?

Enter Gaius Flaminius

Ga. Yes, good lady, wheresoever ye go,
He that listeth to do his diligence
In such manner wise as I have do,
At the last he may come to your presence;
For whosoever oweth obedience
Unto love, he hath great need

462 indifferently] impartially. 472 disslander] speak evil of. 480 perdie] 'par Dieu', certainly.

To attendance if he will speed. 490
Lu. Sir, ye be welcome, what is your mind?
Ga. Why, fair Lucrece, is that your guise
To be so strange and so unkind
To him that oweth you loving service?
I trow I have told you twice or thrice
That mine desire is to marry with you.
Have ye not heard this matter ere now?
Lu. Yes, in very truth I have heard you say
At divers times that ye bare me affection;
To such an intent I say not nay. 500
Ga. What need ye then to ask the question
What I would with you at this season?
Meseemeth ye should therein doubt no more,
Sith ye know well mine errand before:
I wis your strangeness grieveth me sore.
But notwithstanding now will I cease,
And at this time I will chide no more,
Lest I give you cause of heaviness.
I came hither only for your sake, doubtless,
To glad you and please you in all that I can, 510
And not for to chide with you, as I began.
For think it in your mind, I am the man
That would you please in all that I may,
And to that purpose I will do what I can,
Though ye forbid it and say therein nay;
In that point only I will you disobey,
My heart shall ye have in all godly wise,
Whether ye me take or utterly despise.
And to say that I will follow the guise
Of wanton lovers nowaday, 520
Which doth many flattering words devise,
With gifts of rings and brooches gay
Their lemans' hearts for to betray,
Ye must have me therein excused
For it is the thing that I never used.
Therefore I will be short and plain,

493 strange] distant. 523 lemans'] mistresses'.

And I pray you heartily, fair Lucrece,
That ye will be so to me again.
Ye know well I have made labour and business,
And also desired you by words express 530
That ye would vouchsafe in your heart
To be my wife till death us depart.
Lo, this is the matter that I come for,
To know therein your mind and pleasure,
Whether ye set by me any store
To th'effect of my said desire:
And nothing else I will require
But that I may have a plain yea or nay,
Whereto I may trust without delay.

Lu. Methinketh that by that that ye say 540
Ye force not what mine answer be.

Ga. Ah! will ye take it that way?
My lady, I meant not so, perdie;
Th'affirmative were most lief to me,
For, as ye yourself knoweth best,
That was and is my principal request.
But ye may say I am a homely guest
On a gentlewoman so hastily to call.

Lu. Nay, nay, sir, that guise is best,
Ye cannot displease me withal; 550
And according to your desire I shall,
Even as soon as I goodly may,
Answer you therein without delay.
Howbeit, it cannot be done straightway
If I might get a realm thereby.
First will I my father's mind essay
Whether he will thereunto apply;
For if he like you as well as I,
Your mind in this behalf shall be soon eased,
If my said father can be content and pleased. 560

Ga. Gramercy, mine own sweet Lucrece,

532 depart] part, separate. 541 force not] care not. 547 homely guest] ill-mannered fellow. 557 apply] agree.

Of you desire can I no more at all,
Save only that ye do your business
Upon your father busily to call,
So that whatsoever shall befall,
Within few days I may verily know
To what effect this matter shall grow.
Lu. Ye shall know by to-morrow night
What my father will say thereto.
Ga. Then shall ye make mine heart full light, 570
If it please you so to do.
Lu. Yes, doubt ye not it shall be so
And for that cause I will even now depart.
Ga. Now farewell then mine own sweetheart!

Exit Lucrece. A *approaches* Gaius Flaminius *and says to him:*

A. Sir, ye seem a man of great honour,
And that moveth me to be so bold.
I rede you adventure not over much labour
Upon this woman, lest ye take cold:
I tell you the matter is bought and sold;
Without ye take the better heed, 580
For all these fair words ye shall not speed.
Ga. Thinkest thou so in very deed?
A. Yea, so help me God! And I shall tell you why.
Sir, right now this way as I yede,
This gentlewoman came even by
And a fresh gallant in her company;
As God would, near them I stalked
And heard every word that they talked.
Ga. But spake they any word of me?
A. Nay, nay, ye were nothing in her thought. 590
They were as busy as they might be
About such a matter as ye have wrought,
And by God that me dear bought,

577 rede] advise. 579 bought and sold] settled behind your back. 584 yede] went. 593 dear bought] saved at a great price.

Look, what answer that ye now have
Even the same words to him she gave.
I wis, sir, I am but a poor knave,
But yet I would take on me a great pain
Your honesty in this matter to save,
Though it be unto me no profit nor gain;
But therefore I speak and have disdain 600
To see in a woman such dissemblance
Towards a gentleman of your substance.

Ga. Why, hast thou of me any acquaintance?

A. Yea, sir, and some time ye knew me,
Though it be now out of your remembrance.

Ga. By my faith, it may well be,
But nevertheless I thank thee;
Meseemeth thou wouldest that all were well
Betwixt me and yonder fair damsel.

A. Yea, by God, I would fight in the quarrel 610
Rather than ye should lose your intent.

Ga. I pray thee, fellow, where dost thou dwell?

A. By my faith, I am now at mine own commandment,
I lack a master, and that I me repent.
To serve you and please I would be fain,
If it might like you me to retain;
And of one thing I will a certain,
I doubt not I shall do you better stead
Towards this marriage than some other twain,
And if I do not, let me be dead. 620

Ga. Well then, will I do by thy rede,
And in my service thou shalt be,
If thou canst find me any surety.

A. Yes, I can have sureties plenty
For my truth within this place: [*Points to* B.
Here is a gentleman that would trust me
For as much good as he has.

Ga. Yea, and that is but little, percase.

A. By my faith, go where he shall,

598 honesty] credit. 617 a certain] of a certainty.
621 rede] advice. 628 percase] perhaps.

It is as honest a man as any in the reall. 630
I have no more acquaintance within this hall;
If I would any friends essay,
By God, here is one best of all.
I trow he will not say me nay,
For he hath known me many a day.
Sir, will not ye for my truth undertake?

B. Yes, 'fore God, else I would I were bake!
Sir, my master, will ye believe me,
I dare trust him for all that I can make,
If ye find me sufficient surety? 640
As for his truth, doubt not ye
I never could by him anything espy
But that he was as true a man as I.
He and I dwelled many a fair day
In one school, and yet I wot well
From thence he bare never away
The worth of an halfpenny that I can tell;
Therefore he is able with you to dwell.
As for his truth that dare I well say,
Hardily trust him therein ye may. 650

Ga. Upon your word I shall essay.
And, sir, after thy good deserving,
So shall I thy wages pay.
But now, to remember one thing,
Methought thou saidest at the beginning
That Lucrece favoureth better than me
Another lover; what man is he?

A. Cornelius I ween his name should be.

Ga. Ah! Then I know him well, by the rood;
There is not within all this city 660
A man born of a better blood.
But yet Lucrece hath a wit so good
That, as I think, she will before see
Whether his conditions thereto agree;
And if they do not, farewell he!
But therein I have nought ado,

630 reall] realm. 664 conditions] morals.

He shall not be dispraised for me,
Without that I be compelled thereto.
I cannot let him for to woo,
A woman being at her own liberty, 670
For why it is as free for him as for me.
I will forbear never the more
Till I know what shall be the end.
Go thy way unto Lucrece therefore,
And heartily me unto her recommend,
Praying her that she will me send
A ready answer of that thing
That she promised me at her departing.

A. Marry, I shall without any tarrying,
I know mine errand well enow; 680
Ye shall see me appoint a meeting
Where she again shall speak with you.

Ga. Then shall I thy wit allow,
If thou can bring that about.

A. Yes, that I shall do, have ye no doubt.

[*Exit* Gaius Flaminius.

B. Now by my troth, I would not have thought
That thou hadest been half so wise,
For thou hast this matter featly wrought
And conveyed it point devise
To bring thyself to such a service: 690
I see well thou hast some wit in thy head.

A. Yea, a little, but hast thou sped?

B. Even likewise, have thou no dread;
I have gotten a master for my prow,
I never thrived as I shall do now.

A. No, which way?

B. I shall tell thee how.
It is no mastery to thrive at all
Under a man that is so liberal.

669 let him for] prevent him from. 671 For why] wherefore. 683 allow] approve. 689 conveyed it point devise] arranged it perfectly. 694 for my prow] to my advantage. 697 It is no mastery] It needs no skill.

There is now late unto him fall
So great goods by inheritance, 700
That he wot never what to do withal,
But lasheth it forth daily, askance
That he had no daily remembrance
Of time to come, nor maketh no store,
For he careth not which end goeth before.
And by our lady I commend him the more:
Why should he those goods spare
Sith he laboured never therefore?
Nay, an every man should care
For goods, and specially such as are 710
Of gentle blood, it were great sin,
For all liberality in them should begin.
Many a poor man thereby doth win
The chief substance of his living.
My master were worthy to be a king
For liberal expenses in all his dealing.
I trow thou shalt see him come in
Like a rutter somewhat according
In all apparel to him belonging.
How much payeth he, as ye suppose, 720
For the making of a pair of his hose?
A. Marry, twelve pence were a fair thing;
B. Yea, by the rood, twenty times told,
That is even twenty shillings for the making.
A. It cannot be so, without a man would
Make them all with silk and gold.
B. Nay, by yes, none earthly thing
But even the bare cloth and the lining;
Save only that there is in cutting
A new manner of fashion nowaday. 730
Because they should be somewhat strange
They must be stripèd all this way
With small slips of colours gay;

702 lasheth it forth] squanders it. askance] as though. 718 rutter] a cavalier. 727 Nay, by yes] No, by Jesus. 731 strange] out of the common.

A codpiece before, almost thus large,
And therein resteth the greatest charge.
To speak of gowns, and that good change,
Of them he hath store and plenty,
And that the fashions be new and strange,
For none of them passeth the mid thigh,
And yet he putteth in a gown commonly 740
How many broad yards, as ye guess?
A. Marry, two or three.
B. Nay, seven and no less.
A. By my troth, that is like a lie.
B. But it is as true as ye stand there,
And I shall tell you a reason why.
All that doth that fashion wear
They have wings behind ready to fly,
And a sleeve that would cover all the body;
Then forty pleats, as I think in my mind,
They have before, and as many behind. 750
A. Well, as for gentlemen it is full kind
To have their pleasures that may well pay.
B. Yea, but then this grudgeth my mind,
A gentleman shall not wear it a day
But every man will himself array
Of the same fashion even by and by
On the morrow after.
A. Nay, that I defy.
But then I marvel greatly why
You are not garnished after that guise.
B. There is never a knave in the house save I 760
But his gown is made in the same wise,
And for because I am new come to service,
I must for a while be content
To wear still mine old garment.
A. Yea, but abide, to what intent

735 charge] expense. 736 good change] great variety. 751 full kind] very natural. 756 by and by] immediately. 757 defy] deny. 759 garnished] arrayed.

Doth thy master take in hand
To make him so much costly raiment?
B. Marry, that is easy to understand:
All is done for Lucrece's sake.
To wed her he doth his reckoning make. 770
A. Ay, put case that she do him forsake
So that she be my master's wife.
B. By my faith, then I say it will make
Many a man to lose his life,
For thereof will rise a great strife.
A. Marry, I pray God send us peace.
B. By my faith, it will be no less,
If my master have not Lucrece.
A. I can no more; God speed the right!
Lo! These folk will strive and fight 780
For this woman's sake,
And when they have done their uttermost,
I ween verily he shall speed best
That must her forsake.
He is well at ease that hath a wife,
Yet he is better that hath none, by my life;
But he that hath a good wife and will forsake her,
I pray God the devil take her.
B. Now, in good faith, thou art a mad knave,
I see well thou hast wedded a shrew. 790
A. The devil I have!
Nay, I have married two or three
Sith the time that I her lost.
B. And keepest thou them all still with thee?
A. Nay, that would not quit the cost:
To say the truth they found me most.
B. Then they have some manner getting
By some occupation, have they?
A. Sir, they have a pretty way.
The chief means of their living 800
Is lechery—leech-craft I would say—

796 found] provide for.

Wherein they labour night and day,
And ease many a man in some case.
B. And where do they dwell?
A. At the common place,
There thou mayest them all find.
God's mercy, where is my mind?
By God, I shall be shent,
I should have gone to Lucrece
About my master's business, 810
Thitherward I was bent.
B. By my faith, my master is there
All the while that thou art here,
As I verily suppose.
A. I shrew thy face, by Saint Mary,
With thy chattering thou dost me tarry
Even for the same purpose.
B. I say, when thou hast with Lucrece spoken,
I pray thee, will thou deliver me a token
In mine name to her maid? 820
A. Nay, ye must beware of that gear
For I have been afore you there.
B. Why, hast thou her essayed?
A. Yea, yea, that matter is sped full;
I may have her an she wull—
That comfort she me gave.
B. And hast thou none other comfort at all?
I trust to God then yet I shall
All this matter save.
Howbeit I will not the matter begin 830
Without I were sure she were a virgin.
A. By my troth, this comfort shall I put thee in,
I came never on her back in the way of sin.
[*Avoid the place* A.
B. Then all is well and fine.
If the matter be in that case,
I trust that within a little space

815 I shrew] a plague on. 816 tarry] delay.

That wench shall be mine.
I tell you it is a trull of trust
All to quench a man's thrust
Better than any wine. 840
It is a little pretty moucet,
And her voice is as doucet
And as sweet as resty pork;
Her face is somewhat brown and yellow,
But for all that she hath no fellow
In singing hence to York.
But the worst that grieveth me,
She hath no leisure nor liberty,
For an hour or twain,
To be out of her mistress' sight. 850
I watched for her this other night,
But all was in vain;
Howbeit I think that at the last

[*Come in the maiden.*

I shall come within two stones cast
Of her; I ask no more.
And if I do so, then my mate
Shall have no lust therein to prate
As he did before.
Cock's body, here she is!
Now welcome, by heaven's bliss, 860
The last that was in my thought!

Maid. Tush! I pray you let me go,
I have somewhat else to do;
For this hour I have sought
A man that I should speak withal
From my mistress.

B. What do you him call?

Maid. Master Gaius or his man.

B. Am not I he that ye would have?

Maid. No, no, I would have another knave.

839 thrust] thirst. 841 moucet] little mouse. 842 doucet] sweet. 843 resty] rancid. 859 Cock's body] By God's body.

B. Why, am I a knave, than? 870
Maid. Nay, I said not so, perdie,
But where, trow ye, these folks be?
B. I cannot verily say,
His man went even now from me,
And I marvel greatly that ye
Met him not by the way,
For he is gone to speak with Lucrece
From his master.
Maid. What, with my mistress? Nay!
B. Yea, so I heard him say. 880
Maid. God's mercy, and I was sent
Even hither for the same intent,
To bring an answer
Of the errand that he is gone for;
Wherefore now there is no more
But I must go seek him there.
B. Nay, tarry here a while gentle Joan,
For he will come hither anon.
Maid. Tarry? Why should I so?
B. Marry, to laugh and talk with me. 890
Maid. Nay, look where such giglots be,
For I am none of them, I warn thee,
That use so to do.
B. I mean nothing but good and honest
And for your weal, an you list
To assent thereunto.
Maid. For my weal, quotha! how may that be?
That is a thing that I cannot see.
B. Marry, this, lo! is mine intent:
I mean if ye would be content, 900
Or any wise agree
For to be my sacrament of penance—
By God, give it a very vengeance!—
Of wedlock, I would have said.
Maid. Tush! By Saint James, ye do but mock
To speak to me of any wedlock,

891 giglots] wantons.

And I so young a maid.
B. Why, are ye a maid?
Maid. Yea, else I were to blame.
B. Whereby wot ye?
Maid. Marry, for I ame.
B. Ah! That is a thing! 910
[*To the audience.*
Hear ye not, sirs, what she saith?
So reasonable a cause thereto she layeth.
Maid. A straw for your mocking!
Have ye none to mock but me?
B. Mock? Nay, so mote I thee,
I mean even good earnest.
Give me your hand and you shall see
What I will promise you.
Maid. That way were not best for my prow.
Would ye handfast me forth withal? 920
Nay, by the rood, first ye shall
Cheap ere ever you buy;
We must first of the price agree,
For whosoever shall have me,
I promise you faithfully,
He shall me first assure
Of twenty pounds land in jointure.
B. Why, are ye so costly?
Nay, nay, then ye be not for me;
As pretty a woman as ye be 930
I can sometime buy,
For much less wages and hire,
As for the season that I desire
To have her in company.
Therefore if ye can find in your heart
To leave all such jointure apart,
And take me as I am,
I shall do you as great a pleasure,

909 ame] am. 915 mote I thee] may I thrive. 919 for my prow] *See* l. 694. 920 handfast] make a contract of marriage with. 922 Cheap] bargain.

And thereto I will love you out of measure
Else I were to blame. 940
Maid. Yea, but our household shall be full small
But if we have somewhat else withal
Our charges for to bear.
B. Yea, God send us merry weather!
I may not wed and thrive all together,
I look not for that gear.
I shall tell you a marvellous case:
I knew twain married in a place,
Dwelling together in one house,
And I am sure they were not worth a louse 950
At the beginning,
And ere ever the year were do
They were worth an hundred or two.
Maid. That was a marvellous thing,
But yet I can tell thee a greater marvel,
And I knew the persons right well.
Sir, I knew two certain,
That when they were wedded they had in store
Scarce half a bed and no more
That was worth an haw; 960
And within a year or twain
They had so great increase and gain,
That at the last they were fain
To shove their heads in the straw.
B. Tush! ye do but mock and rail,
And I promise you without fail,
If ye list to have me,
I wot where is an hundred pound in store,
And I owe never a groat therefor.
Maid. All that may be. 970
I believe it even as ye say,
But ye tarry me here all day;
I pray you let me go.
And for my marriage, that is a thing

952 do] done, at an end. 960 worth an haw] of the least value. 972 tarry] *See* l. 816.

In the which I purpose to give a sparing
For a year or two.
B. A year or two, quotha, nay, God forbed!
I wis it had been time for you to wed
Seven or eight year ago;
An ye wist how merry a life 980
It is to be a wedded wife,
Ye would change that mind.
Maid. Yea, so it is, as I understand,
If a woman have a good husband,
But that is hard to find;
Many a man blameth his wife, perdie,
And she is more to blame than he.
B. As true as the gospel, now say ye.
But now tell me one thing,
Shall I have none other answer but this 990
Of my desire?
Maid. No, sir, I wis,
Not at this meeting.
B. Will ye now needs be agone? Than
Take your leave honestly. [*Tries to kiss her.*
Maid. See the man!
Let me alone, with sorrow!
B. Marry so be it, but one word,
I will kiss thee ere thou go.
Maid. The devil's turd!
The man is mad, I trow.
B. So mad I am that needs I must 1000
As in this point have my lust
Howsoever I do.
Maid. Perdie, ye may do me that request,
For why it is but good and honest.
[*Kisses her. Enter* A.
A. Now a fellowship, I thee beseech,
Set even such a patch on my breech.

994 honestly] in a seemly way. 995 with sorrow!] sorrow on you! 1005 a fellowship] out of friendly feeling.

B. A wild fire thereon!
Maid. God's mercy! This is he
That I have sought so.
A. Have ye sought me?
Maid. Yea, that have I do; 1010
This gentleman can witness bear
That all this hour I have stand here
Seeking even for you.
A. Have ye two been together so long?
Maid. Yea, why not?
A. Marry, then all is wrong,
I fear me so now.
B. Nay, nay, here be too many witness
For to make any such business
As thou weenest, hardily.
Maid. Why, what is the man's thought? 1020
Suppose ye that I would be naught,
If no man were by?
A. Nay, 'fore God, I meant not so,
But I would no man should have to do
With you, but only I.
Maid. Have to do, quotha, what call ye that?
It soundeth to a thing I wot ne'er what.
A. Eh! God's mercy,
I see well a man must beware
How he speaketh thereas ye are, 1030
Ye take it so strangely;
Nay, I mean nothing but well,
For, by my will, no man shall deal
With you in way of marriage,
But only I—this wise I meant.
Maid. Yea, but though it were your intent,
Yet ye do but rage
To use such words unto me,
For I am yet at my liberty.

1007 A wild fire thereon!] A plague on it!
1021 naught] wanton. 1030 thereas] wherever.
1037 rage] rave.

A. Yea, that I know well, 1040
But nevertheless, sithen I began
To love you long before this man,
I have very great marvel
That ever ye would his mind fulfil
To stand and talk with him still
So long as ye have do.
B. Before me, quotha? Nay, I make avow
I moved this matter long before you,
How say ye thereto?
Maid. I will nothing in the matter say, 1050
Lest I cause you to make a fray,
For thereof I would be loath.
A. By Cock's body, but whosoever it be
That weddeth her besides me
I shall make him wroth.
B. Yea, but he that is so hasty at every word
For a medicine must eat his wife's turd.
Maid. Hold your tongues there I say!
For, an ye make this work for me,
Ye shall both disappointed be, 1060
As far as I may.
A. By my troth, but mark me well,
If ever thou with this man dwell,
As a woman with her make,
Thou shalt find him the most froward man
That ever thou sawest sith the world began;
For I dare undertake
That forty times on a day,
Without any cause, he will thee affray,
And beat thy back and side. 1070
Maid. He shall not need so to do,
For he shall have forty causes and forty too,
If I with him abide.
A. Marry! That is a remedy according;
But I can tell thee another thing,
And it is no lie,

1064 make] mate. 1074 according] suitable.

Thou mayest well be his wedded wife,
But he will never love thee in his life.
Maid. Yet I know a remedy.
A. Howso?
Maid. Marry! I will love him as little again, 1080
For every shrewd turn he shall have twain,
An he were my brother.
B. I wis, Joan, he speaketh but of malice;
There is no man hence to Calais,
Whosoever be the other,
That can himself better apply
To please a woman better than I.
Maid. Yea, so I heard you say,
But yet, be ye never so wroth,
There is never one of you both, 1090
For all your words gay,
That shall be assured of me
Till I may first hear and see
What ye both can do:
And he that can do most mastery,
Be it in cookery or in pastry,
In feats of war or deeds of chivalry,
With him will I go.
A. By my troth, that liketh me well;
There is no mastery that a man can tell 1100
But I am meet thereto:
Wherefore that wager I dare well undertake.
Let me see, wilt thou go quoit for thy lady's sake,
Or what thing shall we do?
B. Nay, if thou wilt her with mastery win,
With boys' game thou mayst not begin,
That is not her intent.
A. What is best that we do, than?
B. Marry, canst thou sing?
A. Yea, that I can,
As well as any man in Kent. 1110

1092 assured of me] betrothed to me.
1103 go quoit] play at quoits.

B. What manner of song shall it be?
A. Whatsoever thou wilt choose thee,
I hold me well content,
And if I meet thee not at the close,
Hardily let me the wager lose
By her own judgement.
Go to now, will ye set in?
B. Nay, by the rood, ye shall begin.
A. By Saint James, I assent.
Abide, Joan, ye can good skill, 1120
And if ye would the song fulfil
With a third part,
It would do right well in my mind.
Maid. Sing on hardily, and I will not be behind,
I pray thee with all my heart.

[*They sing.*

B. I am so hoarse, it will not be.
A. Hoarse, quotha? Nay, so mote I thee,
That was not the thing;
An a man should the truth say,
Ye lost a crochet or two by the way, 1130
To mine understanding.
B. Why, was I a minim before?
A. Yea, by the rood, that ye were and more.
B. Then were ye a minim behind.
Let me see, yet sing again
And mark which of us twain
Pleaseth best your mind.
Maid. Nay, nay, ye shall this matter try
By some other manner of mastery
Than by your singing. 1140
B. Let him essay what mastery he wull.
A. Marry, an my belly were not so full,
I would wrestle with him a fair pull;
That were a game according
For such valiant men as we be.

1121 fulfil] complete.
1127 mote I thee] *See* l. 915.

B. I shrew thine heart an thou spare me!
[*They wrestle.*

Maid. Nay, by my faith, that was no fall.
B. Ah, then I see well ye be partial,
When ye judge so.
Well, I shall do more for your love: 1150
Even here I cast to him my glove
Ere ever I hence go,
On the condition that in the plain field
I shall meet him with spear and shield
My life thereon to jeopardy;
Let me see an he dare take it.
[*Throws down his glove.*

A. Yes, hardily I will not forsake it,
I am not such a coward
But I dare meet thee at all essays;
When shall it be done?
B. Even straightways 1160
Without further delay:
And I shrew his heart that fears
Either with cronal or sharp spears
This bargain to essay.
A. And I beshrew him, for me!
But abide now, let me see.
Where shall I have a horse?
B. Nay, we shall need no horse nor mule,
But let us joust at fart prick in cule.
A. By Saint James, no force, 1170
Even so be it, but where is our gear?
B. By my faith, all thing is ready
That belongeth thereto.
[*To the maid.*] Come forth ye flower of the frying pan,
Help ye to array us as well as ye can,
And howsoever ye do,

1163 cronal] upper part of a lance for unhorsing an opponent. 1169 cule] buttock. 1170 no force] it doesn't matter. 1174 flower of the frying pan] ugly slut.

See that ye judge indifferently
Which of us twain hath the mastery.
Maid. Yes, hardily that I shall,
I shall judge after my mind. 1180
But see ye hold fast behind
Lest ye trouble us in all.
B. Tush, that is the least care of fifteen,
And if I do not, on my game be it seen!
Go to, bind me first hardily:
So—lo now, give me my spear
And put me a staff through here,
Then am I all ready.
A. Abide, who shall help to harness me?
Maid. That shall I do, so mote I thee, 1190
With a right good will.
A. Soft and fair, mine arm is sore,
Ye may not bind me strait therefore.
Maid. Nay, no more I will,
I will not hurt thee for twenty pound.
Come off now, sit down on the ground,
Even upon thy tail.
A. Eh, good lord, when will ye have do?
Maid. Now all is ready hardily, go to,
Bid him baile, baile! 1200
A [*to the audience*]. Fall to prayer, sirs, it is need,
As many of you as would me Good speed,
For this gear standeth me upon.
B. Yea, and that shalt thou find ere we depart,
And if thou spare me, I shrew thy heart:
Let me see, come on! [A *is thrown down.*
A. Out out, alas, for pain!
Let me have a priest, ere I be slain,
My sin to disclose.
B. And because he saith so, it is need, 1210
For he is not in clean life indeed,

1177 indifferently] *See* l. 462. 1189 harness me] put on my armour. 1193 strait] tightly. 1200 Bid him baile] call on him to engage. 1209 disclose] confess.

I feel it at my nose. [*for fo. &c.*
Now ye are mine, lady.
Maid. Nay, never the more!
B. No, why so?
Maid. For I am taken up before.
B. Marry. I beshrew your heart therefore,
It should better content me
That ye had been taken up behind.
Maid. Nay, nay, ye understand not my mind
In that point.
B. It may well be;
But tell me how meant ye than? 1220
Maid. Marry, I am sure to another man
Whose wife I intend to be.
B. Nay, I trow, by Cock's passion,
Ye will not mock us of that fashion,
Ye may not for very shame.
Maid. Shame or not, so shall it be,
And because that for the love of me
Ye two have made this game,
It shall not be done all in vain,
For I will reward you both twain, 1230
And else I were to blame.
Somewhat thereby ye must needs win,
And therefore to each of you will I spin
A new pair of breeches—
Take thee that for thy dole,
And because he is black in the hole,
He shall have as much. [*Maid beats both and exit.*
A. Out alas, what woman was this?
B. It is Lucrece's maid.
A. The devil it is!
I pray God a vengeance take her! 1240
How sayst thou, shall she be thy wife?

1212 *for fo. &c.*] *Apparently a stage-direction,* = faugh, faugh! *with gestures of disgust.* 1214 taken up] pledged. 1221 sure to] betrothed to.

I utterly forsake her.
B. Nay I had liefer she had eaten my knife.

Enter Gaius

Ga. How, sirs, who hath arrayed you this?
A. False thieves, master, I wis,
And all for your quarrel.
Ga. What, and this other man too?
A. Yea, an ye would our hands undo,
The matter we shall tell.
Ga. Yes, marry will I—now tell on, 1250
Who hath you these wrongs done?
A. Marry, that I shall. Cornelius'
Servants, which is your enemy,
Espied me going toward Lucrece's place
That I could bring the matter to pass
Of that gentlewoman, as your desire was:
They laid await for me in the way
And so they left me in this array.
Ga. Yea, but hast thou any deadly wound?
That is the thing that feareth my mind. 1260
A. I' faith, I was left for dead on the ground,
And I have a great gash here behind,
Out of the which there cometh such a wind
That if ye hold a candle thereto,
It will blow it out, that will it do.
Ga. See to it betimes, by mine advice,
Lest the wound fester within.
A. Then have I need of a good surgin,
For it is so deep within the skin
That ye may put your nose therein 1270
Even up to the hard eyes.
Here is a man that quit him as well
For my defence as ever I see;
He took such part that in the quarrel

1242 eaten my knife] been stabbed. 1257 laid await] set an ambush. 1271 to the hard eyes] to the very eyes.

His arm was stricken off by the hard knee,
And yet he slew of them two or three.
Ga. Be they slain? Nay, God forbid!
A. Yes, so help me God, I warrant them dead.
Howbeit I stand in great dread
That, if ever he come in their way, 1280
They will cut off his arm or his head,
For so I heard them all three say.
Ga. Which? They that were slain?
A. Yea, by this day.
What needeth me therefore to lie?
He heard it himself as well as I.
Ga. Well then ye lie both two. [*Exit* B.
But now tell me what hast thou do
As touching my commandment
That I bade thee do to Lucrece?
Spakest thou with her?
A. Yea, sir, doubtless, 1290
And this is her intent:
She commendeth her to you by the same token
That with her father she hath spoken
According to your request;
And so she willeth you to be of good cheer,
Desiring you this night to appear,
Or to-morrow at the furthest,
And she will meet you here in this place
To give you a final answer in this case
Whereto ye shall trust. 1300
Ga. That is the thing that I desire,
But said she so?
A. Yea, by this fire,
I tell you very just,
In so much that she bade me say
And warn you that ye should purvey
For your own business,
For then it shall determined be
Whether Publius Cornelius or ye

1302 this fire] the fire in the hall. 1305 purvey] provide.

Shall have the pre-eminence.
Ga. All that purpose liketh me well; 1310
But who shall be here more, canst thou tell?
A. Marry! Here shall be Fulgens,
And Publius Cornelius himself also,
With divers other many mo
Besides this honourable audience.
Wherefore, if ye will your honour save,
And your intent in this matter have,
It is best that ye go hence
For to study and call to mind
Such arguments as ye can best find 1320
And make yourself all prest.
Ga. Thy counsel is good, be it so,
And even thereafter will I do,
For I hold it best. [*Exit* Gaius. *Enter* B.
B. God's body, sir, this was a fit!
I beshrew the whore's heart yet
When I think thereon;
And yet the strokes be not so sore,
But the shame grieveth me more
Sith that it was done 1330
Before so many as here be present.
But an I might take her,
By my troth, I shall make her
This deed to repent.
A. Yet thou were as good hold thy peace,
For there is no remedy, doubtless;
Therefore let it go.
It is to us both great folly and shame
This matter any more to rehearse or name.
B. Well then, be it so, 1340
And yet because she hath made me smart
I trust once to ride in her cart,
Be it shame or no.
I cannot suffer it patiently
To be rebuked openly

1321 prest] ready.

And to be mocked also.
Another thing grieveth me worst of all,
I shall be shent, that I shall,
Of my master too,
Because I have been so long away 1350
Out of his presence.
A. Nay, nay,
I have heard so much sith I went hence
That he had little mind to thine offence.
B. I pray you tell me why.
A. For as I brought my master on his way,
I heard one of Lucrece' men say
That thy master hath been
All this hour at her place,
And that he his answer has,
This wise as I mean: 1360
She hath appointed him to be here
Soon in the evening about supper
And then he shall have a final answer
What she intendeth to do.
And so then we shall know her intent,
For as I understand she will be content
To have one of them two;
But first she will needs know the certain
Whether is the most noble of them twain,
This she sayeth alway. 1370
B. Why, that is easy to understand
If she be so wise as men bear in hand.
A. Yea, so I heard you say.
Let me see now, what is your opinion
Whether of them is most noble of condition?
B. That can I tell hardily:
He that hath most nobles in store
Him call I the most noble evermore,
For he is most set by.

1368 the certain] certainly. 1369 whether] which of the two. 1372 bear in hand] assert. 1377 nobles] gold coins, each worth 6*s*. 8*d*.

And I am sure Cornelius is able 1380
With his own goods to buy a rabble
Of such as Gaius is:
And over that, if nobleness of kin
May this woman's favour win,
I am sure he cannot miss.
A. Yea, but come hither soon to the end of this play,
And thou shalt see whereto all that will weigh,
It shall be for thy learning.
B. Yea, come again who will, for me,
For I will not be here, so mote I thee! 1390
It is a gentlemanly thing
That I should await and come again
For other men's causes and take such pain—
I will not do it, I make God avow,
Why might not this matter be ended now?
A. Marry! I shall tell thee why:
Lucrece and her father may not attend
At this season to make an end,
So I heard them say;
And also it is a courteous guise 1400
For to respite the matter this wise,
That the parties may
In the meantime advise them well,
For either of them both must tell
And show the best he can
To force the goodness of his own condition,
Both by example and good reason.
I would not for a swan
That thou shouldest be hence at that season,
For thou shalt hear a royal disputation 1410
Betwixt them ere they have do.
Another thing must be considered withal,
These folk that sit here in the hall
May not attend thereto.
We may not with our long play
Let them from their dinner all day,

1406 force] urge. 1416 Let] Keep.

They have not fully dined;
For an this play were once overpast
Some of them would fall to feeding as fast
As they had been almost pined; 1420
But no force hardily an they do.
Usher, get them good wine thereto,
Fill them of the best;
Let it be done or ye will be shent,
For it is the will and commandment
Of the master of the feast.
And therefore we shall the matter forbear,
And make a point even here
Lest we exceed a measure;
And we shall do our labour and true intent 1430
For to play the remnant
At my lord's pleasure.

End of Part One

PART TWO

A *enters and speaks*

Much good do it you every one!
Ye will not believe how fast I have gone,
For fear that I should come too late;
No force I have lost but a little sweat
That I have taken upon this heat
My cold courage to abate.
But now to the matter that I came for,
Ye know the cause thereof before,
Your wits be not so short.
Perdie my fellows and I were here 10

1420 pined] starved. 1421 no force hardily an] it certainly doesn't matter if. 4 No force I have lost] It does not matter that I have lost. 10 Perdie] *See* Part i, l. 480.

To-day when ye were at dinner,
And showed you a little disport
Of one Fulgens and his daughter Lucrece,
And of two men that made great business
Her husband for to be:
She answered to them both than,
Look which was the more noble man
To him she would agree.
This was the substance of the play
That was showed here to-day, 20
Albeit that there was
Divers toys mingled in the same
To stir folk to mirth and game
And to do them solace:
The which trifles be impertinent
To the matter principal,
But nevertheless they be expedient
For to satisfy and content
Many a man withal.
For some there be that looks and gapes 30
Only for such trifles and japes,
And some there be among
That forceth little of such madness
But delighteth them in matter of sadness
Be it never so long.
And every man must have his mind,
Else they will many faults find
And say the play was nought.
But, no force, I care not,
Let them say and spare not, 40
For God knoweth my thought:
It is the mind and intent
Of me and my company to content
The least that standeth here,
And so I trust ye will it allow—
By God's mercy, where am I now?

32 among] at the same time. 33 forceth little of] cares little about. 45 allow] approve.

It were alms to wring me by the ear
Because I make such digression
From the matter that I began
When I entered the hall; 50
For had I made a good continuance,
I should have put you in remembrance
And to your minds call
How Lucrece will come hither again
And her said lovers both twain
To define this question;
Whether of them is the more noble man;
For thereon all this matter began,
It is the chief foundation
Of all this process both all and some. 60
And if these players were once come
Of this matter will they speak:
I marvel greatly in my mind
That they tarry so long behind,
Their hour for to break.

[*To the audience.*

But what, sirs, I pray you everyone,
Have patience, for they come anon,
I am sure they will not fail,
But they will meet in this place
As their promise and appointment was, 70
And else I have marvel.
Let me see what is now a-clock—
Ah! there cometh one, I hear him knock,
He knocketh as he were wood.
One of you go look who it is.

Enter B

B. Nay, nay, all the meinie of them I wis
Cannot so much good:
A man may rap till his nails ache
Or any of them will the labour take

47 alms] a service. 74 wood] mad. 76 meinie] company. 79 Or] Ere.

To give him an answer. 80
A. I have great marvel on thee
That ever thou wilt take upon thee
To chide any man here;
No man is so much to blame as thou
For long tarrying.
B. Yea, God avow!
Will ye play me that?
Marry, that shall be amended anon,
I am late come, and I will soon be gone,
Else I shrew my cat.
Cock's body, sir, it is a fair reason, 90
I am come hither at this season
Only at thy bidding,
And now thou makest to me a quarrel
As though all the matter were in parell
By my long tarrying.
Now, God be with you, so mote I thee,
Ye shall play the knave alone for me.
A. What? I am afraid!
I wis ye are but lewd:
Turn again, all be shrewd! 100
Now are you fair prayed!
B. Why then, is your anger all do?
A. Yea, marry, is it so.
B. So is mine too,
I have done clean.
But now how goeth this matter forth
Of this marriage?
A. By Saint James, right naught worth,
I wot ne'er what they mean,
For I can none otherwise think 110
But that some of them begin to shrink
Because of their long tarriage.
B. Shrink now, quotha! marry, that were marvel.

89 I shrew my cat] I curse my cat. 49 parell] peril. 99 lewd] good for nothing. 101 fair prayed] politely invited.

But one thing of surety I can thee tell
As touching this marriage,
Cornelius my master appointeth him thereupon,
And doubtless he will be here anon
In pain of forty pence,
In so much that he hath devised
Certain strangers freshly disguised 120
At his own expense
For to be here this night also.
A. Strangers, quotha! what to do?
B. Marry, for to glad withal
This gentlewoman at her hither coming.
A. Ah, then, I see well we shall have a mumming.
B. Yea, surely that we shall,
And therefore never think it in thy mind
That my master will be behind
Nor slack at this bargain. 130
[*Enter* Cornelius.
Marry, here he cometh, I have him espied.
No more words, stand thou aside,
For it is he plain.
Cor. My friend, whereabout goest thou all day?
B. Marry, sir, I came hither to essay
Whether these folk had been here,
And yet they be not come,
So help me God and halidom!
Of that I have much marvel that they tarry so.
Cor. Marry, go thy way, and wit where they will
or no. 140
B. Yea, God avow, shall I so?
Cor. Yea, marry, so I say.
B. Yet in that point, as seemeth me,
Ye do not according to your degree.
Cor. I pray thee tell me why.
B. Marry, it would become them well enow

116 appointeth him thereupon] is determined upon it.
120 freshly] gaily. 138 halidom] *See* Part i, l. 190.
140 where] whether.

To be here afore and to wait upon you,
And not you to tarry
For their leisure, and abide them here
As it were one that were led by the ear, 150
For that I defy.
By this means you should be their drudge,
I tell you troth, I,
And yet the worst that grieveth me
Is that your adversary should in you see
So notable a folly—
Therefore withdraw you for a season.

Cor. By Saint John, thou sayest but reason.

B. Yea, do so hardily,
And when the time draweth upon 160
That they be come every one
And all thing ready,
Then shall I come straight away
For to seek you without delay.

Cor. Be it so hardily.
But one thing while I think thereon,
Remember this when I am gone—
If it happen so
That Lucrece come in first alone,
Go in hand with her anon, 170
Howsoever thou do,
For to feel her mind toward me,
And by all means possible to be
Induce her thereunto.

B. Then some token you must give me,
For else she will not believe me
That I came from you.

Cor. Marry, that is even wisely spoken.
Commend me to her by the same token,
She knoweth it well enow, 180
That as she and I walked once together
In her garden hither and thither
There happened a strange case;
For at the last we did see

A bird sitting on a hollow tree,
An ash I trow it was.
Anon she prayed me for to essay
If I could start the bird away.
B. And did ye so? alas, alas!
Cor. Why the devil sayst thou so? 190
B. By Cock's bones, for it was a cuckoo,
And men say among,
He that throweth stone or stick
At such a bird he is like
To sing that bird's song.
Cor. What the devil reck I therefor?
Hear what I say to thee evermore,
And mark thine errand well.
Sir, I had no stone to throw withal,
And therefore she took me her musk-ball, 200
And thus it befell—
I kyst it as straight as any pole
So that it lighted even in the hole
Of the hollow ash.
Now canst thou remember all this?
B. By God, I would be loth to do amiss
For some time I am full rash.
Ye say that ye kyst it even in the hole
Of the hollow ash as straight as a pole?
Said ye not so? 210
Cor. Yes.
B. Well, then let me alone!
As for this errand it shall be done
As soon as ye be go.
Cor. Farewell then! I leave thee here
And remember well all this gear
Howsoever thou do. [*Exit* Cornelius.
B. Yes, hardly this errand shall be spoken.
[*To the audience.*] But how say you, sirs, by this token,
Is it not a quaint thing?

192 among] commonly. 202 kyst] cast. So in l. 208.

I weened he had been a sad man, 220
But I see well he is a mad man
In this message doing.
But what, choose he for me!
I am but as a messenger, perdie;
The blame shall not be mine but his,
For I will his token report,
Whether she take it in earnest or sport,
I will not thereof miss.
Be she wroth or well apaid, 229
I will tell her even as he said. [*Enter* Lucrece.
God avow! Here she is,
It is time for me to be wise.
Now welcome, lady, flower of price,
I have sought you twice or thrice
Within this hour, I wis.
Luc. Me, sir, have ye sought me?
B. Yea, that I have, by God that bought me.
Luc. To what intent?
B. Marry, for I have things a few
The which I must to you shew 240
By my master's commandment.
Publius Cornelius is his name,
Your very lover in pain of shame,
And if ye love him not ye be to blame;
For this dare I say,
And on a book make it good,
He loved you better than his own heart' blood.
Luc. His hard blood? nay, nay,
Half that love would serve for me.
B. Yet sith he did you first see 250
In the place where he dwells,
He had loved you so in his heart
That he setteth not by himself a fart
Nor by no man else;

220 sad] serious, sane. 229 apaid] *See* Part i, l. 136. 237 bought] redeemed. 248 His hard blood] His very blood—*with a play on* h(e)art *and* hard.

And because ye should give credence
Unto my saying in his absence
And trust to that I say,
He told me tokens, two or three,
Which I know well, as he told me.
Luc. Tokens, what be they? 260
B. Let me see, now I had need to be wise,
For one of his tokens is very nice
As ever I heard tell:
He prayed you for to believe me
By the same token that ye and he
Walked together by a hollow tree.
Luc. All that I know well.
B. Ah, then I am yet in the right way,
But I have some other thing to say
Touching my credence, 270
Which as I think were best to be spared,
For haply ye would not have it declared
Before all this audience.
Luc. Nay, nay, hardily spare not.
As for my deeds I care not
If all the world it heard.
B. Marry, then shall I proceed.
He showed me also in very deed
How there sat a bird,
And then ye delivered him your musk-ball 280
For to throw at the bird withal,
And then, as he said, ye did no worse
But even fair kyst him on the nook of the arse.
Luc. Nay, there thou liest falsely, by my fay.
B. Troth, it was on the hole of th'arse I should say,
I wist well it was one of the two,
The nook or the hole.
Luc. Nay, nor yet so!
B. By my faith, ye kyst him or he kyst you
On the hole of th'arse, choose you now,

283 kyst] kissed. *So in* l. 288. B *confuses two meanings of the word. See* l. 202. nook] corner, part.

This he told me sure. 290
Howbeit I speak it not in reprove,
For it was done but for good love
And for no sinful pleasure.
Luc. Nay, nay, man thou art far amiss;
I know what thine errand is,
Though thou be negligent;
Of thy folly thou mayst well abash,
For thou shouldst have said the hollow ash,
That hole thy master meant.
B. By God avow, I trow it was, 300
I cry you mercy, I have done you trespass,
But I pray you take it in patience
For I mistook it by negligence,
A mischief come thereon!
He might have sent you this gear in a letter.
But I shall go learn mine errand better
And come again anon. [*Exit.*
Luc. Yea, so do hardily!
Now forsooth this was a lewd message
As ever I heard sith I was bore, 310
And if his master have thereof knowledge,
He will be angry with him therefore.
Howbeit, I will speak thereof no more,
For it hath been my condition alway
No man to hinder but to help where I may.

Enter A

A. Fair mistress liketh it you to know
That my master commends me to you?
Luc. Commendeth you to me?
A. Nay, commendeth you to him.
Luc. Well amended, by Saint Sim. 320
A. Commendeth he to you, I would say,
Or else you to he, now choose ye may
Whether liketh you better;

297 mayst well abash] may well feel ashamed.
323 Whether] which of the two.

And here he sendeth you a letter—
God's mercy I had it right now.
[*To the audience.*
Sirs, is there none there among you
That took up such a writing?
I pray you, sirs, let me have it again.
Luc. Ye are a good messenger, for certain,
But I pray you, sir, of one thing, 330
Who is your master? tell me that.
A. Master, what call ye him? perdie ye wot
Whom I mean well and fine.
Luc. Yet I know not, so mote I go!
A. What? yes, perdie, he that would have you so.
Luc. I suppose there be many of tho,
If I would incline.
But yet know I not who ye mean,
I hold best that ye go again
To learn your master's name. 340
A. By my faith, and I hold it best,
Ye may say I am a homely guest
In earnest and in game.
Luc. Abide, I shall go to you near hand.
What is your own name, I would understand?
Tell me that ere I go,
I trow thou canst not well tell.
A. By my faith, not verily well
Because ye say so.
[*Scratching his head and pausing.*
By this light I have forgotten. 350
Howbeit by that time I have spoken
With some of my company,
I shall be ascertained of this gear.
But shall I find you again here?
[*Enter* Publius Cornelius.
Luc. Yea, that thou shalt haply. [*Exit* A.
Cor. Now, fair Lucrece, according to th'appointment
That ye made with me here this day

342 homely guest] *See* Part i, l. 547.

Because ye shall not find me there negligent,
Here I am come your will to obey,
And ready am I for myself to say 360
That as touching the degree of noble condition
Betwixt me and Gaius there may be no comparison:
And that shall I show you by apparent reason
If it shall like you that I now begin.

Luc. Nay, ye shall spare it for a little season
Till such time that Gaius, your adversary, come in,
For I will give you therein none audience
Till ye be both together in presence.
And in any wise keep well your patience,
Like as I have bound you both to the peace: 370
I forbid you utterly all manner of violence
During this matter, and also that ye cease
Of all such words as may give occasion
Of brawling or other ungodly condition.

Cor. There shall be in me no such abusion
In word nor deed, I you promise.
But now let me see, what occupation
Or what manner of pastime will ye devise
While that these folk doth tarry this wise?
Will ye see a base dance after the guise 380
Of Spain, while ye have nothing to do?
All things have I purveyed that belong thereto.

Luc. Sir, I shall give you the looking on.

Cor. Will ye do so? I ask no more.
Go soon and bid them come thence anon,
And cause the minstrels to come in before.

Enter B *with* Mummers

B. Marry, as for one of them his lip is sore,
I trow he may not pipe, he is so sick.
Spele up tamborine, ik bide owe, frelike.

[*They dance.*

380 base dance] slow, stately dance. 389 Spele . . . frelike] Play up, tabor, I bid you, merrily. *On the Flemish words see Introduction.*

Luc. Forsooth, this was a goodly recreation. 390
But I pray you of what manner nation
Be these godly creatures?
Were they of England or of Wales?
B. Nay, they be wild Irish Portingales
That did all these pleasures.
Howbeit it was for my master's sake,
And he will deserve it, I undertake,
On the largest wise.
Cor. Go thyself, why standest thou so?
And make them cheer, let it be do, 400
The best thou canst devise.
B. Yes, they shall have cheer heaven high,
But one thing I promise you faithfully,
They get no drink thereto. [*Exit* B.

Enter Gaius Flaminius.

Luc. Lo, here this man is come now.
Now may ye in your matter proceed.
Ye remember both what I said to you
Touching mine answer, I trow it is no need
Any more to rehearse it.
Cor. No, in very deed,
For much rehearsal would let the speed 410
Of all this matter, it needeth no more;
Let us roundly to the matter we come for.
Luc. Yea, that, I pray you, as heartily as I can.
But first me seemeth it were expedient
That ye both name some indifferent man
For to give betwixt you the foresaid judgement.
Cor. Nay, as for that, by mine assent
No man shall have that office but ye.
Ga. And I hold me well content that it so be.
Luc. Yea, but notwithstanding that ye thereto agree
That I should this question of noblesse define, 421
It is a great matter which, as seemeth me,

394 Portingales] Portuguese. 410 let] interfere with. 415 indifferent] impartial.

Pertaineth to a philosopher or else a divine.
Howbeit, sith the choice of this matter is mine,
I can be content under certain protestation,
When that I have heard you, to say mine opinion.
Lo, this wise I mean and thus I do intend,
That whatsoever sentence I give betwixt you two
After mine own fantasy, it shall not extend
To any other person, I will that it be so, 430
For why no man else hath therein ado:
It may not be noted for a general precedent,
Albeit that for your parts ye do thereto assent.

Ga. As touching that point we hold us well content;
Your sentence shall touch no man but us twain,
And sith ye shall give it by our own agreement,
None other man ought to have thereat disdain.
Wherefore all this doubt ye may well refrain,
And in the matter principal this time would be spent.

Cor. Then will I begin.

Ga. I hold me well content. 440

Cor. Sith ye have promised, fair Lucrece, heretofore
That to the more noble man ye will incline,
Vary not from that word, and I ask no more,
For then shall the victory of this cause be mine,
As it shall be easy to judge and define
For every creature that any reason has.
Meseemeth I durst make himself judge in this case,
Save that I fear me the beauty of your face
Should therein blind him so that he ne might
Equally discern the wrong from the right. 450
And if he were half so wise a man indeed
As he reputeth himself for to be
Upon your said answer he should not need
To gainsay in this matter or traverse with me.
My nobleness is known through all the city;
He knoweth himself the nobleness of my kin,
And at that one point my process I will begin.

447 himself] Gaius Flaminius. 449 he ne might] he might not. 454 traverse with me] go counter to me.

Among all the stories of Romans that ye read,
Where find ye any blood of so great nobleness
As hath been the Cornelii whereof I am bred? 460
And if so be that I would therein hold my peace
Yet all your chronicles beareth good witness
That my progenitors and ancestors have be
The chief aid and defence of this noble city.

How oft have mine ancestors in times of necessity
Delivered this city from deadly peril,
As well by their manhood as by their policy!
What jeopardy and pain they have suffered in the quarrel
Th'empire to increase and for the commonweal!
It needeth not the specialities to rehearse or name,
Sith every true Roman knoweth the same. 471

In every man's house those histories be rife
And written in books, as in some places be
The gests of Arthur, or of Alexander's life,
In the which stories ye may evidently see
And read how Carthage, that royal city,
By Scipio of Afric, my great-grandsire,
Subdued was and also ascribed to his empire.

And many other cities that did conspire,
Against the noble senator making resistence, 480
As often as necessity did it require,
They were reduced unto due obedience
Either by the policy or by the violence
Of my said ancestors; the stories be plain
And witness that I speak not these words in vain.

My blood hath ever taken such pain
To safeguard the commonweal from ruin and decay
That by one advice the Senate did ordain

474 gests] deeds. 478 ascribed . . . empire] brought beneath his dominion. 486 blood] family. 488 advice] decision.

Them to be named the fathers of the country,
And so were mine authors reputed alway 490
For in every need they did upon them call
For help as the child doth on the father natural.

Howbeit to pray them it was no need at all,
For of their own minds they were ready alway.
In token of the same, for a memorial
Of their deserts, the city did edify
Triumphal arches whereupon ye may
To my great honour see at this day
Th'images of mine ancestors even by and by
Because that their nobleness should never die. 500

In token also that they were worthy
Great honour and praise of all the country,
It is commanded and used generally
That every citizen that passeth that way
By the said images he must obey,
And to those figures make a due reverence,
And else to the laws he doth great offence.

Sith it is so then that of convenience
Such honour and homage must needs be do
To these dead images, then much more reverence
To me should be given, I trow ye think so, 511
For I am their very image and relic too
Of their flesh and blood, and very inheritor
As well of their goods as of their said honour.

To me they have left many a castle and tower
Which in their triumphs they rightfully wan;
To me they have also left all their treasure
In such abundance, that I trow no man
Within all Rome, sith it first began,
Had half the store, as I understand, 520
That I have even now at once in my hand.

490 authors] ancestors. 499 by and by] here at hand. 505 obey] bow.

Lo, in these things my nobleness doth stand
Which in mine opinion sufficeth for this intent,
And I trow there is no man through all this land
Of Italy but if he were here present
He would to my saying in this matter assent,
And give unto me the honour and pre-eminence
Rather than make against me resistence.

[*To* Gaius Flaminius.

I marvel greatly what should thy mind incense
To think that thy title therein should be good: 530
Perdie thou canst not say for thy defence
That ever there was gentleman of thy kin or blood,
And if there were one it would be understood,
Without it be thyself which now of late
Among noble gentlemen playest checkmate.

Luc. No more thereof, I pray you! such words I hate,
And I did forbid you them at the beginning,
To eschew th'occasion of strife and debate.

Ga. Nay, let him alone, he speaketh after his learning,
For I shall answer him to everything 540
When he hath all said, if ye will hear me,
As I think ye will of your equity.

Cor. Abide, I must make an end first, perdie.
To you, sweet Lucrece, I would have said before
That if ye will to my desire in this matter agree
Doubtless ye shall bless the time that ever ye were bore,
For riches shall ye have at your will evermore,
Without care or study of laborious business,
And spend all your days in ease and pleasant idleness.

About your own apparel ye can do none excess 550
In my company that should displease my mind;
With me shall ye do none other manner of business
But hunt for your solace at the hart and hind,
And sometime, where we convenient game find,

529 incense] incite. 535 Among . . . playest checkmate] bringest defeat on.

Our hawks shall be ready to show you a flight
Which shall be right pleasant and cheerful to your sight.

And if so be that in hunting ye have no delight,
Then may ye dance awhile for your disport,
Ye shall have at your pleasure both day and night
All manner of minstrelsy to do you comfort. 560
Do what thing ye will, I have to support
Our charges, and over that I may sustain
At mine own finding a pound or twain.

And as for him, I am certain
His ancestors were of full poor degree,
Albeit that now within a year or twain,
Because that he would a gentleman be,
He hath him gotten both office and fee,
Which, after the rate of his wretched sparing,
Sufficeth scarcely for his bare living. 570

Wherefore, sweet Lucrece, it were not according
For your great beauty with him to dwell,
For there should ye have a threadbare living
With wretched scarceness, and I have heard tell
That maidens of your age love not right well
Such manner of husbands without it be they
That forceth little to cast themselves away.

I mean specially for such of them as may
Speed better if they will, as ye be in the case,
And therefore, Lucrece, whatsoever he will say, 580
His title against you to force and embrace,
Ye shall do your own self too great a trespass
If ye follow his part and incline thereto.
Now say what ye will, sir, for I have all do.

561–2 I have . . . charges] I have enough to defray our expenses. 577 That forceth . . . away] That care little about casting themselves away. 581 embrace] fix with a brace, fasten.

Ga. With right good will I shall go to,
So that ye will hear me with as great patience
As I have heard you, reason would so.
[*To the audience.*] And whatsoever I shall speak in this audience,
Either of mine own merits or of his insolence,
Yet first unto you all, sirs, I make this request, 590
That it would like you to construe it to the best.

For loth would I be as any creature
To boast of mine own deeds, it was never my guise;
On that other side, loth I am to make any reporture
Of this man's folly or him to despise,
But nevertheless this matter toucheth me in such wise
That, whatsoever ye think in me, I must proceed
Unto the very truth thereof, as the matter is indeed.

To make a great rehearsal of that ye have said,
The time will not suffer, but nevertheless 600
Two things for yourself in substance ye have laid
Which, as ye suppose, maketh for your noblesse,
Upon the which things dependeth all your process.
First of your ancestors ye allege the noble gests,
Secondly, the substance that ye have of their bequests.

In the which things only, by your own confession,
Standeth all your nobleness, this said ye before:
Whereunto this I say, under the correction 608
Of Lucrece, our judge, here, that ye are never the more
Worthy in mine opinion to be called noble therefore,
And without ye have better causes to show than these,
Of reason ye must the victory of this matter lese.

To the first part, as touching your ancestors' deeds,
Some of them were noble like as ye declare,
The stories beareth witness, I must grant them needs,

594 reporture] mention. 603 process] argument.
612 lese] lose.

But yet, for all that some of them ware
Of contrary disposition, like as ye are,
For they did no profit, no more do ye,
To the commonweal of this noble city.

If ye will the title of nobleness win, 620
Show what have ye done yourself therefore:
Some of your own merits let see bring in,
If ever ye did any sith ye were bore;
But surely ye have no such thing in store
Of your own merits, whereby of right
Ye should appear noble to any man's sight.

But nevertheless, I will you not blame
Though ye speak not of your own deeds at all;
And, to say the truth, ye may not for shame,
Your life is so voluptuous and so bestial 630
In following of every lust sensual,
That I marvel nothing in my mind
If ye leave your own deeds behind.

[*To* Lucrece.

He weeneth that by his proud countenance
Of word and deed with nice array,
His great oaths and open maintenance
Of thefts and murders every day,
Also his riotous disports and play,
His sloth, his cowardice and other excess,
His mind disposed to all uncleanness, 640
By these things only he shall have nobleness.

Nay, the title of nobleness will not ensue
A man that is all given to such insolence,
But it groweth of long continued virtue,
As I trust, lady, that your indifference
Can well define by your sentence.
His ancestors were not of such condition,
But all contrary to his disposition;

616 ware] were. 635 nice] elegant. 645 indifference] impartiality. 646 define] decide.

And therefore they were noble without fail,
And did great honour to all the country. 650
But what can their said nobleness avail
To him that taketh a contrary way,
Of whom men speaketh every day
So great dishonour that it is marvel
The country suffereth him therein to dwell?

And where he too witeth me of poor kin,
He doth me therein a wrongful offence,
For no man shall thanks or praising win
By the gifts that he hath of nature's influence:
Likewise I think by a contrary sense 660
That if a man be born blind or lame,
Not he himself but nature therein is to blame.

Therefore he doth not me therein repreve,
And as for that point this I wot well
That both he and I came of Adam and Eve;
There is no difference that I can tell
Which maketh one man another to excel
So much as doth virtue and godly manner,
And therein I may well with him compare.

Howbeit I speak it not for mine own praise, 670
But certainly this hath ever been my condition:
I have borne unto God all my days
His laud and praise with my due devotion,
And next that I bear always
To all my neighbours charitable affection;
Incontinency and uncleanness I have had in abomination,
Loving to my friend and faithful withal,
And ever I have withstood my lusts sensual.

One time with study my time I spend
To eschew idleness, the causer of sin, 680
Another time my country manly I defend,

656 witeth me of] reproaches me with.
663 repreve] reprove, refute.

And for the victories that I have done therein
Ye have seen yourself, sir, that I have come in
To this noble city twice or thrice
Crownèd with laurel, as it is the guise.

By these ways, lo, I do arise
Unto great honour from low degree,
And if mine heirs will do likewise,
They shall be brought to noblesse by me;
But, Cornelius, it seemeth by thee 690
That the noblesse of thine ancestors every one
Shall utterly starve and die in thee alone.

And where he too witeth me on that other side
Of small possession and great scarceness,
For all that, lady, if ye will with me abide,
I shall assure you of moderate riches,
And that sufficient for us both, doubtless.
Ye shall have also a man according
To your own conditions in everything.

Now, Lucrece, I have showèd unto you a part 700
Of my title that I claim you by,
Beseeching you therefore with all my heart
To consider us both twain indifferently,
Which of us twain ye will rather allow
More worthy for noblesse to marry with you.

Luc. Sirs, I have heard you both at large—
Cor. Nay abide, Lucrece, I pray you heartily,
Sith he layeth many things to my charge,
Suffer that I may thereunto reply.
Luc. I wis replication shall not be necessary 710
Without that ye have some other thing in store
To show for yourself than ye did before.
Cor. Why, lady, what thing will ye desire more
Than I have showed to make for nobleness?
Luc. Yes, something there is that maketh therefore

692 starve] perish. 710 replication] rejoinder.

Better than ye have showèd in your process.
But now let me see what man of witness,
Or what other proofs will ye forth bring
By the which either of you may justify his saying.
Ga. As for my part, I will stand gladly 720
To the common voice of all the country.
Luc. And ye likewise, sir?
Cor. Yea, certainly,
I shall in no wise your word disobey.
Luc. Then will I betwixt you both take this way:
I shall go inquire as fast as I may
What the common fame will therein report,
And when I have thereof a due evidence,
Then shall I again to you resort
To show you the opinion of my sentence,
Whom I will judge to have the pre-eminence. 730
Cor. Nay, fair Lucrece, I you require
Let me not now depart in vain
Not knowing th'effect of my desire.
Luc. Sir, although it be to you a pain
Yet must ye do so even both twain.
Each of you depart hence to his own place,
And take no more labour or pain in this case,
For as touching th'effect of my sentence,
I shall go write it by good advisement
Soon after that I am departed from hence; 740
And then to either of you both shall be sent
A copy of the same to this intent
That of none other person it shall be sayn
Sith it concerneth but only unto you twain.
Ga. This is a good way, as in my mind;
Are not ye, sir, content in likewise?
Cor. I wot ne'er yet, I will praise as I find
And as I have cause—that is ever my guise.
Ga. Well, Lucrece, will ye command me any service
Luc. No service at all, sir, why say ye so? 750

729 sentence] decision. 739 by good advisement] after good consideration. 743 sayn] seen.

Our Lord speed you both wheresoever ye go!
[*Exeunt* Publius Cornelius *and* Gaius Flaminius.
Now some maid haply, an she were in my case,
Would not take that way that I do intend,
For I am fully determined with God's grace
So that to Gaius I will condescend,
For in this case I do him commend
As the more noble man, sith he this wise
By means of his virtue to honour doth arise.
And for all that I will not despise
The blood of Cornelius, I pray you think not so: 760
God forbid that ye should note me that wise,
For truly I shall honour them wheresoever I go,
And all other that be of like blood also,
But unto the blood I will have little respect
Where the conditions be sinful and abject.
[*To the audience.*
I pray you all, sirs, as many as be here,
Take not my words by a sinister way.

Enter B

B. Yes, by my troth, I shall witness bear,
Wheresoever I become another day,
How such a gentlewoman did openly say 770
That by a churl's son she would set more
Than she would do by a gentleman bore.
Luc. Nay, sir, then ye report me amiss.
B. I pray you tell me how said ye than?
Luc. Fore God, sir, the substance of my words was this—
I say even as I said when I began—
That for virtue excellent I will honour a man
Rather than for his blood, if it so fall
That gentle conditions agree not withal.
B. Then I put case that a gentleman bore 780
Have godly manners to his birth according.
Luc. I say of him is to be set great store:
Such one is worthy more laud and praising
Than many of them that hath their beginning

Of low kindred, else God forbid!
I will not affirm the contrary for my head,
For in that case there may be no comparison.
But nevertheless I said this before,
That a man of excellent virtuous conditions,
Although he be of a poor stock bore, 790
Yet I will honour and commend him more
Than one that is descended of right noble kin
Whose life is all dissolute and rotted in sin.
And therefore I have determined utterly
That Gaius Flaminius shall have his intent;
To him only I shall myself apply
To use me in wedlock at his commandment;
So that to Cornelius I will never assent,
Although he had as great possession
As any one man in Christian region: 800
I shall in no wise favour or love his condition,
Howbeit that his blood requireth due reverence,
And that shall I give him with all submission,
But yet shall he never have the pre-eminence,
To speak of very noblesse, by my sentence.
[*To* B.] Ye be his servant, sir, go your way
And report to your master even as I say.

B. Shall I do that errand? Nay let be,
By the rood, ye shall do it yourself for me!
[*Exit* Lucrece.
I promise you faithfully, 810
I would my master had been in Scotland
When he did put this matter in her hand
To stand to her judgement.
But forasmuch as it is so
That this wrong to him is do
By a woman, he must let it go
And hold him content.
But he is of such disposition
That when he heareth of this conclusion,
He will be stark mad, 820

796 apply] attach.

Yea, by my troth, as mad as an hare:
It shall make him so full of care
That he will with himself fare
Even as it were a lad.
And so would not I, so mote I thee!
For this matter, an I were as he,
It should never anger me;
But this would I do,
I would let her go in the mare's name.

Enter A

A. What now, sirs, how goeth the game? 830
What is this woman go?
B. Yea, yea, man.
A. And what way hath she taken?
B. By my faith, my master is forsaken
And needs she will agree
Unto thy master, thus she sayeth,
And many causes therefore she layeth
Why it should so be.
A. I marvel greatly whereof that grew.
B. By my faith, she said, I tell thee true,
That she would needs have him for his virtue, 840
And for none other thing.
A. Virtue, what the devil is that?
An I can tell, I shrew my cat,
To mine understanding.
B. By my faith, no more can I
But this she said here openly,
All these folk can tell. [*To the audience.*
A. How say ye, good women, is it your guise
To choose all your husbands that wise?
By my troth, then I marvel. 850
B. Nay, this is the fear, so mote I go,
That men choose not their wives so
In places where I have be,

825 mote I thee] may I thrive. 843 I . . . cat] *See* l. 89.

For wives may well complain and groan,
Albeit that cause have they none
That I can hear or see.
But of wedded men there be right few
That will not say the best is a shrew,
Therein they all agree.
I warn you wedded men every one 860
That other remedy have ye none
So much for your ease,
An ye would study till to-morrow,
But let them even alone with sorrow,
When they do you displease.
A. Tush! here is no man that setteth a blank
By thy counsel or conneth thee thank,
Speak thereof no more;
They know that remedy better than thou.
But what shall we twain do now? 870
I care most therefore,
Methinketh that matter would be wist.
B. Marry, we may go hence when we list,
No man saith us nay.
A. Why, then, is the play all done?
B. Yea, by my faith, an we were once gone,
It were done straightway.
A. And I would have thought in very deed
That this matter should have proceed
To some other conclusion. 880
B. Yea, thou art a master merry man,
Thou shall be wise I wot ne'er whan.
Is not the question
Of nobleness now fully defined,
As it may be so by a woman's mind?
What wouldst thou have more?
Thou toldest me that other day
That all the substance of this play

864 let . . . sorrow] let them go to the devil. 866 setteth a blank] sets a farthing's value. 867 conneth thee thank] gives thee thanks. 881 a master merry man] a chief jester.

Was done specially therefore,
Not only to make folk mirth and game, 890
But that such as be gentlemen of name
May be somewhat moved
By this example for to eschew
The way of vice and favour virtue,
For sin is to be reproved
More in them, for their degree,
Than in other persons such as be
Of poor kin and birth.
This was the cause principal,
And also for to do withal 900
This company some mirth.
And though the matter that we have played
Be not percase so well conveyed
And with so great reason
As the history itself requireth,
Yet the author thereof desireth
That for this season
At the least ye will take it in patience;
And if there be any offence—
Show us wherein ere we go hence— 910
Done in the same,
It is only for lack of cunning,
And not he but his wit running
Is thereof to blame.
And glad would he be and right fain
That some man of stable brain
Would take on him the labour and pain
This matter to amend.
And so he willed me for to say,
And that done, of all this play 920
Shortly here we make an end.

Imprinted at London by Iohan Rastell
dwelling on the south side of Paul's
Church beside Paul's Chain.

903 percase] perchance.

¶ The playe called the foure PP.

¶ A newe and a very mery enterlude of
A palmer.
A pardoner.
A potycary.
A pedler.

Made by Johñ Heewood

AN INTERLUDE OF

A PALMER. A POTHECARY.
A PARDONER. A PEDLAR.

Enter the Palmer

Palm. Now God be here! Who keepeth this place?
Now, by my faith, I cry you mercy!
Of reason I must sue for grace,
My rudeness showeth me now so homely.
Whereof your pardon axed and won,
I sue you, as courtesy doth me bind,
To tell this which shall be begun
In order as may come best in mind.
I am a palmer, as ye see,
Which of my life much part hath spent 10
In many a fair and far country,
As pilgrims do of good intent.
At Jerusalem have I been
Before Christ's blessèd sepulture;
The Mount of Calvary have I seen,
A holy place, ye may be sure;
To Josophat and Olivet
On foot, God wot, I went right bare,
Many a salt tear did I sweat
Before this carcase could come there. 20
Yet have I been at Rome also,
And gone the stations all arow,
Saint Peter's shrine, and many mo
Than, if I told, all ye do know,
Except that there be any such
That hath been there and diligently
Hath taken heed and markèd much,

5 axed] asked. 22 all arow] one after another.

Then can they speak as much as I.
Then at the Rhodes also I was,
And round about to Amias; 30
At Saint Toncomber; and Saint Trunnion;
At Saint Botolph; and Saint Anne of Buxton;
On the hills of Armony, where I see Noe's ark;
With holy Job; and Saint George in Southwark;
At Waltham; and at Walsingham;
And at the good Rood of Dagenham;
At Saint Cornelius; at Saint James in Gales;
And at Saint Winifred's Well in Wales;
At Our Lady of Boston; at Saint Edmundsbury;
And straight to Saint Patrick's Purgatory; 40
At Redburne; and at the Blood of Hales,
Where pilgrims' pains right much avails;
At Saint Davy's; and at Saint Denis;
At Saint Matthew; and Saint Mark in Venice;
At Master John Shorn; at Canterbury;
The great God of Catwade; at King Henry;
At Saint Saviour's; at Our Lady of Southwell;
At Crome; at Willesden; and at Muswell;
At Saint Richard; and at Saint Roke;
And at Our Lady that standeth in the oak. 50
To these, with other many one,
Devoutly have I prayed and gone,
Praying to them to pray for me
Unto the Blessed Trinity;
By whose prayers and my daily pain
I trust the sooner to obtain
For my salvation grace and mercy.
For, be ye sure, I think surely
Who seeketh saints for Christ's sake
And namely such as pain do take 60
On foot to punish their frail body
Shall thereby merit more highly
Than by anything done by man.

29–50] For these saints and shrines see p. 342.
60 namely] especially.

Enter the Pardoner *speaking*

Pard. And when ye have gone as far as ye can,
For all your labour and ghostly intent
Yet welcome home as wise as ye went!
Palm. Why, sir, despise ye pilgrimage?
Pard. Nay, 'fore God, sir! Then did I rage!
I think ye right well occupied
To seek these saints on every side. 70
Also your pain I not dispraise it;
But yet I discommend your wit;
And, ere we go, even so shall ye,
If ye in this will answer me:
I pray you, show what the cause is
Ye went all these pilgrimages.
Palm. Forsooth, this life I did begin
To rid the bondage of my sin;
For which these saints, rehearsed ere this,
I have both sought and seen, iwis, 80
Beseeching them to be record
Of all my pain unto the Lord
That giveth all remission
Upon each man's contrition.
And by their good mediation,
Upon mine humble submission,
I trust to have in very deed
For my soul's health the better speed.
Pard. Now is your own confession likely
To make yourself a fool quickly! 90
For I perceive ye would obtain
None other thing for all your pain
But only grace your soul to save.
Now, mark in this what wit ye have
To seek so far, and help so nigh!
Even here at home is remedy,
For at your door myself doth dwell,
Who could have saved your soul as well

68 Then did I rage] Then I would be mad.

As all your wide wandering shall do,
Though ye went thrice to Jericho. 100
Now, since ye might have sped at home,
What have ye won by running at Rome?
Palm. If this be true that ye have moved,
Then is my wit indeed reproved!
But let us hear first what ye are.
Pard. Truly, I am a pardoner.
Palm. Truly a pardoner, that may be true,
But a true pardoner doth not ensue!
Right seldom is it seen, or never,
That truth and pardoners dwell together; 110
For, be your pardons never so great,
Yet them to enlarge ye will not let
With such lies that oft-times, Christ wot,
Ye seem to have that ye have not.
Wherefore I went myself to the self thing
In every place, and, without faining,
Had as much pardon there assuredly
As ye can promise me here doubtfully.
Howbeit, I think ye do but scoff.
But if ye had all the pardon ye speak of, 120
And no whit of pardon graunted
In any place where I have haunted,
Yet of my labour I nothing repent.
God hath respect how each time is spent;
And, as in his knowledge all is regarded,
So by his goodness all is rewarded.
Pard. By the first part of this last tale
It seemeth you come late from the ale!
For reason on your side so far doth fail
That ye leave reasoning and begin to rail; 130
Wherein ye forget your own part clearly,
For ye be as untrue as I;
And in one point ye are beyond me,
For ye may lie by authority,

103 moved] propounded. 112 enlarge] magnify let] forbear. 115 the self thing] the thing itself.

And all that hath wandered so far
That no man can be their controller.
And, where ye esteem your labour so much,
I say yet again my pardons be such
That, if there were a thousand souls on a heap,
I would bring them all to heaven as good cheap 140
As ye have brought yourself on pilgrimage
In the last quarter of your voyage,
Which is far a this side heaven, by God!
There your labour and pardon is odd,
With small cost and without any pain,
These pardons bringeth them to heaven plain.
Give me but a penny or two pence,
And as soon as the soul departeth hence,
In half an hour—or three quarters at most—
The soul is in heaven with the Holy Ghost! 150

While he is speaking, enter the Pothecary

Pot. Send ye any souls to heaven by water?
Pard. If we did, sir, what is the matter?
Pot. By God, I have a dry soul should thither!
I pray you let our souls go to heaven togither.
So busy you twain be in souls' health,
May not a pothecary come in by stealth?
Yes, that I will, by Saint Anthony!
And, by the leave of this company,
Prove ye false knaves both, ere we go,
In part of your sayings, as this, lo: 160
[*To the* Palmer.
Thou by thy travel thinkest heaven to get;
[*To the* Pardoner.
And thou by pardons and relics countest no let

136 controller] contradictor. 140 as good cheap] at as low a rate. 143 far a this side] far on this side of, far away from. 144 There . . . odd] Whereas your labour is out of proportion to the pardon obtained. 158 this company] the audience. 162 countest no let] reckonest there will be no obstacle.

To send thine own soul to heaven sure,
And all other whom thou list to procure.
If I took an action, then were they blank;
For, like thieves, the knaves rob away my thank.
All souls in heaven having relief,
Shall they thank your crafts? Nay, thank mine, chief!
No soul, ye know, entereth heaven-gate
Till from the body he be separate; 170
And whom have ye known die honestly
Without help of the pothecary?
Nay, all that cometh to our handling,
Except ye hap to come to hanging—
That way, perchance, ye shall not mister
To go to heaven without a glister!
But, be ye sure, I would be woe
If ye should chance to beguile me so.
As good to lie with me a-night
As hang abroad in the moonlight! 180
There is no choice to flee my hand
But, as I said, into the band.
Since of our souls the multitude
I send to heaven, when all is viewed,
Who should but I, then, altogither
Have thank of all their coming thither?

Pard. If ye killed a thousand in an hour's space,
When come they to heaven, dying from state of grace?

Pot. If a thousand pardons about your necks were tied,
When come they to heaven if they never died? 190

Palm. Long life after good works, indeed,
Doth hinder man's receipt of meed,
And death before one duty done
May make us think we die too soon.
Yet better tarry a thing, then have it,
Than go too soon and vainly crave it.

175 mister] find it needful. 176 glister] clyster, purge.
182 the band] the rope. 192 meed] reward.
195 tarry . . . have it] wait for a thing and then get it.

Pard. The longer ye dwell in communication,
The less shall you like this imagination;
For ye may perceive, even at the first chop,
Your tale is trapped in such a stop 200
That, at the least, ye seem worse than we.
Pot. By the Mass, I hold us naught, all three!

While he is speaking, enter the Pedlar

Ped. By Our Lady, then have I gone wrong!
And yet to be here I thought long.
Pot. Brother, ye have gone wrong no whit.
I praise your fortune and your wit
That can direct you so discreetly
To plant you in this company:
Thou a palmer, and thou a pardoner,
I a pothecary.
Ped. And I a pedlar! 210
Pot. Now, on my faith, full well matched!
Where the devil were we four hatched?
Ped. That maketh no matter, since we be matched.
I could be merry if that I catched
Some money for part of the ware in my pack.
Pot. What the devil hast thou there at thy back?
Ped. Why, dost thou not know that every pedler
In every trifle must be a meddler,
Specially in women's triflings,
Those use we chief above all things. 220
Which things to see, if ye be disposed,
Behold what ware here is disclosed.
This gear showeth itself in such beauty
That each man thinketh it saith: 'Come, buy me!'
Look, where yourself can like to be chooser,
Yourself shall make price, though I be loser!
Is here nothing for my father Palmer?
Have ye not a wanton in a corner
For your walking to holy places?

199 at the first chop] at the very outset.

By Christ, I have heard of as strange cases! 230
Who liveth in love, or love would win,
Even at this pack he must begin,
Where is right many a proper token,
Of which by name part shall be spoken:
Gloves, pins, combs, glasses unspotted,
Pomanders, hooks, and laces knotted,
Brooches, rings, and all manner beads,
Lace, round and flat, for women's heads,
Needles, thread, thimbles, shears, and all such knacks—
Where lovers be, no such things lacks— 240
Cypress, swathbands, ribands, and sleevelaces,
Girdles, knives, purses, and pincases.
Pot. Do women buy their pincases of you?
Ped. Yea, that they do, I make God avow!
Pot. So mote I thrive, then, for my part,
I beshrew thy knave's naked heart
For making my wife's pincase so wide,
The pins fall out, they cannot abide.
Great pins must she have, one or other;
If she lose one, she will find another! 250
Wherein I find cause to complain,
New pins to her pleasure and my pain!
Pard. Sir, ye seem well seen in women's causes.
I pray you, tell me what causeth this,
That women, after their arising,
Be so long in their apparelling?
Ped. Forsooth, women have many lets,
And they be masked in many nets,
As frontlets, fillets, partlets and bracelets;
And then their bonnets, and their poignets. 260
By these lets and nets the let is such
That speed is small when haste is much.
Pot. Another cause why they come not forward,

241 Cypress] a fine lawn material. swathbands] swaddling clothes. 257 lets] hindrances. 259 partlets] ruffs. 260 poignets] wristlets.

Which maketh them daily to draw backward,
And yet is a thing they cannot forbear—
The trimming and pinning up their gear,
Specially their fiddling with the tail-pin;
And, when they would have it prick in,
If it chance to double in the cloth
Then be they wood and sweareth an oath, 270
Till it stand right, they will not forsake it.
Thus, though it may not, yet would they make it.
But be ye sure they do but defar it,
For, when they would make it, oft-times mar it.
But prick them and pin them as much as ye will,
And yet will they look for pinning still!
So that I durst hold you a joint
Ye shall never have them at a full point.

Ped. Let women's matters pass, and mark mine!
Whatever their points be, these points be fine. 280
Wherefore, if ye be willing to buy,
Lay down money! Come off quickly!

Palm. Nay, by my troth, we be like friars:
We are but beggars, we be no buyers.

Pard. Sir, ye may show your ware for your mind,
But I think ye shall no profit find.

Ped. Well, though this journey acquit no cost,
Yet think I not my labour lost;
For, by the faith of my body,
I like full well this company. 290
Up shall this pack, for it is plain
I came not hither all for gain.
Who may not play one day in a week
May think his thrift is far to seek!
Devise what pastime ye think best,
And make ye sure to find me prest.

Pot. Why, be ye so universal
That you can do whatsoever ye shall?

270 wood] mad. 277 hold] wager. 287 acquit no cost] do not pay for any expense. 296 prest] ready.

Ped. Sir, if ye list to appose me,
What I can do then shall ye see. 300
Pot. Then tell me this: be ye perfect in drinking?
Ped. Perfect in drinking as may be wished by thinking!
Pot. Then after your drinking, how? Fall ye to winking?
Ped. Sir, after drinking, while the shot is tinking,
Some heads be swinking, but mine will be sinking,
And upon drinking mine eyes will be pinking,
For winking to drinking is alway linking.
Pot. Then drink and sleep ye can well do.
But, if ye were desired thereto,
I pray you, tell me, can you sing? 310
Ped. Sir, I have some sight in singing.
Pot. But is your breast anything sweet?
Ped. Whatever my breast be, my voice is meet.
Pot. That answer showeth you a right singing man!
Now what is your will, good father, than?
Palm. What helpeth will where is no skill?
Pard. And what helpeth skill where is no will?
Pot. For will or skill, what helpeth it
Where froward knaves be lacking wit?
Leave of this curiosity; 320
And who that list, sing after me! [*Here they sing.*
Ped. This liketh me well, so mote I thee!
Pard. So help me God, it liketh not me!
Where company is met and well agreed,
Good pastime doth right well indeed;
But who can set in dalliance
Men set in such a variance
As we were set ere ye came in?

299 appose] question. 303 winking] sleeping. 304 the shot is tinking] the money for the bill is clinking. 305 swinking] swimming. 306 pinking] blinking. 311 sight] skill. 312 breast] breath in singing. 320 curiosity] quibbling. 322 mote I thee] may I thrive.

Which strife this man did first begin,
[*Points to the* Palmer.
Alleging that such man as use, 330
For love of God, and not refuse
On foot to go from place to place
A pilgrimage, calling for grace,
Shall in that pain with penitence
Obtain discharge of conscience,
Comparing that life for the best
Induction to our endless rest.
Upon these words our matter grew;
For, if he could avow them true,
As good to be a gardener 340
As for to be a pardoner.
But, when I heard him so far wide,
I then approached and replied,
Saying this: that this indulgence,
Having the foresaid penitence,
Dischargeth man of all offence
With much more profit than this pretence.
I ask but twopence at the most,
Iwis, this is not very great cost,
And from all pain, without despair, 350
My soul for his—keep even his chair,
And when he dieth he may be sure
To come to heaven, even at pleasure.
And more than heaven he cannot get,
How far soever he list to jet.
Then is his pain more than his wit
To walk to heaven, since he may sit!
Sir, as we were in this contention,
In came this daw with his invention,
[*Points to the* Pothecary.
Reviling us, himself avaunting, 360

330 use] are accustomed. 351 keep . . . chair] he may even sit at his ease. 355 jet] sally forth. 359 daw] dolt.

That all the souls to heaven ascending
Are most bound to the pothecary,
Because he helpeth most men to die;
Before which death he sayeth, indeed,
No soul in heaven can have his meed.
Ped. Why, do pothecaries kill men?
Pot. By God, men say so now and then!
Ped. And I thought ye would not have mist
To make men live as long as ye list.
Pot. As long as we list? Nay, long as they can! 370
Ped. So might we live without you than.
Pot. Yea, but yet it is necessary
For to have a pothecary;
For when ye feel your conscience ready,
I can send you to heaven quickly.
Wherefore, concerning our matter here,
Above these twain I am best, clear.
And, if ye list to take me so,
I am content you, and no mo,
Shall be our judge as in this case, 380
Which of us three shall take the best place.
Ped. I neither will judge the best nor worst;
For, be ye blest or be ye curst,
Ye know it is no whit my sleight
To be a judge in matters of weight.
It behoveth no pedlars nor proctors
To take on them judgement as doctors.
But if your minds be only set
To work for soul's health, ye be well met,
For each of you somewhat doth show 390
That souls toward heaven by you do grow.
Then, if ye can so well agree
To continue together all three,
And all you three obey one will,
Then all your minds ye may fulfil:
As, if ye came all to one man

384 sleight] skill. 386 proctors] *probably here* alms-collectors.

Who should go pilgrimage more than he can,
[*To the* Palmer.
In that ye, palmer, as debite,
May clearly discharge him, perdie;
[*To the* Pardoner.
And for all other sins, once had contrition, 400
Your pardons giveth him full remission;
[*To the* Pothecary.
And then ye, master pothecary,
May send him to heaven by-and-by.
Pot. If he taste this box nigh about the prime,
By the Mass, he is in heaven ere evensong time!
My craft is such that I can right well
Send my friends to heaven and myself to hell.
But, sirs, mark this man, for he is wise
Who could devise such a device;
For if we three may be as one, 410
Then be we Lords every one;
Between us all could not be missed
To save the souls of whom we list.
But, for good order, at a word,
Twain of us must wait on the third;
And unto that I do agree,
For both you twain shall wait on me!
Pard. What chance is this that such an elf
Command two knaves, beside himself?
Nay, nay, my friend, that will not be; 420
I am too good to wait on thee!
Palm. By Our Lady, and I would be loth
To wait on the better of you both!
Ped. Yet be ye sure, for all this doubt,
This waiting must be brought about.
Men cannot prosper, wilfully led;

398 debite] *a corruption of* deputy. 403 by-and-by] immediately. 404 the prime] the service for the first hour of the day. 418 What chance . . . elf] What a misfortune that such a poor devil should. 419 knaves] servants.

All thing decayeth where is no head.
Wherefore, doubtless, mark what I say:
To one of you three twain must obey;
And, since ye cannot agree in voice — 430
Who shall be head, there is no choice
But to devise some manner thing
Wherein ye all be like cunning;
And in the same who can do best,
The other twain to make them prest
In every thing of his intent
Wholly to be at commandment.
And now have I found one mastery
That ye can do indifferently,
And is neither selling nor buying, — 440
But even only very lying!
And all ye three can lie as well
As can the falsest devil in hell.
And, though afore ye heard me grudge
In greater matters to be your judge,
Yet in lying I can some skill;
And, if I shall be judge, I will.
And, be ye sure, without flattery,
Where my conscience findeth the mastery,
There shall my judgement strait be found, — 450
Though I might win a thousand pound.

Palm. Sir, for lying, though I can do it,
Yet am I loth for to go to it.

Ped. [*To the* Palmer.] Ye have not cause to fear to be bold,
For ye may be here uncontrolled.

[*To the* Pardoner.

And ye in this have good advantage,
For lying is your common usage.

[*To the* Pothecary.

435 prest] *see* l. 296. 438 mastery] art. 439 indifferently] equally. 449 Where . . . mastery] Where I conscientiously find the superiority. 450 strait] strict, impartial. 455 uncontrolled] uncontradicted.

And you in lying be well sped,
For all your craft doth stand in falsehead.

[*To all three.*

Ye need not care who shall begin, 460
For each of you may hope to win.
Now speak, all three, even as ye find:
Be ye agreed to follow my mind?

Palm. Yea, by my troth, I am content.

Pard. Now, in good faith, and I assent.

Pot. If I denied, I were a noddy,
For all is mine, by God's body!

[*Here the* Pothecary *hoppeth.*

Palm. Here were a hopper to hop for the ring!
But, sir, this gear goeth not by hopping.

Pot. Sir, in this hopping I will hop so well 470
That my tongue shall hop as well as my heel;
Upon which hopping I hope, and not doubt it,
To hope so that ye shall hope without it.

Palm. Sir, I will neither boast nor brawl,
But take such fortune as may fall;
And, if ye win this mastery,
I will obey you quietly.
And sure I think that quietness
In any man is great riches,
In any manner company, 480
To rule or be ruled indifferently.

Pard. By that boast thou seemest a beggar indeed.
What can thy quietness help us at need?
If we should starve, thou hast not, I think,
One penny to buy us one pot of drink.
Nay, if riches might rule the roast,
Behold what cause I have to boast!

[*He opens his pack.*

Lo, here be pardons half a dozen.
For ghostly riches they have no cozen;
And, moreover, to me they bring 490

481 indifferently] equally. 489 ghostly] spiritual.

Sufficient succour for my living.
And here be relics of such a kind
As in this world no man can find.
Kneel down, all three, and, when ye leave kissing,
Who list to offer shall have my blissing!
Friends, here shall ye see even anone
Of All-Hallows the blessed jaw-bone,
Kiss it hardily, with good devotion!
Pot. This kiss shall bring us much promotion.
Fogh! by Saint Saviour, I never kissed a worse! 500
Ye were as good kiss All-Hallows' arse!
For, by All-Hallows, methinketh
That All-Hallows' breath stinketh.
Palm. Ye judge All-Hallows' breath unknown;
If any breath stink, it is your own.
Pot. I know mine own breath from All-Hallows',
Or else it were time to kiss the gallows.
Pard. Nay, sirs, behold, here may ye see
The great-toe of the Trinity.
Who to this toe any money vow'th, 510
And once may roll it in his mouth,
All his life after, I undertake,
He shall be rid of the tooth-ache.
Pot. I pray you, turn that relic about!
Either the Trinity had the gout,
Or else, because it is three toes in one,
God made it much as three toes alone.
Pard. Well, let that pass, and look upon this;
Here is a relic that doth not miss
To help the least as well as the most. 520
This is a buttock-bone of Pentecost!
Pot. By Christ, and yet, for all your boast,
This relic hath beshitten the roast!
Pard. Mark well this relic—here is a whipper!
My friends, unfeigned, here is a slipper
Of one of the Seven Sleepers, be sure.

498 hardily] assuredly. 524 a whipper] one that beats everything.

Doubtless this kiss shall do you great pleasure,
For all these two days it shall so ease you
That none other savours shall displease you.
Pot. All these two days! Nay, all this two year! 530
For all the savours that may come here
Can be no worse; for, at a word,
One of the Seven Sleepers trod in a turd.
Ped. Sir, methinketh your devotion is but small.
Pard. Small? Marry, methinketh he hath none at all!
Pot. What the devil care I what ye think?
Shall I praise relics when they stink?
Pard. Here is an eye-tooth of the Great Turk.
Whose eyes be once set on this piece of work
May haply lose part of his eyesight, 540
But not all till he be blind outright.
Pot. Whatsoever any other man see'th,
I have no devotion to Turks' teeth;
For, although I never saw a greater,
Yet methinketh I have seen many better.
Pard. Here is a box full of humble-bees
That stung Eve as she sat on her knees
Tasting the fruit to her forbidden.
Who kisseth the bees within this hidden
Shall have as much pardon, of right, 550
As for any relic he kissed this night.
Palm. Sir, I will kiss them, with all my heart.
Pot. Kiss them again, and take my part,
For I am not worthy—nay, let be!
Those bees that stung Eve shall not sting me!
Pard. Good friends, I have yet herein this glass,
Which on the drink at the wedding was
Of Adam and Eve undoubtedly.
If ye honour this relic devoutly,
Although ye thirst no whit the less, 560
Yet shall ye drink the more, doubtless,
After which drinking ye shall be as meet
To stand on your head as on your feet.
Pot. Yea, marry, now I can ye thank!

In presence of this the rest be blank.
Would God this relic had come rather!
Kiss that relic well, good father!
Such is the pain that ye palmers take
To kiss the pardon-bowl for the drink's sake.
O holy yeast, that looketh full sour and stale, 570
For God's body help me to a cup of ale!
The more I behold thee, the more I thirst;
The oftener I kiss thee, more like to burst!
But since I kiss thee so devoutly,
Hire me, and help me with drink till I die!
What, so much praying and so little speed?
Pard. Yea, for God knoweth when it is need
To send folks drink; but, by Saint Anthony,
I ween he hath sent you too much already.
Pot. If I have never the more for thee, 580
Then be the relics no riches to me,
Nor to thyself, except they be
More beneficial than I can see.
Richer is one box of this triacle
Than all thy relics that do no miracle.
If thou hadst prayed but half so much to me
As I have prayed to thy relics and thee,
Nothing concerning mine occupation
But straight should have wrought in operation.
And, as in value I pass you an ace, 590
Here lieth much riches in little space—
I have a box of rhubarb here,
Which is as dainty as it is dear.
So help me God and halidom,
Of this I would not give a dram
To the best friend I have in England's ground,
Though he would give me twenty pound;
For, though the stomach do it abhor,
It purgeth you clean from the color,

566 rather] sooner. 584 triacle] balsam.
590 pass you an ace] surpass you by the value of an ace.
599 color] choler, bile.

And maketh your stomach sore to walter, 600
That ye shall never come to the halter.
Ped. Then is that medicine a sovereign thing
To preserve a man from hanging.
Pot. If ye will taste but this crumb that ye see,
If ever ye be hanged, never trust me!
Here have I diapompholicus—
A special ointment, as doctors discuss;
For a fistula or a canker
This ointment is even sheet-anchor,
For this medicine helpeth one and other, 610
Or bringeth them in case that they need no other.
Here is syrapus de Byzansis—
A little thing is enough of this,
For even the weight of one scruple
Shall make you strong as a cripple.
Here be other: as, diosfialios,
Diagalanga, and sticados,
Blanka manna, diospoliticon,
Mercury sublime, and metridaticon,
Pelitory, and arsefetita, 620
Cassy, and colloquintita.
These be the things that break all strife
Between man's sickness and his life.
From all pain these shall you deliver,
And set you even at rest for ever!
Here is a medicine—no more like the same
Which commonly is called thus by name
Alikakabus or alkakengy—
A goodly thing for dog's that be mangy.
Such be these medicines that I can 630
Help a dog as well as a man.
Not one thing here particularly
But worketh universally,
For it doth me as much good when I sell it
As all the buyers that taste it or smell it.
Now, since my medicines be so special,

600 walter] be upset.

And in operation so general,
And ready to work whensoever they shall,
So that in riches I am principal,
If any reward may entreat ye, 640
I beseech your maship be good to me,
And ye shall have a box of marmalade
So fine that ye may dig it with a spade.

Ped. Sir, I thank you; but your reward
Is not the thing that I regard.
I must, and will, be indifferent:
Wherefore proceed in your intent.

Pot. Now, if I wist this wish no sin,
I would to God I might begin!

Pard. I am content that thou lie first. 650

Palm. Even so am I; and say thy worst!
Now let us hear of all thy lies
The greatest lie thou mayst devise,
And in the fewest words thou can.

Pot. Forsooth, ye be an honest man.

Palm. There said ye much! but yet no lie.

Pard. Now lie ye both, by Our Lady!
Thou liest in boast of his honesty,
And he hath lied in affirming thee.

Pot. If we both lie, and ye say true, 660
Then of these lies your part adieu!
And if ye win, make none avaunt;
For ye are sure of one ill servaunt.

[*To the* Palmer.

Ye may perceive by the words he gave
He taketh your maship but for a knave.
But who told true, or lied indeed,
That will I know ere we proceed.
Sir, after that I first began
To praise you for an honest man,
When ye affirmed it for no lie— 670
Now, by our faith, speak even truly—
Thought ye your affirmation true?

641 maship] mastership. 646 indifferent] impartial.

Palm. Yea, marry, aye! for I would ye knew
I think myself an honest man.
Pot. What, thought ye in the contrary than?
Pard. In that I said the contrary,
I think from truth I did not vary.
Pot. And what of my words?
Pard. I thought ye lied.
Pot. And so thought I, by God that died!
Now have you twain each for himself laid 680
That none hath lied aught, but both true said;
And of us twain none hath denied,
But both affirmed, that I have lied:
Now since ye both your truth confess,
And that we both my lie so witness
That twain of us three in one agree—
And that the liar the winner must be—
Who could provide such evidence
As I have done in this pretence? [*To the* Pedlar.
Methinketh this matter sufficient 690
To cause you to give judgement,
And to give me the mastery,
For ye perceive these knaves cannot lie.
Palm. Though neither of us as yet had lied,
Yet what we can do is untried;
For yet we have devised nothing,
But answered you and given hearing.
Ped. Therefore I have devised one way
Whereby all three your minds may say:
For each of you one tale shall tell; 700
And which of you telleth most marvel
And most unlike to be true,
Shall most prevail, whatever ensue.
Pot. If ye be set in marvelling,
Then shall ye hear a marvellous thing;
And though, indeed, all be not true,
Yet sure the most part shall be new.
I did a cure, no longer ago
But *Anno Domini millesimo*,

On a woman, young and so fair 710
That never have I seen a gayer.
God save all women from that likeness!
This wanton had the falling sickness,
Which by descent came lineally,
For her mother had it naturally.
Wherefore, this woman to recure
It was more hard, ye may be sure.
But, though I boast my craft is such
That in such things I can do much,
How oft she fell were much to report; 720
But her head so giddy and her heels so short
That, with the twinkling of an eye,
Down would she fall even by and by.
But, ere she would arise again,
I showed much practice, much to my pain;
For the tallest man within this town
Should not with ease have broken her sown.
Although for life I did not doubt her,
Yet did I take more pain about her
Than I would take with my own sister; 730
Sir, at the last I gave her a glister,
I thrust a tampion in her tewel
And bade her keep it for a jewel.
But I knew it so heavy to carry
That I was sure it would not tarry;
For where gunpowder is once fired
The tampion will no longer be hired.
Which was well seen in time of this chance;
For, when I had charged this ordinance,
Suddenly, as it had thundered, 740
Even at a clap loosed her bombard.
Now mark, for here beginneth the revel:
This tampion flew ten long mile level,

716 recure] recover. 723 by and by] at once. 726 tallest] doughtiest. 727 sown] swoon. 731 glister] *see* l. 176. 732 tampion] plug. tewel] a vent, or opening, here the anus. 737 hired] employed.

To a fair castle of lime and stone—
For strength I know not such a one—
Which stood upon an hill full high,
At foot whereof a river ran by,
So deep, till chance had it forbidden,
Well might the Regent there have ridden.
But when this tampion on this castle light, 750
It put the walls so far to flight
That down they came each upon other,
No stone left standing, by God's Mother!
But rolled down so fast the hill
In such a number, and so did fill,
From bottom to brim, from shore to shore,
This foresaid river, so deep before,
That who list now to walk thereto,
May wade it over and wet no shoe.
So was this castle laid wide open 760
That every man might see the token.
But—in a good hour may these words be spoken!—
After the tampion on the walls was wroken,
And piece by piece in pieces broken,
And she delivered with such violence
Of all her inconvenience,
I left her in good health and lust,
And so she doth continue, I trust!

Ped. Sir, in your cure I can nothing tell;
But to our purpose ye have said well. 770

Pard. Well, sir, then mark what I can say!
I have been a pardoner many a day,
And done greater cures ghostly
Than ever he did bodily;
Namely, this one which ye shall hear,
Of one departed within this seven year,
A friend of mine, and likewise I

749 the Regent] one of Henry VIII's largest ships of war. 751 walls] *conjectural for* castels *in the early texts.* 765 she] the pothecary's patient. 773 ghostly] spiritually. 775 Namely] especially.

To her again was as friendly—
Who fell so sick so suddenly
That dead she was even by-and-by, 780
And never spake with priest nor clark,
Nor had no whit of this holy wark,
For I was thence, it could not be;
Yet heard, I say, she asked for me.
But when I bethought me how this chanced,
And that I have to heaven advanced
So many souls to me but strangers
And could not keep my friend from dangers,
But she to die so dangerously
For her soul's health especially, 790
That was the thing that grieved me so
That nothing could release my woe
Till I had tried even out of hand
In what estate her soul did stand.
For which trial, short tale to make,
I took this journey for her sake.
Give ear, for here beginneth the story!
From hence I went to purgatory,
And took with me this gear in my fist,
Whereby I may do there what I list. 800
I knocked, and was let in quickly;
But, Lord, how low the souls made curtsy!
And I to every soul again
Did give a beck them to retain,
And axed them this question than:
If that the soul of such a woman
Did late among them there appear.
Whereto they said she came not here.
Then feared I much it was not well.
Alas! thought I, she is in hell! 810
For with her life I was so acquainted
That sure I thought she was not sainted.
With this it chanced me to sneeze;
'Christ help!' quoth a soul that lay for his fees.

814 lay . . . fees] lay in purgatory for want of fees.

'Those words,' quoth I, 'thou shalt not lees!'
Then with these pardons of all degrees
I paid his toll, and set him so quite
That straight to heaven he took his flight.
And I from thence to hell that night,
To help this woman, if I might, 820
Not as who saith by authority,
But by the way of entreaty.
And first to the devil that kept the gate
I came, and spake after this rate:
'All hail, sir devil!' and made low curtsy.
'Welcome!' quoth he, this smilingly:
He knew me well, and I at last
Remembered him since long time past,
For, as good hap would have it chance,
This devil and I were of old acquaintance, 830
For oft in the play of Corpus Christi
He hath played the devil at Coventry.
By his acquaintance and my behaviour
He showed to me right friendly favour.
And—to make my return the shorter—
I said to this devil: 'Good master porter,
For all old love, if it lie in your power,
Help me to speak with my lord and your.'
'Be sure,' quoth he, 'no tongue can tell
What time thou couldest have come so well, 840
For this day Lucifer fell,
Which is our festival in hell.
Nothing unreasonable craved this day
That shall in hell have any nay.
But yet beware thou come not in
Till time thou may thy passport win.
Wherefore stand still, and I will wit
If I can get thy safe-conduit.'

815 lees] lose, find vain. 817 quite] quit of obligations. 831–2 the play of Corpus Christi . . . at Coventry] the miracle play acted at Coventry on the festival of Corpus Christi. 844 nay] denial.

He tarried not, but shortly gat it,
Under seal, and the devil's hand at it, 850
In ample wise, as ye shall hear.
Thus it began: 'Lucifer,
By the power of God chief devil of hell,
To all the devils that there do dwell,
And every of them, we send greeting,
Under straight charge and commanding,
That they aiding and assistant be
To such a pardoner'—and named me—
'So that he may at liberty
Pass safe without his jeopardy 860
Till that he be from us extinct
And clearly out of hell's precinct.
And, his pardons to keep safeguard,
We will they lie in the porter's ward.
Given in the furnace of our palace,
In our high court of matters of malice,
Such a day and year of our reign.'
'God save the devil!' quoth I, 'for plain,
I trust this writing to be sure.'
'Then put thy trust,' quoth he, 'in ure, 870
Since thou art sure to take no harm.'
This devil and I walked arm in arm,
So far till he had brought me thither
Where all the devils of hell togither
Stood in array in such apparel
As for that day there meetly fell:
Their horns well gilt, their claws full clean,
Their tails well kempt, and, as I ween,
With sothery butter their bodies anointed—
I never saw devils so well appointed. 880
The master devil sat in his jacket,
And all the souls were playing at racket.
None other rackets they had in hand

861 extinct] passed away. 870 ure] use, practice.
878 kempt] combed. 879 sothery] *the meaning is uncertain. Perhaps a formation from* soot = *sweet.*

Save every soul a good firebrand;
Wherewith they played so prettily
That Lucifer laughed merrily,
And all the residue of the fiends
Did laugh full well together like friends.
But of my friend I saw no whit,
Nor durst not axe for her as yet. 890
Anon all this rout was brought in silence,
And I by an usher brought in presence.
Then to Lucifer low as I could
I knelt. Which he so well allowed
That thus he becked; and, by Saint Anthony,
He smiled on me well-favouredly,
Bending his brows, as broad as barn-durs,
Shaking his ears, as rugged as burs,
Rolling his eyes, as round as two bushels,
Flashing the fire out of his nose-thrills, 900
Gnashing his teeth so vaingloriously
That methought time to fall to flattery.
Wherewith I told, as I shall tell:
'O pleasant picture ! O prince of hell!
Featured in fashion abominable!
And since that it is inestimable
For me to praise thee worthily,
I leave off praise, unworthy
To give thee praise, beseeching thee
To hear my suit, and then to be 910
So good to grant the thing I crave.
And, to be short, this would I have—
The soul of one which hither is flitted
Delivered hence, and to me remitted.
And in this doing, though all be not quit,
Yet some part I shall deserve it,
As thus: I am a pardoner,
And over souls, as a controller,
Throughout the earth my power doth stand,
Where many a soul lieth on my hand, 920

895 becked] nodded. 915 quit] made even.

That speed in matters as I use them,
As I receive them or refuse them;
Whereby, what time thy pleasure is
Ye shall require any part of this,
The least devil here that can come thither
Shall choose a soul and bring him hither.'
'Now,' quoth the devil, 'we are well pleased!
What is his name thou wouldest have eased?'
'Nay,' quoth I, 'be it good or evil,
My coming is for a she devil.' 930
'What callest her?' quoth he, 'thou whoreson!'
'Forsooth,' quoth I, 'Margery Coorson.'
'Now, by our honour,' said Lucifer,
'No devil in hell shall withhold her!
And if thou wouldest have twenty mo,
Were not for justice, they should go.
For all we devils within this den
Have more to do with two women
Than with all the charge we have beside.
Wherefore, if thou our friend will be tried, 940
Apply thy pardons to women so
That unto us there come no mo.'
To do my best I promised by oath.
Which I have kept; for, as the faith go'th,
At these days to heaven I do procure
Ten women to one man, be sure.
Then of Lucifer my leave I took,
And straight unto the master cook.
I was had into the kitchen,
For Margery's office was therein. 950
All things handled there discreetly,
For every soul beareth office meetly,
Which might be seen to see her sit
So busily turning of the spit;
For many a spit here hath she turned,
And many a good spit hath she burned,
And many a spit full hot hath toasted
Before the meat could be half roasted.

And, ere the meat were half roasted indeed,
I took her then from the spit for speed. 960
But when she saw this brought to pass,
To tell the joy wherein she was,
And of all the devils, for joy how they
Did roar at her delivery,
And how the chains in hell did ring,
And how all the souls therein did sing,
And how we were brought to the gate,
And how we took our leave thereat—
Be sure lack of time suffereth nat
To rehearse the twentieth part of that! 970
Wherefore, this tale to conclude briefly,
This woman thanked me chiefly
That she was rid of this endless death;
And so we departed on Newmarket Heath.
And if that any man do mind her,
Who list to seek her, there shall he find her!
Ped. Sir, ye have sought her wondrous well;
And, where ye found her, as ye tell,
To hear the chance ye found in hell,
I find ye were in great parell. 980
Palm. His tale is all much parellous;
But part is much more marvellous.
As where he said the devils complain
That women put them to such pain
By their conditions so crooked and crabbed,
Frowardly fashioned, so wayward and wrabbed,
So far in division, and stirring such strife,
That all the devils be weary of their life!
This in effect he told for truth;
Whereby much marvel to me ensu'th, 990
That women in hell such shrews can be,
And here so gentle, as far as I see.
Yet have I seen many a mile,
And many a woman in the while—

974 departed] separated. 980 parell] peril.
986 wrabbed] perverse.

Not one good city, town, nor borough
In Christendom but I have been thorough,
And this I would ye should understand:
I have seen women five hundred thousand
Wives and widows, maids and married,
And oft with them have long time tarried, 1000
Yet in all places where I have been,
Of all the women that I have seen,
I never saw, nor knew, in my conscience,
Any one woman out of patience.

Pot. By the Mass, there is a great lie!

Pard. I never heard a greater, by Our Lady!

Ped. A greater? nay, know ye any so great?

Palm. Sir, whether that I lose or get,
For my part, judgement shall be prayed.

Pard. And I desire as he hath said. 1010

Pot. Proceed, and ye shall be obeyed.

Ped. Then shall not judgement be delayed.
Of all these three, if each man's tale
In Paul's Churchyard were set on sale
In some man's hand that hath the sleight,
He should sure sell these tales by weight.
For, as they weigh, so be they worth.
But which weigheth best? to that now forth!
[*To the* Pothecary.
Sir, all the tale that ye did tell
I bear in mind; [*to the* Pardoner] and yours as well; 1020
And, as ye saw the matter meetly,
So lied ye both well and discreetly.
Yet were your lies with the least, trust me!
[*To the* Pothecary.
For, if ye had said ye had made flee
Ten tampions, out of ten women's tails,
Ten times ten mile, to ten castles or jails,

1009 prayed] asked for. 1014 Paul's Churchyard] Booksellers' Row. 1015 the sleight] the skill of the trade.

And fill ten rivers, ten times so deep
As ten of that which your castle stones did keep—
[*To the* Pardoner.
Or if ye ten times had bodily
Fet ten souls out of purgatory, 1030
And ten times so many out of hell,
Yet, by these ten bones, I could right well
Ten times sooner all that have believed
Than the tenth part of that he hath meved.

Pot. Two knaves before one lacketh two knaves of five;
Then one, and then one, and both knaves alive;
Then two, and then two, and three at a cast;
Thou knave, and thou knave, and thou knave, at last! [*To the* Pedlar.
Nay, knave, if ye try me by number,
I will as knavishly you accumber. 1040
Your mind is all on your privy tithe,
For all in ten methinketh your wit lithe.
Now ten times I beseech Him that high sits
Thy wife's ten commandments may search thy five wits;
Then ten of my turds in ten of thy teeth,
And ten on thy nose, which every man see'th.
And twenty times ten this wish I wold,
That thou hadest been hanged at ten year old!
For thou goest about to make me a slave.
I will thou know that I am a gentleman, knave! 1050
[*Points to the* Pardoner.
And here is another shall take my part.

Pard. Nay, first I beshrew your knave's heart
Ere I take part in your knavery!

1028 keep] hold back. 1030 Fet] Fetched.
1032 ten bones] ten fingers. 1034 he] the Palmer.
meved] moved, propounded. 1037 cast] reckoning.
1040 accumber] overwhelm. 1042 lithe] lieth.
1044 Thy wife's ten commandments] Thy wife's ten finger-nails.

I will speak fair, by Our Lady! [*To the* Pedlar.
Sir, I beseech your maship to be
As good as ye can be to me.
Ped. I would be glad to do you good,
And him also, be he never so wood.
But doubt you not I will now do
The thing my conscience leadeth me to. 1060
Both your tales I take far impossible,
Yet take I his farther incredible.
Not only the thing itself alloweth it,
But also the boldness thereof avoweth it.
[*To the* Pothecary.
I know not where your tale to try,
[*To the* Pardoner.
Nor yours, but in hell or purgatory;
But his boldness hath faced a lie
That may be tried even in this company,
As, if ye list, to take this order:
Among the women in this border, 1070
Take three of the youngest and three of the oldest,
Three of the hottest and three of the coldest,
Three of the wisest and three of the shrewdest,
Three of the chastest and three of the lewdest,
Three of the lowest and three of the highest,
Three of the farthest and three of the nighest,
Three of the fairest and three of the maddest,
Three of the foulest and three of the saddest—
And when all these threes be had asunder,
Of each three, two, justly by number, 1080
Shall be found shrews, except this fall,
That ye hap to find them shrews all!
Himself for truth all this doth know,
And oft hath tried some of this row;
And yet he sweareth, by his conscience,
He never saw woman break patience!

1055 maship] mastership. 1058 wood] mad. 1062 his] the Palmer's; *so in* l. 1067. 1063 alloweth] proves. 1078 saddest] most serious.

Wherefore, considered with true intent,
His lie to be so evident,
And to appear so evidently
That both you affirmed it a lie, 1090
And that my conscience so deeply
So deep hath sought this thing to try,
And tried it with mind indifferent,
Thus I award, by way of judgement—
Of all the lies ye all have spent
His lie to be most excellent.

Palm. Sir, though ye were bound of equity
To do as ye have done to me,
Yet do I thank you of your pain,
And will requite some part again. 1100

Pard. Marry, sir, ye can no less do
But thank him as much as it cometh to.
And so will I do for my part: [*To the* Pedlar.
Now a vengeance on thy knave's heart!
I never knew pedlar a judge before,
Nor never will trust peddling-knave more!
[*The* Pothecary *begins to curtsy to the* Palmer.
What doest thou there, thou whoreson noddy?

Pot. By the Mass, learn to make curtsy!
Curtsy before, and curtsy behind him,
And then on each side—the devil blind him! 1110
Nay, when I have it perfectly,
Ye shall have the devil and all of curtsy!
But it is not soon learned, brother,
One knave to make curtsy to another.
Yet, when I am angry, that is the worst,
I shall call my master knave at the first.

Palm. Then would some master perhaps clout ye!
But, as for me, ye need not doubt ye;
For I had liefer be without ye
Than have such business about ye. 1120

Pard. So help me God, so were ye better!
What, should a beggar be a jetter?

1122 jetter] swaggerer.

It were no whit your honesty
To have us twain jet after ye.
Pot. Sir, be ye sure he telleth you true.
If we should wait, this would ensue:
It would be said—trust me at a word—
Two knaves made curtsy to the third.
Ped. [*To the* Palmer.] Now, by my troth, to speak my mind,
Since they be so loth to be assigned, 1130
To let them loose I think it best,
And so shall ye live best in rest.
Palm. Sir, I am not on them so fond
To compel them to keep their bond.
[*To the* Pothecary *and* Palmer.
And, since ye list not to wait on me,
I clearly of waiting discharge ye.
Pard. Marry, sir, I heartily thank you!
Pot. And I likewise, I make God avow!
Ped. Now be ye all even as ye begun;
No man hath lost, nor no man hath won. 1140
Yet in the debate wherewith ye began,
By way of advice I will speak as I can:
[*To the* Palmer.
I do perceive that pilgrimage
Is chief the thing ye have in usage;
Whereto, in effect, for love of Christ
Ye have, or should have, been enticed.
And who so doth, with such intent,
Doth well declare his time well spent.
[*To the* Pardoner.
And so do ye in your pretence,
If ye procure thus indulgence 1150
Unto your neighbours charitably
For love of them in God only.
All this may be right well applied
To show you both well occupied;

1126 wait] act as attendants. 1130 assigned] appointed to give service.

For, though ye walk not both one way,
Yet, walking thus, this dare I say,
That both your walks come to one end.
And so for all that do pretend,
By aid of God's grace, to ensue
Any manner kind of virtue: 1160
As, some great alms for to give,
Some in wilful poverty to live,
Some to make highways and such other warks,
And some to maintain priests and clarks
To sing and pray for soul departed—
These, with all other virtues well marked,
Although they be of sundry kinds,
Yet be they not used with sundry minds;
But, as God only doth all those move,
So every man, only for His love, 1170
With love and dread obediently
Worketh in these virtues uniformly.
Thus every virtue, if we list to scan,
Is pleasant to God and thankful to man;
And who that by grace of the Holy Ghost
To any one virtue is moved most,
That man, by that grace, that one apply,
And therein serve God most plentifully!
Yet not that one so far wide to wrest,
So liking the same to mislike the rest; 1180
For who so wresteth his work is in vain.
And even in that case I perceive you twain,
Liking your virtue in such wise
That each other's virtue you do despise.
Who walketh this way for God would find him,
The farther they seek him, the farther behind him.
One kind of virtue to despise another
Is like as the sister might hang the brother.
Pot. For fear lest such perils to me might fall,
I thank God I use no virtue at all! 1190

1159 ensue] follow. 1179 wide to wrest] over-strain.

Ped. That is of all the very worst way!
For more hard it is, as I have heard say,
To begin virtue where none is pretended
Than, where it is begun, the abuse to be mended.
Howbeit, ye be not all to begin;
One sign of virtue ye are entered in,
As this I suppose ye did say true,
In that ye said ye use no virtue;
In the which words, I dare well report,
Ye are well beloved of all this sort, 1200
By your railing here openly
At pardons and relics so lewdly.
Pot. In that I think my fault not great;
For all that he hath I know counterfeit.
Ped. For his, and all other that ye know feigned,
Ye be neither counselled nor constrained
To any such thing in any such case
To give any reverence in any such place;
But where ye doubt the truth, not knowing,
Believing the best, good may be growing. 1210
In judging the best, no harm at the lest,
In judging the worst, no good at the best.
But best in these things, it seemeth to me,
To take no judgement upon ye;
But, as the Church doth judge or take them,
So do ye receive or forsake them;
And so, be sure, ye cannot err,
But may be a fruitful follower.
Pot. Go ye before, and, as I am true man,
I will follow as fast as I can. 1220
Pard. And so will I; for he hath said so well,
Reason would we should follow his counsel.
[*To the audience.*
Palm. Then to our reason God give us His grace,
That we may follow with faith so firmly
His commandments that we may purchase

1193 pretended] purposed. 1195 not all to begin] not an entire beginner.

His love, and so consequently
To believe his Church fast and faithfully;
So that we may, according to his promise,
Be kept out of error in any wise.
And all that hath 'scaped us here by negligence, 1230
We clearly revoke and forsake it.
To pass the time in this without offence
Was the cause why the maker did make it;
And so we humbly beseech you take it;
Beseeching Our Lord to prosper you all
In the faith of his Church Universal!

Imprinted at London in Fleet Street at
the sign of the George by William
Middleton.

FINIS.

RALPH ROISTER DOISTER

A COMEDY

BY

NICHOLAS UDALL

Dramatis Personae

Ralph Roister Doister.
Matthew Merrygreek.
Gawyn Goodluck, *affianced to Dame Custance.*
Tristram Trusty, *his friend.*
Dobinet Doughty } *servants to Ralph Roister Doister.*
Harpax }

Tom Truepenny, *servant to Dame Custance.*
Sim Suresby, *servant to Goodluck.*
Scrivener.
Dame Christian Custance, *a widow.*
Margery Mumblecrust, *her nurse.*
Tibet Talkapace } *her maidens.*
Annot Alyface }

RALPH ROISTER DOISTER

THE PROLOGUE

What creature is in health, either young or old,
But some mirth with modesty will be glad to use—
As we in this interlude shall now unfold?
Wherein all scurrility we utterly refuse,
Avoiding such mirth wherein is abuse;
Knowing nothing more commendable for a man's recreation
Than mirth which is used in an honest fashion.

For mirth prolongeth life, and causeth health,
Mirth recreates our spirits, and voideth pensiveness,
Mirth increaseth amity, not hindering our wealth; 10
Mirth is to be used both of more and less,
Being mixed with virtue in decent comeliness—
As we trust no good nature can gainsay the same.
Which mirth we intend to use, avoiding all blame.

The wise poets long time heretofore,
Under merry comedies secrets did declare,
Wherein was contained very virtuous lore,
With mysteries and forewarnings very rare.
Such to write neither Plautus nor Terence did spare,
Which among the learned at this day bears the bell: 20
These with such other therein did excel.

Our comedy or interlude which we intend to play
Is named 'Roister Doister', indeed,
Which against the vain-glorious doth inveigh,
Whose humour the roisting sort continually doth feed.
Thus by your patience, we intend to proceed
In this our interlude by God's leave and grace,
And here I take my leave for a certain space.

FINIS

9 voideth] gets rid of. 20 bears the bell] is the bell-wether, takes the lead. 25 roisting] roistering.

ACT I

SCENE I

Enter Matthew Merrygreek

As long liveth the merry man, they say,
As doth the sorry man, and longer by a day;
Yet the grasshopper, for all his summer piping,
Starveth in winter with hungry griping.
Therefore another said saw doth men advise
That they be together both merry and wise.
This lesson must I practise, or else ere long,
With me, Matthew Merrygreek, it will be wrong.
Indeed, men so call me; for, by Him that us bought,
Whatever chance betide, I can take no thought; 10
Yet wisdom would that I did myself bethink
Where to be provided this day of meat and drink;
For know ye, that, for all this merry note of mine,
He might appose me now that should ask where I dine.
My living lieth here, and there, of God's grace
Sometime with this good man, sometime in that place,
Sometime Lewis Loiterer biddeth me come near;
Somewhiles Watkin Waster maketh us good cheer;
Sometime Davy Diceplayer, when he hath well cast,
Keepeth revel-rout as long as it will last; 20
Sometimes Tom Titivile maketh us a feast;
Sometime with Sir Hugh Pye I am a bidden guest,
Sometime at Nicol Neverthrive's I get a sop,
Sometime I am feasted with Bryan Blinkinsop,
Sometime I hang on Hankyn Hoddydody's sleeve,
But this day, on Ralph Roister Doister's, by his leave.
For truly of all men he is my chief banker
Both for meat and money, and my chief sheet-anchor.

9 Him that us bought] our Redeemer. 14 appose] put in a quandary. 21 Titivile] originally, as Tutiville, the name of a devil in Towneley Miracle cycle.

For, sooth Roister Doister in that he doth say,
And require what ye will; ye shall have no nay. 30
But now of Roister Doister somewhat to express,
That ye may esteem him after his worthiness:
In these twenty towns, and seek them throughout,
Is not the like stock whereon to graff a lout.
All the day long is he facing and craking
Of his great acts in fighting and fraymaking:
But, when Roister Doister is put to his proof,
To keep the Queen's peace is more for his behoof.
If any woman smile, or cast on him an eye,
Up is he to the hard ears in love by-and-by! 40
And in all the hot haste must she be his wife,
Else farewell his good days, and farewell his life!
Master Ralph Roister Doister is but dead and gone
Except she on him take some compassion,
Then chief of counsel must be Matthew Merrygreek,
'What if I for marriage to such an one seek?'
Then must I sooth it, whatever it is:
For what he saith or doth cannot be amiss.
Hold up his yea and nay, be his nown white son;
Praise and rouse him well, and ye have his heart
won, 50
For so well liketh he his own fond fashions
That he taketh pride of false commendations.
But such sport have I with him as I would not lese,
Though I should be bound to live with bread and
cheese.
For exalt him, and have him as ye lust, indeed—
Yea, to hold his finger in a hole for a need.
I can, with a word, make him fain or loth;
I can, with as much, make him pleased or wroth;

29 sooth] humour, flatter. 34 graff] graft. 35 facing and craking] swaggering and boasting. 40 to the hard ears] to the very ears. by-and-by] at once. 47 sooth it] assent to it. 49 his nown] his own, *in comic analogy to* my nown *for* mine own. white son] pet, favourite. 51 fond] foolish. 53 lese] lose.

I can, when I will, make him merry and glad,
I can, when me lust, make him sorry and sad; 60
I can set him in hope, and eke in despair;
I can make him speak rough, and make him speak fair.
But I marvel I see him not all this same day;
I will seek him out—But, lo! he cometh this way.
I have yond espied him sadly coming,
And in love, for twenty pound, by his glumming.

SCENE II

Merrygreek. *Enter* Ralph Roister Doister

Roister Doister. Come, death, when thou wilt, I am weary of my life!
Merrygreek. I told you, I, we should woo another wife!
Roister Doister. Why did God make me such a goodly person?
Merrygreek. He is in by the week. We shall have sport anon.
Roister Doister. And where is my trusty friend, Matthew Merrygreek?
Merrygreek. I will make as I saw him not. He doth me seek.
Roister Doister. I have him espied, methinketh; yond is he.
Ho! Matthew Merrygreek, my friend, a word with thee!
Merrygreek. I will not hear him, but make as I had haste.
Farewell, all my good friends! The time away doth waste, 10
And the tide, they say, tarrieth for no man!
Roister Doister. Thou must with thy good counsel help me if thou can.

66 glumming] scowling. 2 you] the audience.
4 in by the week] head over heels in love.

Merrygreek. God keep thee, worshipful Master Roister Doister!
And farewell the lusty Master Roister Doister!
Roister Doister. I must needs speak with thee a word or twain.
Merrygreek. Within a month or two I will be here again.
Negligence in great affairs, ye know, may mar all.
Roister Doister. Attend upon me now, and well reward thee I shall.
Merrygreek. I have take my leave, and the tide is well spent.
Roister Doister. I die except thou help! I pray thee, be content. 20
Do thy part well, now, and ask what thou wilt;
For without thy aid my matter is all spilt.
Merrygreek. Then, to serve your turn, I will some pains take,
And let all mine own affairs alone for your sake.
Roister Doister. My whole hope and trust resteth only in thee.
Merrygreek. Then can ye not do amiss, whatever it be.
Roister Doister. Gramercies, Merrygreek! most bound to thee I am.
Merrygreek. But up with that heart, and speak out like a ram!
Ye speak like a capon that had the cough now:
Be of good cheer! Anon ye shall do well enow. 30
Roister Doister. Upon thy comfort I will all things well handle.
Merrygreek. So, lo! that is a breast to blow out a candle!
But what is this great matter, I would fain know?
We shall find remedy therefore, I trow.
Do ye lack money? Ye know mine old offers;
Ye have always a key to my purse and coffers.
Roister Doister. I thank thee! Had ever man such a friend?
Merrygreek. Ye give unto me; I must needs to you lend.

22 spilt] ruined. 29 capon] cock. 32 breast] breath.

Roister Doister. Nay, I have money plenty all things to discharge.
Merrygreek. That knew I right well when I made offer so large. [*Aside.*
Roister Doister. But it is no such matter.
Merrygreek. What is it than?
Are ye in danger of debt to any man? 41
If ye be, take no thought, nor be not afraid.
Let them hardily take thought how they shall be paid.
Roister Doister. Tut! I owe nought!
Merrygreek. What then? Fear ye imprisonment?
Roister Doister. No.
Merrygreek. No, I wist, ye offend not so to be shent.
But if ye had, the Tower could not you so hold
But to break out at all times ye would be bold.
What is it? Hath any man threatened you to beat?
Roister Doister. What is he that durst have put me in that heat? 50
He that beateth me—by His arms!—shall well find,
That I will not be far from him, nor run behind.
Merrygreek. That thing know all men ever since ye overthrew
The fellow of the lion which Hercules slew.
But what is it, then?
Roister Doister. Of love I make my moan.
Merrygreek. Ah, this foolish love! Wilt ne'er let us alone?
But, because ye were refused the last day,
Ye said ye would ne'er more be entangled that way.
I would meddle no more, since I find all so unkind.
Roister Doister. Yea, but I cannot so put love out of my mind. 60
Merrygreek. But is your love—tell me first, in any wise—
In the way of marriage, or of merchandise?

41 than] then. 44 hardily] surely. 46 shent] disgraced. 51 by His arms!] by God's arms! 57 the last day] yesterday.

If it may otherwise than lawful be found,
Ye get none of my help for a hundred pound.

Roister Doister. No, by my troth; I would have her to my wife.

Merrygreek. Then are ye a good man, and God save your life!
And what, or who is she, with whom ye are in love?

Roister Doister. A woman, whom I know not by what means to move.

Merrygreek. Who is it?

Roister Doister. A woman, yond.

Merrygreek. What is her name?

Roister Doister. Her, yonder.

Merrygreek. Whom?

Roister Doister. Mistress—ah—

Merrygreek. Fie, fie, for shame!
Love ye, and know not whom but 'her, yond', 'a woman'? 71
We shall then get you a wife I cannot tell whan.

Roister Doister. The fair woman that supped with us yesternight;
And I heard her name twice or thrice, and had it right.

Merrygreek. Yea, ye may see ye ne'er take me to good cheer with you;
If ye had, I could have told you her name now.

Roister Doister. I was to blame indeed; but the next time, perchance—
And she dwelleth in this house.

Merrygreek. What! Christian Custance?

Roister Doister. Except I have her to my wife, I shall run mad.

Merrygreek. Nay, unwise perhaps, but I warrant you for mad! 80

Roister Doister. I am utterly dead unless I have my desire.

80 for mad] against madness.

Merrygreek. Where be the bellows that blew this sudden fire?

Roister Doister. I hear she is worth a thousand pound and more.

Merrygreek. Yea, but learn this one lesson of me afore:
An hundred pound of marriage-money, doubtless,
Is ever thirty pound sterling, or somewhat less,
So that her thousand pound, if she be thrifty,
Is much near about two hundred and fifty,
Howbeit, wooers and widows are never poor!

Roister Doister. Is she a widow? I love her better therefore. 90

Merrygreek. But I hear she hath made promise to another.

Roister Doister. He shall go without her, an he were my brother.

Merrygreek. I have heard say—I am right well advised—
That she hath to Gawyn Goodluck promised.

Roister Doister. What is that Gawyn Goodluck?

Merrygreek. A merchant man.

Roister Doister. Shall he speed afore me? Nay, sir, by sweet Saint Anne!
Ah, sir, 'Backare', quoth Mortimer to his sow.
I will have her mine own self, I make God a vow.
For, I tell thee, she is worth a thousand pound!

Merrygreek. Yet a fitter wife for your maship might be found. 100
Such a goodly man as you might get one with land,
Besides pounds of gold a thousand, and a thousand,
And a thousand, and a thousand, and a thousand,
And so to the sum of twenty hundred thousand.
Your most goodly personage is worthy of no less.

Roister Doister. I am sorry God made me so comely, doubtless;
For that maketh me eachwhere so highly favoured,
And all women on me so enamoured.

97 Backare] Back there! 100 maship] mastership.

Merrygreek. 'Enamoured,' quoth you? Have ye spied out that?
Ah, sir, marry, now I see you know what is what. 110
'Enamoured,' ka? Marry, sir, say that again!
But I thought not ye had marked it so plain.

Roister Doister. Yes, eachwhere they gaze all upon me and stare.

Merrygreek. Yea, Malkin, I warrant you as much as they dare.
And ye will not believe what they say in the street,
When your maship passeth by, all such as I meet,
That sometimes I can scarce find what answer to make.
'Who is this?', saith one, 'Sir Launcelot du Lake?'
'Who is this? Great Guy of Warwick?', saith another.
'No,' say I, 'it is the thirteenth Hercules' brother.'
'Who is this? Noble Hector of Troy?', saith the third. 121
'No, but of the same nest,' say I, 'it is a bird.'
'Who is this? Great Goliath, Samson, or Colbrand?'
'No,' say I, 'but it is a Brute of the Alie Land.'
'Who is this? Great Alexander? or Charlemagne?'
'No, it is the tenth Worthy,' say I to them again.
I know not if I said well.

Roister Doister. Yes; for so I am.

Merrygreek. Yea, for there were but nine Worthies before ye came.
To some others, the third Cato I do you call.

111 ka] quotha. 114 Malkin] slut, *apparently addressed contemptuously to* Roister Doister *in an aside.* 123 Colbrand] the Danish giant in the romance of *Guy of Warwick.* 124 Brute] Brutus, the legendary great-grandson of Aeneas and ancestor of the British kings. Alie] ? Hali, Holy. 126 the tenth Worthy] an addition to the traditional nine; cf. l. 128. 129 the third Cato] the successor to Cato the Censor and Cato of Utica.

And so, as well as I can, I answer them all. 130
'Sir, I pray you, what lord, or great gentleman, is this?'
'Master Ralph Roister Doister, dame,' say I, iwis.
'O Lord!' saith she then, 'What a goodly man it is,
Would Christ I had such a husband as he is!'
'O Lord!' say some, 'that the sight of his face we lack!'
'It is enough for you,' say I, 'to see his back;
His face is for ladies of high and noble parages,
With whom he hardly 'scapeth great marriages;'
With much more than this—and much otherwise.

Roister Doister. I can thee thank that thou canst such answers devise. 140
But I perceive thou dost me throughly know.

Merrygreek. I mark your manners for mine own learning, I trow.
But such is your beauty, and such are your acts,
Such is your personage, and such are your facts,
That all women, fair and foul, more and less,
That eye you, they lub you, they talk of you doubtless.
Your pleasant look maketh them all merry;
Ye pass not by, but they laugh till they be weary,
Yea, and money could I have, the truth to tell,
Of many, to bring you that way where they dwell.

Roister Doister. Merrygreek, for this thy reporting well of me— 151

Merrygreek. What should I else, sir? it is my duty, perdie.

Roister Doister. I promise thou shalt not lack, while I have a groat.

Merrygreek. Faith, sir, and I ne'er had more need of a new coat.

Roister Doister. Thou shalt have one to-morrow, and gold for to spend.

132 iwis] assuredly. 137 parages] lineage.
144 facts] deeds. 146 lub] love.

Merrygreek. Then I trust to bring the day to a good end;
For, as for mine own part, having money enow,
I could live only with the remembrance of you.
But now to your widow, whom you love so hot.
Roister Doister. By Cock, thou sayest truth! I had almost forgot. 160
Merrygreek. What if Christian Custance will not have you? what?
Roister Doister. Have me? yes, I warrant you, never doubt of that,
I know she loveth me, but she dare not speak.
Merrygreek. Indeed, meet it were some body should it break.
Roister Doister. She looked on me twenty times yesternight,
And laughed so—
Merrygreek. That she could not sit upright?
Roister Doister. No, faith, could she not.
Merrygreek. No, even such a thing I cast.
Roister Doister. But, for wooing, thou knowest, women are shamefast.
But an she knew my mind, I know she would be glad,
And think it the best chance that ever she had. 170
Merrygreek. To her, then, like a man, and be bold forth to start,
Wooers never speed well, that have a false heart.
Roister Doister. What may I best do?
Merrygreek. Sir, remain ye awhile here;
Ere long one or other of her house will appear.
Ye know my mind.
Roister Doister. Yea, now, hardily, let me alone.
Merrygreek. In the meantime, sir, if you please, I will home,
And call your musicians; for in this your case
It would set you forth, and all your wooing grace;

160 Cock] God. 164 break] disclose. 167 cast] guessed.

Ye may not lack your instruments to play and sing.
Roister Doister. Thou knowest I can do that.
Merrygreek. As well as anything. 180
Shall I go call your folks, that ye may show a cast?
Roister Doister. Yea, run, I beseech thee, in all possible haste.
Merrygreek. I go. [*Exit.*
Roister Doister. Yea, for I love singing out of measure,
It comforteth my spirits, and doth me great pleasure.
But who cometh forth yond from my sweetheart Custance?
My matter frameth well; this is a lucky chance.

SCENE III

Roister Doister *in the background.* *Enter* Margery Mumblecrust, *spinning on the distaff, and* Tibet Talkapace, *sewing*

M. Mumblecrust. If this distaff were spun, Margery Mumblecrust—
Tib. Talkapace. Where good stale ale is, will drink no water, I trust.
M. Mumblecrust. Dame Custance hath promised us good ale and white bread—
Tib. Talkapace. If she keep not promise I will beshrew her head!
But it will be stark night before I shall have done.
Roister Doister. I will stand here awhile, and talk with them anon.
I hear them speak of Custance, which doth my heart good;
To hear her name spoken doth even comfort my blood.
M. Mumblecrust. Sit down to your work, Tibet, like a good girl.

181 cast] specimen of your skill.

Tib. Talkapace. Nurse, meddle you with your spindle and your whirl! 10
No haste but good, Madge Mumblecrust; for whip and whur,
The old proverb doth say, never made good fur.
M. Mumblecrust. Well, ye will sit down to your work anon, I trust.
Tib. Talkapace. Soft fire maketh sweet malt, good Madge Mumblecrust.
M. Mumblecrust. And sweet malt maketh jolly good ale for the nones.
Tib. Talkapace. Which will slide down the lane without any bones. [*Sings.*
Old brown bread-crusts must have much good mumbling,
But good ale down your throat hath good easy tumbling.
Roister Doister. The jolliest wench that ere I heard! little mouse!
May I not rejoice that she shall dwell in my house? 20
Tib. Talkapace. So, sirrah, now this gear beginneth for to frame.
M. Mumblecrust. Thanks to God, though your work stand still, your tongue is not lame!
Tib. Talkapace. And, though your teeth be gone, both so sharp and so fine,
Yet your tongue can run on pattens as well as mine.
M. Mumblecrust. Ye were not for nought named Tib Talkapace.
Tib. Talkapace. Doth my talk grieve you? Alack, God save your grace!
M. Mumblecrust. I hold a groat ye will drink anon for this gear.
Tib. Talkapace. And I will pray you the stripes for me to bear.

10 whirl] wheel. 11 whur] whirr, hurry. 21 sirrah] *addressed to* Margery, *in a Tudor use of the word.* 27 hold] wager.

M. Mumblecrust. I hold a penny, ye will drink without a cup.

Tib. Talkapace. Wherein so e'er ye drink, I wot ye drink all up. 30

Enter Annot Alyface, *knitting*

Ann. Alyface. By Cock! and well sewed, my good Tibet Talkapace!

Tib. Talkapace. And e'en as well knit, my nown Annot Alyface!

Roister Doister. See what a sort she keepeth that must be my wife.

Shall not I, when I have her, lead a merry life?

Tib. Talkapace. Welcome, my good wench, and sit here by me just.

Ann. Alyface. And how doth our old beldame here, Madge Mumblecrust?

Tib. Talkapace. Chide, and find faults, and threaten to complain.

Ann. Alyface. To make us poor girls shent, to her is small gain.

M. Mumblecrust. I did neither chide, nor complain, nor threaten.

Roister Doister. It would grieve my heart to see one of them beaten. 40

M. Mumblecrust. I did nothing but bid her work and hold her peace.

Tib. Talkapace. So would I, if you could your clattering cease;

But the devil cannot make old trot hold her tong.

Ann. Alyface. Let all these matters pass, and we three sing a song!

So shall we pleasantly both the time beguile now

And eke dispatch all our works ere we can tell how.

Tib. Talkapace. I shrew them that say nay, and that shall not be I.

32 my nown] mine own. 33 sort] company.
43 tong] tongue.

M. Mumblecrust. And I am well content.
Tib. Talkapace. Sing on then, by-and-by.
Roister Doister. And I will not away, but listen to their song,
Yet Merrygreek and my folks tarry very long. 50

Tib. Talkapace, Ann. Alyface, *and* Margery, *do sing here*

Pipe, merry Annot, &c.
Trilla, trilla, trillary.
Work, Tibet; work, Annot; work, Margery!
Sew, Tibet; knit, Annot; spin, Margery!
Let us see who shall win the victory.

Tib. Talkapace. This sleeve is not willing to be sewed, I trow.
A small thing might make me all in the ground to throw!

Then they sing again

Pipe, merry Annot, &c.
Trilla, trilla, trillary.
What, Tibet? what, Annot? what, Margery? 60
Ye sleep, but we do not; that shall we try.
Your fingers be numbed, our work will not lie.

Tib. Talkapace. If ye do so again, well, I would advise you nay.
In good sooth, one stop more, and I make holiday.

They sing the third time

Pipe, merry Annot, &c.
Trilla, trilla, trillary.
Now, Tibet; now, Annot; now, Margery;
Now whippet apace for the mastery,
But it will not be, our mouth is so dry.

Tib. Talkapace. Ah, each finger is a thumb to-day methink, 70
I care not to let all alone, choose it swim or sink.

64 stop] stitch. 68 whippet] *apparently for* whip it, be up and doing.

They sing the fourth time

Pipe, merry Annot, &c.
Trilla, trilla, trillary.
When, Tibet? when, Annot? when, Margery?
I will not! I cannot, no more can I!
Then give we all over, and there let it lie.

[*Let her cast down her work.*

Tib. Talkapace. There it lieth! The worst is but a curried coat,
Tut, I am used thereto; I care not a groat!
Ann. Alyface. Have we done singing since? Then will I in again. 79
Here I found you, and here I leave both twain. [*Exit.*
M. Mumblecrust. And I will not be long after. Tib Talkapace [*Spying* Roister Doister.
Tib. Talkapace. What is the matter?
M. Mumblecrust. Yond stood a man all this space,
And hath heard all that ever we spake together.
Tib. Talkapace. Marry! the more lout he for his coming hither!
And the less good he can, to listen maidens' talk!
I care not an I go bid him hence for to walk.
It were well done to know what he maketh here away.
Roister Doister. Now might I speak to them, if I wist what to say.
M. Mumblecrust. Nay, we will go both off, and see what he is.
Roister Doister [*advancing*]. One that hath heard all your talk and singing, iwis. 90
Tib. Talkapace. The more to blame you! a good thrifty husband
Would elsewhere have had some better matters in hand.
Roister Doister. I did it for no harm, but for good love I bear

74 when] an exclamation of impatience. 77 a curried coat] a beating. 91 husband] housekeeper.

To your dame mistress Custance, I did your talk hear.
And, mistress nurse, I will kiss you for acquaintance.

M. Mumblecrust. I come anon, sir.

Tib. Talkapace. Faith, I would our dame Custance
Saw this gear!

M. Mumblecrust. I must first wipe all clean, yea, I must.

Tib. Talkapace. Ill 'chieve it, doting fool, but it must be cust!

M. Mumblecrust. God yield you, sir! Chad not so much i-chotte not whan,
Ne'er since chwas bore, chwine, of such a gay gentleman! 100

Roister Doister. I will kiss you too, maiden, for the good will I bear you.

Tib. Talkapace. No, forsooth, by your leave, ye shall not kiss me!

Roister Doister. Yes; be not afeard; I do not disdain you a whit.

Tib. Talkapace. Why should I fear you? I have not so little wit,
Ye are but a man, I know very well.

Roister Doister. Why, then?

Tib. Talkapace. Forsooth, for I will not, I use not to kiss men.

Roister Doister. I would fain kiss you too, good maiden, if I might.

Tib. Talkapace. What should that need?

Roister Doister. But to honour you, by this light!
I use to kiss all them that I love, to God I vow.

Tib. Talkapace. Yea, sir, I pray you, when did ye last kiss your cow? 110

Roister Doister. Ye might be proud to kiss me, if ye were wise.

98 cust] kissed. 99 God yield] God reward.
99–100 Chad . . . i-chotte . . . chwas bore, chwine] I(ch) had . . . I(ch) wot . . . I(ch) was born, I(ch) ween; *in the conventional stage rustic dialect.*

Tib. Talkapace. What promotion were therein?
Roister Doister. Nurse is not so nice.
Tib. Talkapace. Well, I have not been taught to kissing and licking.
Roister Doister. Yet I thank you, mistress nurse, ye made no sticking.
M. Mumblecrust. I will not stick for a kiss with such a man as you!
Tib. Talkapace. They that lust! I will again to my sewing now.

Enter Ann. Alyface

Ann. Alyface. Tidings, ho! tidings! Dame Custance greeteth you well.
Roister Doister. Whom? me?
Ann. Alyface. You, sir? No, sir; I do no such tale tell.
Roister Doister. But, an she knew me here—
Ann. Alyface. Tibet Talkapace,
Your mistress, Custance, and mine, must speak with your grace. 120
Tib. Talkapace. With me?
Ann. Alyface. Ye must come in to her, out of all doubts.
Tib. Talkapace. And my work not half done! A mischief on all louts! [*Exeunt* Ann. *and* Tib.
Roister Doister. Ah, good sweet nurse!
M. Mumblecrust. A good sweet gentleman!
Roister Doister. What?
M. Mumblecrust. Nay, I cannot tell, sir; but what thing would you?
Roister Doister. How doth sweet Custance, my heart of gold, tell me how?
M. Mumblecrust. She doth very well, sir, and commends me to you.
Roister Doister. To me?
M. Mumblecrust. Yea, to you, sir.

112 nice] coy. 126 commends me] *Margery should say* commends her, sends her remembrances.

Roister Doister. To me? Nurse, tell me plain, To me?

M. Mumblecrust. Yea.

Roister Doister. That word maketh me alive again!

M. Mumblecrust. She commended me to one last day, whoe'er it was.

Roister Doister. That was e'en to me and none other, by the Mass. 130

M. Mumblecrust. I cannot tell you surely, but one it was.

Roister Doister. It was I and none other. This cometh to good pass.
I promise thee, nurse, I favour her.

M. Mumblecrust. E'en so, sir.

Roister Doister. Bid her sue to me for marriage.

M. Mumblecrust. E'en so, sir.

Roister Doister. And surely for thy sake, she shall speed.

M. Mumblecrust. E'en so, sir.

Roister Doister. I shall be contented to take her.

M. Mumblecrust. E'en so, sir.

Roister Doister. But at thy request, and for thy sake.

M. Mumblecrust. E'en so, sir.

Roister Doister. And, come, hark in thine ear what to say.

M. Mumblecrust. E'en so, sir.

[*Here let him tell her a great, long tale in her ear.*

SCENE IV

Roister Doister *and* M. Mumblecrust
Enter Merrygreek, Dobinet Doughty, *and* Harpax

Merrygreek. Come on, sirs, apace; and quit yourselves like men.
Your pains shall be rewarded.

Doughty. But I wot not when.

Merrygreek. Do your master worship as ye have done in time past.

Doughty. Speak to them; of mine office he shall have a cast.

Merrygreek. Harpax, look that thou do well, too, and thy fellow.

Harpax. I warrant, if he will mine example follow.

Merrygreek. Curtsy, whoresons; duck you and crouch at every word.

Doughty. Yes, whether our master speak earnest or bord.

Merrygreek. For this lieth upon his preferment indeed.

Doughty. Oft is he a wooer, but never doth he speed. 10

Merrygreek. But with whom is he now so sadly rounding yond?

Doughty. With *Nobs nicebecetur miserere* fond.

Merrygreek. God be at your wedding! Be ye sped already?
I did not suppose that your love was so greedy.
I perceive now ye have chose of devotion;
And joy have ye, lady, of your promotion!

Roister Doister. Tush, fool, thou art deceived; this is not she.

Merrygreek. Well, mock much of her, and keep her well, I 'vise ye.
I will take no charge of such a fair piece keeping.

M. Mumblecrust. What aileth this fellow? He driveth me to weeping. 20

Merrygreek. What! weep on the wedding day? Be merry, woman!
Though I say it, ye have chose a good gentleman.

Roister Doister. Kock's nowns! what meanest thou man? tut a whistle!

4 cast] specimen. 8 bord] jest. 11 sadly rounding] seriously whispering. 12 With *Nobs . . . miserere* fond] *Probably either* (1) foolish with 'dear darling, pity me'; or (2) infatuated with this woe-begone dear darling, i.e. Margery Mumblecrust. 18 mock] make (*an unusual form, probably with a play on* mock *in its ordinary sense*). 23 Kock's nowns] God's wounds. a whistle] a worthless thing.

Merrygreek. Ah, sir, be good to her; she is but a gristle!
Ah, sweet lamb and cony!
Roister Doister. Tut, thou art deceived!
Merrygreek. Weep no more, lady; ye shall be well received.
Up with some merry noise, sirs, to bring home the bride!
Roister Doister. Gog's arms, knave! Art thou mad?
I tell thee thou art wide.
Merrygreek. Then ye intend by night to have her home brought.
Roister Doister. I tell thee, no!
Merrygreek. How then?
Roister Doister. 'Tis neither meant nor thought. 30
Merrygreek. What shall we then do with her?
Roister Doister. Ah, foolish harebrain!
This is not she!
Merrygreek. No is? Why then, unsaid again!
And what young girl is this with your maship so bold?
Roister Doister. A girl?
Merrygreek. Yea; I dare say; scarce yet threescore year old.
Roister Doister. This same is the fair widow's nurse, of whom ye wot.
Merrygreek. Is she but a nurse of a house? Hence home, old trot!
Hence at once!
Roister Doister. No! no!
Merrygreek. What! an please your maship,
A nurse talk so homely with one of your worship?
Roister Doister. I will have it so: it is my pleasure and will.
Merrygreek. Then I am content. Nurse, come again; tarry still. 40
Roister Doister. What! she will help forward this my suit for her part.

24 a gristle] a young pig, or tender thing. 28 wide] mistaken. 32 No is?] is it not she? 38 homely] familiarly.

Merrygreek. Then is't mine own pigsny, and blessing on my heart.
Roister Doister. This is our best friend, man!
Merrygreek. Then teach her what to say.
M. Mumblecrust. I am taught already.
Merrygreek. Then go, make no delay!
Roister Doister. Yet hark, one word in thine ear.
Merrygreek. Back, sirs, from his tail!
Roister Doister. Back, villains! Will ye be privy of my counsail?
Merrygreek. Back, sirs! so! I told you afore ye would be shent.
Roister Doister. She shall have the first day a whole peck of argent.
M. Mumblecrust. A peck? *Nomine Patris!* have ye so much spare?
Roister Doister. Yea, and a cart-load thereto, or else were it bare, 50
Besides other movables, household stuff, and land.
M. Mumblecrust. Have ye lands too?
Roister Doister. An hundred marks.
Merrygreek. Yea, a thousand!
M. Mumblecrust. And have ye cattle too? and sheep too?
Roister Doister. Yea, a few.
Merrygreek. He is ashamed the number of them to show.
E'en round about him, as many thousand sheep goes,
As he and thou, and I too have fingers and toes.
M. Mumblecrust. And how many years old be you?
Roister Doister. Forty at least.
Merrygreek. Yea, and thrice forty to them!
Roister Doister. Nay, now thou dost jest.
I am not so old; thou misreckonest my years.
Merrygreek. I know that; but my mind was on bullocks and steers. 60
M. Mumblecrust. And what shall I show her your mastership's name is?

42 pigsny] (pig's eye), darling. 48 argent] silver.

Roister Doister. Nay, she shall make suit ere she know that, iwis.
M. Mumblecrust. Yet let me somewhat know.
Merrygreek. This is he, understand,
That killed the Blue Spider in Blanchepowder land.
M. Mumblecrust. Yea, Jesus! William! Zee law! Did he zo? law!
Merrygreek. Yea, and the last elephant that ever he saw;
As the beast passed by, he start out of a busk,
And e'en with pure strength of arms plucked out his great tusk.
M. Mumblecrust. Jesus! *Nomine Patris!* what a thing was that!
Roister Doister. Yea, but, Merrygreek, one thing thou hast forgot. 70
Merrygreek. What?
Roister Doister. Of th'other elephant.
Merrygreek. Oh, him that fled away.
Roister Doister. Yea.
Merrygreek. Yea! he knew that his match was in place that day.
Tut, he beat the King of Crickets on Christmas day,
That he crept in a hole, and not a word to say!
M. Mumblecrust. A sore man, by zembletee!
Merrygreek. Why, he wrung a club
Once, in a fray, out of the hand of Belzebub.
Roister Doister. And how when Mumfision?
Merrygreek. Oh, your custreling
Bore the lantern a-field so before the gosling—
Nay that is too long a matter now to be told:
Never ask his name, nurse, I warrant thee, be bold. 80
He conquered in one day from Rome to Naples,
And won towns, nurse, as fast as thou canst make apples.
M. Mumblecrust. O Lord! My heart quaketh for fear! He is too sore!

67 busk] bush. 75 sore] fierce. by zembletee] in appearance. 77 custreling] young esquire.

Roister Doister. Thou makest her too much afeard. Merrygreek, no more!
This tale would fear my sweetheart Custance right evil.
Merrygreek. Nay, let her take him, nurse, and fear not the devil!
But thus is our song dashed. Sirs, ye may home again.
Roister Doister. No, shall they not! I charge you all here to remain.
The villain slaves! a whole day ere they can be found!
Merrygreek. Couch! On your marrowbones, whoresons! Down to the ground! 90
Was it meet he should tarry so long in one place
Without harmony of music, or some solace?
Whoso hath such bees as your master in his head,
Had need to have his spirits with music to be fed.
By your mastership's licence!
Roister Doister. What is that? a mote?
Merrygreek. No; it was a fowl's feather had light on your coat.
Roister Doister. I was nigh no feathers since I came from my bed.
Merrygreek. No, sir, it was a hair that was fall from your head.
Roister Doister. My men come when it please them—
Merrygreek. By your leave!
Roister Doister. What is that?
Merrygreek. Your gown was foul spotted with the foot of a gnat. 100
Roister Doister. Their master to offend they are nothing afeard.
What now?
Merrygreek. A lousy hair from your mastership's beard.
All the Servants. And sir, for nurse's sake, pardon this one offence.

90 marrowbones] *here used for* knees. 96 fowl's] *the quarto has* fooles, *with a double meaning.*

We shall not after this show the like negligence.
Roister Doister. I pardon you this once; and come sing ne'er the worse!
Merrygreek. How like you the goodness of this gentleman, nurse?
M. Mumblecrust. God save his mastership that so can his men forgive!
And I will hear them sing ere I go, by his leave.
Roister Doister. Marry, and thou shalt, wench! Come, we two will dance!
M. Mumblecrust. Nay, I will by mine own self foot the song perchance. 110
Roister Doister. Go to it, sirs, lustily!
M. Mumblecrust. Pipe up a merry note.
Let me hear it played, I will foot it, for a groat!

They sing

Whoso to marry a minion wife
Hath had good chance and hap,
Must love her and cherish her all his life,
And dandle her in his lap.

If she will fare well, if she will go gay,
A good husband ever still,
Whatever she lust to do or to say,
Must let her have her own will. 120

About what affairs soever he go,
He must show her all his mind;
None of his counsel she may be kept fro,
Else is he a man unkind.

Roister Doister. Now, nurse, take this same letter here to thy mistress;
And as my trust is in thee, ply my business.
M. Mumblecrust. It shall be done.
Merrygreek. Who made it?
Roister Doister. I wrote it, each whit.
Merrygreek. Then needs it no mending.

113 minion] darling.

Roister Doister. No, no!
Merrygreek. No; I know your wit;
I warrant it well.
M. Mumblecrust. It shall be delivered.
But, if ye speed, shall I be considered? 130
Merrygreek. Whough! dost thou doubt of that?
M. Mumblecrust. What shall I have?
Merrygreek. An hundred times more than thou canst devise to crave.
M. Mumblecrust. Shall I have some new gear? for my old is all spent.
Merrygreek. The worst kitchen wench shall go in ladies' raiment.
M. Mumblecrust. Yea?
Merrygreek. And the worst drudge in the house shall go better
Than your mistress doth now.
M. Mumblecrust. Then I trudge with your letter.
Roister Doister. Now, may I repose me, Custance is mine own.
Let us sing and play homeward, that it may be known.
Merrygreek. But are you sure that your letter is well enough?
Roister Doister. I wrote it myself!
Merrygreek. Then sing we to dinner!
[*Here they sing, and go out singing.*

SCENE V

Enter Christian Custance *and* M. Mumblecrust

Dame Custance. Who took thee this letter, Margery Mumblecrust?
M. Mumblecrust. A lusty gay bachelor took it me of trust,
And if ye seek to him he will 'low your doing.

1 took] gave. 3 'low] allow, approve.

Dame Custance. Yea, but where learned he that manner of wooing?
M. Mumblecrust. If to sue to him you will any pains take,
He will have you to his wife, he saith, for my sake.
Dame Custance. Some wise gentleman, belike! I am bespoken;
And I thought, verily, this had been some token
From my dear spouse Gawyn Goodluck; whom, when him please,
God luckily send home to both our hearts' ease. 10
M. Mumblecrust. A jolly man it is, I wot well by report,
And would have you to him for marriage resort.
Best open the writing, and see what it doth speak.
Dame Custance. At this time, nurse, I will neither read nor break.
M. Mumblecrust. He promised to give you a whole peck of gold.
Dame Custance. Perchance lack of a pint, when it shall be all told!
M. Mumblecrust. I would take a gay rich husband, an I were you.
Dame Custance. In good sooth, Madge, e'en so would I, if I were thou.
But no more of this fond talk now, let us go in.
And see thou no more move me folly to begin. 20
Nor bring me no more letters for no man's pleasure,
But thou know from whom.
M. Mumblecrust. I warrant ye shall be sure!
[*Exeunt*.

ACT II

SCENE I

Enter Dobinet Doughty

Doughty. Where is the house I go to? before or behind?
I know not where, nor when, nor how, I shall it find.

If I had ten men's bodies and legs and strength,
This trotting that I have must needs lame me at length.
And now that my master is new set on wooing,
I trust there shall none of us find lack of doing.
Two pairs of shoes a day will now be too little
To serve me, I must trot to and fro so mickle.
'Go bear me this token!' 'Carry me this letter!' 9
'Now this is the best way,' 'now that way is better!'
Up before day, sirs, I charge you, an hour or twain!
'Trudge! Do me this message, and bring word quick again!'
If one miss but a minute, then: 'His arms and wounds,
I would not have slacked for ten thousand pounds!
Nay, see, I beseech you, if my most trusty page
Go not now about to hinder my marriage!'
So fervent hot wooing, and so far from wiving,
I trow never was any creature living.
With every woman is he in some love's pang.
Then up to our lute at midnight, twangledom twang; 20
Then twang with our sonnets, and twang with our dumps,
And heigho from our heart, as heavy as lead lumps;
Then to our recorder with toodleloodle poop,
As the howlet out of an ivy bush should whoop;
Anon to our gittern, thrumpledum, thrumpledum thrum,
Thrumpledum, thrumpledum, thrumpledum, thrumpledum, thrum.
Of songs and ballads also he is a maker,
And that can he as finely do as Jack Raker;
Yea, and extempore will he ditties compose—
Foolish Marsyas ne'er made the like, I suppose! 30

13 His] God's. 21 dumps] mournful songs. 23 recorder] flute. 24 howlet] owl. 25 gittern] guitar. 28 Jack Raker] an imaginary composer of bad verse. 30 Marsyas] the Phrygian flute-player, who challenged Apollo.

Yet must we sing them; as good stuff, I undertake,
As for such a pen-man is well fitting to make.
'Ah, for these long nights! heigho! when will it be
day?
I fear, ere I come, she will be wooed away.'
Then, when answer is made that it may not be,
'O death, why comest thou not by-and-by?' saith he.
But then, from his heart to put away sorrow,
He is as far in with some new love next morrow.
But in the mean season we trudge and we trot;
From dayspring to midnight, I sit not, nor rest not.
And now am I sent to Dame Christian Custance; 41
But I fear it will end with a mock for pastance.
I bring her a ring, with a token in a clout;
And, by all guess, this same is her house out of doubt.
I know it now perfect, I am in my right way.
And lo yond the old nurse that was with us last day!

SCENE II

Doughty. *Enter* M. Mumblecrust

M. Mumblecrust. I was ne'er so shook up afore since I
was born.
That our mistress could not have chid, I would have
sworn;
And I pray God I die, if I meant any harm,
But for my life-time, this shall be to me a charm!

Doughty. God you save and see, nurse! And how is it
with you?

M. Mumblecrust. Marry, a great deal the worse it is, for
such as thou!

Doughty. For me? Why so?

M. Mumblecrust. Why, were not thou one of them, say,
That sang and played here with the gentleman last
day?

36 by-and-by] at once. 42 pastance] pastime.
43 clout] piece of cloth.

Doughty. Yes; and he would know if you have for him spoken,
And prays you to deliver this ring and token. 10
M. Mumblecrust. Now, by the token that God tokened, brother,
I will deliver no token, one nor other!
I have once been so shent for your master's pleasure,
As I will not be again for all his treasure.
Doughty. He will thank you, woman.
M. Mumblecrust. I will none of his thank. [*Exit.*
Doughty. I ween I am a prophet! this gear will prove blank!
But what! should I home again without answer go?
It were better go to Rome on my head than so.
I will tarry here this month, but some of the house
Shall take it of me; and then I care not a louse. 20
But yonder cometh forth a wench—or a lad;
If he have not one Lombard's touch, my luck is bad.

SCENE III

Dobinet Doughty. *Enter* Tom Truepenny

Truepenny. I am clean lost for lack of merry company!
We 'gree not half well within, our wenches and I.
They will command like mistresses; they will forbid,
If they be not served, Truepenny must be chid.
Let them be as merry now as ye can desire,
With turning of a hand our mirth lieth in the mire!
I cannot skill of such changeable mettle;
There is nothing with them but 'in dock, out nettle!'
Doughty. Whether is it better that I speak to him first,
Or he first to me? it is good to cast the worst. 10

11 the token that God tokened] token *is here used in the Biblical sense of* sign, miracle. 22 one Lombard's touch] one quality of a Lombard, or money-changer, that of keeping gold, here the gold ring for Custance. 8 'in dock, out nettle!'] the dock-leaf, the remedy for the nettle-sting, is the greatest contrast to it.

If I begin first, he will smell all my purpose;
Otherwise, I shall not need anything to disclose.

Truepenny. What boy have we yonder? I will see what he is.

Doughty. He cometh to me. It is hereabout, iwis.

Truepenny. Wouldest thou aught, friend, that thou lookest so about?

Doughty. Yea; but whether ye can help me or no, I doubt.
I seek to one mistress Custance house, here dwelling.

Truepenny. It is my mistress ye seek to, by your telling.

Doughty. Is there any of that name here but she?

Truepenny. Not one in all the whole town that I know, perdie. 20

Doughty. A widow she is, I trow?

Truepenny. And what an she be?

Doughty. But ensured to an husband?

Truepenny. Yea, so think we.

Doughty. And I dwell with her husband that trusteth to be.

Truepenny. In faith, then must thou needs be welcome to me,
Let us for acquaintance shake hands togither;
And whate'er thou be, heartily welcome hither.

Enter Tib. Talkapace *and* Ann. Alyface

Tib. Talkapace. Well, Truepenny, never but flinging!

Ann. Alyface. And frisking!

Truepenny. Well, Tibet and Annot, still swinging and whisking!

Tib. Talkapace. But ye roil abroad.

Ann. Alyface. In the street, everywhere!

Truepenny. Where are ye twain, in chambers, when ye meet me there? 30
But come hither, fools; I have one now by the hand,

22 ensured] contracted to. 27 flinging] rushing about. 28 whisking] dashing here and there. 29 roil] gad about.

Servant to him that must be our mistress' husband,
Bid him welcome.

Ann Alyface. To me truly is he welcome!

Tib. Talkapace. Forsooth, and as I may say, heartily welcome!

Doughty. I thank you, mistress maids.

Ann. Alyface. I hope we shall better know.

Tib. Talkapace. And when will our new master come?

Doughty. Shortly, I trow.

Tib. Talkapace. I would it were to-morrow: for till he resort,
Our mistress, being a widow, hath small comfort,
And I heard our nurse speak of an husband to-day
Ready for our mistress, a rich man and a gay; 40
And we shall go in our French hoods every day,
In our silk cassocks, I warrant you, fresh and gay,
In our trick ferdegews and biliments of gold;
Brave in our suits of change, seven double fold.
Then shall ye see Tibet, sirs, tread the moss so trim.
Nay, why said I 'tread'? ye shall see her glide and swim,
Not lumperdee clumperdee like our spaniel Rig.

Truepenny. Marry, then, prick-me-dainty, come toast me a fig!
Who shall then know our Tib. Talkapace, trow ye?

Ann. Alyface. And why not Annot Alyface as fine as she?

Truepenny. And what? had Tom Truepenny a father, or none? 51

Ann. Alyface. Then our pretty new come man will look to be one.

Truepenny. We four, I trust, shall be a jolly merry knot.
Shall we sing a fit to welcome our friend, Annot?

Ann. Alyface. Perchance he cannot sing.

Doughty. I am at all essays.

Tib. Talkapace. By Cock, and the better welcome to us always!

43 trick . . . biliments] trim farthingales and head-dresses. 48 prick-me-dainty] my fine lady.

Here they sing

A thing very fit
For them that have wit,
And are fellows knit,
Servants in one house to be, 60
Is fast for to sit,
And not oft to flit,
Nor vary a whit,
But lovingly to agree.

No man complaining,
No other disdaining
For loss or for gaining,
But fellows or friends to be;
No grudge remaining,
No work refraining, 70
Nor help restraining,
But lovingly to agree.

No man for despite,
By word or by write
His fellow to twite,
But further in honesty;
No good turns entwite,
Nor old sores recite,
But let all go quite,
And lovingly to agree. 80

After drudgery,
When they be weary,
Then to be merry,
To laugh and sing they be free;
With chip and cherry
Heigh derry derry,
Trill on the berry,
And lovingly to agree.

Finis.

77 entwite] rebuke. 87 Trill on the berry] the refrain of a song.

Tib. Talkapace. Will you now in with us unto our mistress go?
Doughty. I have first for my master an errand or two. 90
But I have here from him a token and a ring,
They shall have most thank of her that first doth it bring.
Tib. Talkapace. Marry, that will I!
Truepenny. See, an Tibet snatch not now!
Tib. Talkapace. And why may not I, sir, get thanks as well as you? [*Exit.*
Ann. Alyface. Yet get ye not all; we will go with you both,
And have part of your thanks, be ye never so loth!
[*Exeunt* Ann. *and* Truepenny.
Doughty. So my hands are rid of it; I care for no more.
I may now return home; so durst I not afore. [*Exit.*

SCENE IV

Enter Dame Custance, Tib. Talkapace, Ann. Alyface, *and* Truepenny

Dame Custance. Nay, come forth all three! and come hither, pretty maid!
Will not so many forewarnings make you afraid?
Tib. Talkapace. Yes, forsooth.
Dame Custance. But still be a runner up and down?
Still be a bringer of tidings and tokens to town?
Tib. Talkapace. No, forsooth, mistress.
Dame Custance. Is all your delight and joy
In whisking and ramping abroad like a tomboy?
Tib. Talkapace. Forsooth, these were there too, Annot and Truepenny.
Truepenny. Yea, but ye alone took it, ye cannot deny.
Ann. Alyface. Yea, that ye did.
Tib. Talkapace. But if I had not, ye twain would.
Dame Custance. You great calf! ye should have more wit, so ye should! 10

But why should any of you take such things in hand?
Tib. Talkapace. Because it came from him that must be your husband.
Dame Custance. How do ye know that?
Tib. Talkapace. Forsooth, the boy did say so.
Dame Custance. What was his name?
Ann. Alyface. We asked not.
Dame Custance. Did ye? no?
Ann. Alyface. He is not far gone, of likelihood.
Truepenny. I will see.
Dame Custance. If thou canst find him in the street, bring him to me.
Truepenny. Yes. [*Exit.*
Dame Custance. Well, ye naughty girls, if ever I perceive
That henceforth you do letters or tokens receive
To bring unto me from any person or place,
Except ye first show me the party face to face, 20
Either thou, or thou, full truly aby thou shalt.
Tib. Talkapace. Pardon this, and the next time powder me in salt!
Dame Custance. I shall make all girls by you twain to beware.
Tib. Talkapace. If ever I offend again, do not me spare.
But if ever I see that false boy any more
By your mistress-ship's licence, I tell you afore,
I will rather have my coat twenty times swinged,
Than on the naughty wag not to be avenged.
Dame Custance. Good wenches would not so ramp abroad idly.
But keep within doors, and ply their work earnestly.
If one would speak with me that is a man likely, 31
Ye shall have right good thank to bring me word quickly;
But otherwise with messages to come in post

14 Did ye? no?] *the quarto has* No, did?, *which does not rhyme.* 21 aby] pay for it. 22 powder] preserve.

From henceforth, I promise you, shall be to your cost.
Get you in to your work!
Tib. Talkapace. Yes, forsooth.
Dame Custance. Hence, both twain;
And let me see you play me such a part again!

Re-enter Truepenny

Truepenny. Mistress, I have run past the far end of the street,
Yet can I not yonder crafty boy see nor meet.
Dame Custance. No?
Truepenny. Yet I looked as far beyond the people
As one may see out of the top of Paul's steeple. 40
Dame Custance. Hence in at doors, and let me no more be vexed!
Truepenny. Forgive me this one fault, and lay on for the next. [*Exit.*
Dame Custance. Now will I in too; for I think, so God me mend,
This will prove some foolish matter in the end! [*Exit.*

ACT III

SCENE I

Enter Matthew Merrygreek

Merrygreek. Now say this again:—he hath somewhat to doing
Which followeth the trace of one that is wooing,
Specially that hath no more wit in his head
Than my cousin Roister Doister withal is led.
I am sent in all haste to espy and to mark
How our letters and tokens are likely to wark.

2 Which] Who.

Master Roister Doister must have answer in haste,
For he loveth not to spend much labour in waste.
Now as for Christian Custance, by this light,
Though she had not her troth to Gawyn Goodluck plight, 10
Yet rather than with such a loutish dolt to marry,
I daresay would live a poor life solitary.
But fain would I speak with Custance, if I wist how,
To laugh at the matter. Yond cometh one forth now.

SCENE II

Merrygreek. *Enter* Tib. Talkapace

Tib. Talkapace. Ah, that I might but once in my life have a sight
Of him that made us all so ill shent: by this light,
He should never escape if I had him by the ear,
But even from his head I would it bite or tear;
Yea, and if one of them were not enow,
I would bite them both off, I make God avow!

Merrygreek. What is he, whom this little mouse doth so threaten?

Tib. Talkapace. I would teach him, I trow, to make girls shent or beaten.

Merrygreek. I will call her. Maid, with whom are ye so hasty?

Tib. Talkapace. Not with you, sir, but with a little wagpasty, 10
A deceiver of folks by subtle craft and guile.

Merrygreek. I know where she is: Dobinet hath wrought some wile.

Tib. Talkapace. He brought a ring and token which he said was sent
From our dame's husband; but I wot well I was shent!
For it liked her as well, to tell you no lies,

10 wagpasty] mischievous rogue. 12 where she is] what she means.

As water in her ship, or salt cast in her eyes.
And yet whence it came neither we nor she can tell.

Merrygreek. We shall have sport anon; I like this very well!—
And dwell ye here with Mistress Custance, fair maid?

Tib. Talkapace. Yea, marry do I, sir. What would ye have said? 20

Merrygreek. A little message unto her by word of mouth.

Tib. Talkapace. No messages, by your leave, nor tokens, forsooth!

Merrygreek. Then help me to speak with her.

Tib. Talkapace. With a good will that.

[*Enter* Christian Custance.

Here she cometh forth. Now speak—ye know best what.

Dame Custance. None other life with you, maid, but abroad to skip?

Tib. Talkapace. Forsooth, here is one would speak with your mistress-ship.

Dame Custance. Ah, have ye been learning of more messages now?

Tib. Talkapace. I would not hear his mind, but bade him show it to you.

Dame Custance. In at doors!

Tib. Talkapace. I am gone. [*Exit.*

Merrygreek. Dame Custance, God ye save!

Dame Custance. Welcome, friend Merrygreek: and what thing would ye have? 30

Merrygreek. I am come to you a little matter to break.

Dame Custance. But see it be honest, else better not to speak.

Merrygreek. How feel ye yourself affected here of late?

Dame Custance. I feel no manner change but after the old rate.
But whereby do ye mean?

Merrygreek. Concerning marriage.

Doth not love lade you?

Dame Custance. I feel no such carriage.

Merrygreek. Do ye feel no pangs of dotage? answer me right.

Dame Custance. I dote so that I make but one sleep all the night.

But what need all these words?

Merrygreek. Oh Jesus! will ye see

What dissembling creatures these same women be?

The gentleman ye wot of, whom ye do so love 41

That ye would fain marry him, if ye durst it move,

Among other rich widows, which are of him glad,

Lest ye for losing of him perchance might run mad,

Is now contented that upon your suit making,

Ye be as one in election of taking.

Dame Custance. What a tale is this! that I wot of? Whom I love?

Merrygreek. Yea, and he is as loving a worm, again, as a dove.

E'en of very pity he is willing you to take,

Because ye shall not destroy yourself for his sake. 50

Dame Custance. Marry, God yield his maship! Whatever he be,

It is gentmanly spoken.

Merrygreek. Is it not, trow ye?

If ye have the grace now to offer yourself, ye speed.

Dame Custance. As much as though I did, this time it shall not need.

But what gentman is it, I pray you tell me plain,

That wooeth so finely?

Merrygreek. Lo where ye be again,

As though ye knew him not!

Dame Custance. Tush, ye speak in jest!

Merrygreek. Nay, sure, the party is in good knacking earnest;

And have you he will, he saith, and have you he must.

36 lade] load. carriage] burden. 58 knacking earnest] downright earnest.

Dame Custance. I am promised during my life; that is just. 60
Merrygreek. Marry, so thinketh he, unto him alone.
Dame Custance. No creature hath my faith and troth but one—
That is Gawyn Goodluck: and if it be not he,
He hath no title this way, whatever he be,
Nor I know none to whom I have such word spoken.
Merrygreek. Ye know him not, you, by his letter and token?
Dame Custance. Indeed, true it is that a letter I have;
But I never read it yet, as God me save!
Merrygreek. Ye a woman, and your letter so long unread?
Dame Custance. Ye may thereby know what haste I have to wed. 70
But now who it is for my hand, I know by guess.
Merrygreek. Ah, well I say.
Dame Custance. It is Roister Doister, doubtless.
Merrygreek. Will ye never leave this dissimulation?
Ye know him not?
Dame Custance. But by imagination;
For no man there is but a very dolt and lout
That to woo a widow would so go about.
He shall never have me his wife while he do live.
Merrygreek. Then will he have you if he may, so mote I thrive!
And he biddeth you send him word by me,
That ye humbly beseech him ye may his wife be, 80
And that there shall be no let in you, nor mistrust,
But to be wedded on Sunday next, if he lust;
And biddeth you to look for him.
Dame Custance. Doth he bid so?
Merrygreek. When he cometh, ask him whether he did or no.
Dame Custance. Go, say that I bid him keep him warm at home!

81 let] obstacle.

For, if he come abroad, he shall cough me a mome.
My mind was vexed, I shrew his head! Sottish dolt!
Merrygreek. He hath in his head—
Dame Custance. As much brain as a bird-bolt!
Merrygreek. Well, Dame Custance, if he hear you thus play choploge—
Dame Custance. What will he?
Merrygreek. Play the devil in the horologe. 90
Dame Custance. I defy him, lout!
Merrygreek. Shall I tell him what ye say?
Dame Custance. Yea; and add whatsoever thou canst, I thee pray,
And I will avouch it, whatsoever it be.
Merrygreek. Then let me alone! we will laugh well, ye shall see.
It will not be long ere he will hither resort.
Dame Custance. Let him come when him lust, I wish no better sport.
Fare ye well. I will in and read my great letter;
I shall to my wooer make answer the better. [*Exit.*

SCENE III

Merrygreek

Merrygreek. Now that the whole answer in my devise doth rest,
I shall paint out our wooer in colours of the best;
And all that I say shall be on Custance's mouth;
She is author of all that I shall speak, forsooth.
But yond cometh Roister Doister now, in a trance.

Enter Roister Doister

Roister Doister. Juno send me this day good luck and good chance!

86 cough me a mome] prove himself a fool to me. 88 bird-bolt] blunt-headed arrow. 89 choploge] chop-logic. 90 Play . . . horologe] strike; *from* the Jack that strikes the hour upon a bell.

I cannot but come see how Merrygreek doth speed.
Merrygreek. I will not see him, but give him a jut, indeed.
I cry your mastership mercy!
Roister Doister. And whither now?
Merrygreek. As fast as I could run, sir, in post against you. 10
But why speak ye so faintly? or why are ye so sad?
Roister Doister. Thou knowest the proverb—because I cannot be had.
Hast thou spoken with this woman?
Merrygreek. Yea, that I have!
Roister Doister. And what, will this gear be?
Merrygreek. No, so God me save!
Roister Doister. Hast thou a flat answer?
Merrygreek. Nay, a sharp answer!
Roister Doister. What?
Merrygreek. Ye shall not, she saith, by her will marry her cat!
Ye are such a calf! such an ass! such a block!
Such a lilburn! such a hoball! such a lobcock!
And, because ye should come to her at no season,
She despised your maship out of all reason. 20
'Bawawe what ye say,' ko I, 'of such a gentman!'
'Nay, I fear him not,' ko she, 'do the best he can.
He vaunteth himself for a man of prowess great,
Whereas a good gander, I daresay, may him beat.
And, where he is louted, and laughed to scorn,
For the veriest dolt that ever was born,
And veriest lubber, sloven, and beast
Living in this world from the west to the east,
Yet of himself hath he such opinion
That in all the world is not the like minion. 30
He thinketh each woman to be brought in dotage

8 a jut] a push. 18 lilburn . . . hoball . . . lobcock] lubber . . . clown . . . bumpkin. 21 Bawawe] Beware. ko] quoth. 25 louted] mocked. 30 minion] gallant.

With the only sight of his goodly personage;
Yet none that will have him. We do him lout and flock,
And make him among us our common sporting-stock.
And so would I now,' ko she, 'save only because'—
'Better nay,' ko I, 'I lust not meddle with daws.'
'Ye are happy,' ko I, 'that ye are a woman!
This would cost you your life in case ye were a man.'

Roister Doister. Yea, an hundred thousand pound should not save her life!

Merrygreek. No, but that ye woo her to have her to your wife. 40
But I could not stop her mouth.

Roister Doister. Heigh-ho, alas!

Merrygreek. Be of good cheer, man, and let the world pass!

Roister Doister. What shall I do, or say now that it will not be?

Merrygreek. Ye shall have choice of a thousand as good as she.
And ye must pardon her; it is for lack of wit.

Roister Doister. Yea, for were not I an husband for her fit?
Well, what should I now do?

Merrygreek. In faith I cannot tell.

Roister Doister. I will go home and die!

Merrygreek. Then shall I bid toll the bell?

Roister Doister. No.

Merrygreek. God have mercy on your soul!
Ah, good gentleman,
That e'er ye should thus die for an unkind woman! 50
Will ye drink once ere ye go?

Roister Doister. No, no, I will none.

Merrygreek. How feel your soul to God?

Roister Doister. I am nigh gone.

Merrygreek. And shall we hence straight?

33 flock] jeer at.

Roister Doister. Yea.
Merrygreek. *Placebo dilexi:*
Master Roister Doister will straight go home and die,
Our Lord Jesus Christ his soul have mercy upon:
Thus you see to-day a man, to-morrow John.
Yet saving for a woman's extreme cruelty,
He might have lived yet a month or two or three.
Roister Doister. Heigh-ho, alas, the pangs of death my heart do break!
Merrygreek. Hold your peace! For shame, sir! A dead man may not speak! 60
Ne quando. What mourners and what torches shall we have?
Roister Doister. None.
Merrygreek. *Dirige.* He will go darkling to his grave,
Neque lux, *neque crux*, *neque* mourners, *neque* clink,
He will steal to heaven, unknowing to God, I think,
A porta inferi. Who shall your goods possess?
Roister Doister. Thou shalt be my sectour, and have all, more and less.
Merrygreek. *Requiem aeternam!* Now, God reward your mastership!
And I will cry halfpenny-dole for your worship.
Come forth, sirs, hear the doleful news I shall you tell!
[*He calls* Roister Doister's *servants.*
Our good master here will no longer with us dwell. 70
But in spite of Custance, which hath him wearied,
Let us see his maship solemnly buried;
And while some piece of his soul is yet him within,
Some part of his funerals let us here begin.
Audivi vocem. All men take heed by this one gentleman
How you set your love upon an unkind woman!
For these women be all such mad peevish elves,
They will not be won except it please themselves.

53 *Placebo dilexi*] *On this and the other Latin phrases between this line and* l. 96 *see note* 2, p. 342. 63 clink] clinking of the bell. 66 sectour] executor.

But, in faith, Custance, if ever ye come in hell,
Master Roister Doister shall serve you as well. 80
And will ye needs go from us thus, in very deed?
Roister Doister. Yea, in good sadness.
Merrygreek. Now Jesus Christ be your speed!
Good-night, Roger, old knave! farewell, Roger, old knave!
Good-night, Roger, old knave! knave, knap!
Nequando. Audivi vocem. Requiem aeternam.
Pray for the late master Roister Doister's soul!
And come forth, parish clerk, let the passing bell toll.
[*To* Roister Doister's *servants.*
Pray for your master, sirs, and for him ring a peal.
He was your right good master while he was in heal.

The Peal of Bells rung by the Parish Clerk and Roister Doister's *four men*

The first Bell, a Triple. When died he? When died he?
The second. We have him! we have him! 91
The third. Roister Doister! Roister Doister!
The fourth Bell. He cometh! he cometh!
The great Bell. Our own! our own!
Qui Lazarum.
Roister Doister. Heigh-ho!
Merrygreek. Dead men go not so fast
In Paradisum.
Roister Doister. Heigh-ho!
Merrygreek. Soft, hear what I have cast!
Roister Doister. I will hear nothing, I am passed.
Merrygreek. Whough, wellaway!
Ye may tarry one hour, and hear what I shall say.
Ye were best, sir, for a while to revive again
And quite them ere ye go.
Roister Doister. Trowest thou so?
Merrygreek. Yea, plain. 100
Roister Doister. How may I revive, being now so far passed?

84 knap] rogue.

Merrygreek. I will rub your temples, and fetch you again at last.
Roister Doister. It will not be possible.
Merrygreek. Yes, for twenty pound.
Roister Doister. Arms! what dost thou?
Merrygreek. Fetch you again out of your sound.
By this cross, ye were nigh gone indeed! I might feel
Your soul departing within an inch of your heel.
Now follow my counsel.
Roister Doister. What is it?
Merrygreek. If I were you,
Custance should eft seek to me ere I would bow.
Roister Doister. Well, as thou wilt have me, even so will I do.
Merrygreek. Then shall ye revive again for an hour or two? 110
Roister Doister. As thou wilt; I am content, for a little space.
Merrygreek. Good hap is not hasty; yet in space cometh grace.
To speak with Custance yourself should be very well;
What good thereof may come, nor I nor you can tell.
But now the matter standeth upon your marriage,
Ye must now take unto you a lusty courage,
Ye may not speak with a faint heart to Custance,
But with a lusty breast and countenance,
That she may know she hath to answer to a man.
Roister Doister. Yes, I can do that as well as any can. 120
Merrygreek. Then, because ye must Custance face to face woo,
Let us see how to behave yourself ye can do.
Ye must have a portly brag, after your estate.
Roister Doister. Tush, I can handle that after the best rate.

104 Arms!] God's arms! sound] swoon. 123 portly brag . . . estate] dignified bearing suitable to your rank.

Merrygreek. Well done! So lo! Up, man, with your head and chin!
Up with that snout, man! So lo! now ye begin!
So! that is somewhat like! But, pranky-coat, nay, whan?
That is a lusty brute! Hands under your side, man!
So lo! Now is it even as it should be!
That is somewhat like, for a man of your degree! 130
Then must ye stately go, jetting up and down.
Tut! can ye no better shake the tail of your gown?
There, lo! such a lusty brag it is ye must make!

Roister Doister. To come behind and make curtsy, thou must some pains take.

Merrygreek. Else were I much to blame, I thank your mastership.
The lord one day all to begrime you with worship!
Back, sir sauce! let gentlefolks have elbow room!
Void, sirs! see ye not Master Roister Doister come?
Make place, my masters!

Roister Doister. Thou jostlest now too nigh.

Merrygreek. Back, all rude louts!

Roister Doister. Tush!

Merrygreek. I cry your maship mercy! 140
Hoighdagh! if fair, fine mistress Custance saw you now,
Ralph Roister Doister were her own, I warrant you.

Roister Doister. Ne'er an M by your girdle?

Merrygreek. Your good Mastership's
Mastership were her own Mistress-ship's Mistress-ships,
Ye were take up for hawks, ye were gone, ye were gone!

127 pranky-coat] that 's a dandy! 128 brute] gallant; cf. I. ii. 124. 131 jetting] strutting. 136 all to begrime] altogether besmear. 137 sir sauce] saucy fellow. 143 Ne'er . . . girdle?] Have you not a respectful M (Master) to address me by? 145 Ye were take up for hawks] You would be snapped up as a husband for hawk's meat (a proverbial phrase).

But now one other thing more yet I think upon.
Roister Doister. Show what it is.
Merrygreek. A wooer, be he never so poor,
Must play and sing before his best-beloved's door;
How much more, then, you?
Roister Doister. Thou speakest well, out of doubt.
Merrygreek. And perchance that would make her the sooner come out. 150
Roister Doister. Go call my musicians; bid them hie apace.
Merrygreek. I will be here with them ere ye can say *trey ace.* [*Exit.*
Roister Doister. This was well said of Merrygreek! I 'low his wit.
Before my sweetheart's door we will have a fit,
That, if my love come forth, that I may with her talk,
I doubt not but this gear shall on my side walk.
But lo, how well Merrygreek is returned sence!

Re-enter Merrygreek *with the musicians*

Merrygreek. There hath grown no grass on my heel since I went hence!
Lo, here have I brought that shall make you pastance.
Roister Doister. Come, sirs, let us sing, to win my dear love Custance. 160

They sing

I mun be married a Sunday;
I mun be married a Sunday;
Whosoever shall come that way,
  I mun be married a Sunday.

Roister Doister is my name,
Roister Doister is my name;
A lusty brute, I am the same,
  I mun be married a Sunday.

152 *trey ace*] a throw at dice that turns up trey, three pips, with one dice and ace with the other. 153 'low] allow, approve. 154 fit] strain of music. 157 sence] since, already.

Christian Custance have I found,
Christian Custance have I found, 170
A widow worth a thousand pound.
I mun be married a Sunday.

Custance is as sweet as honey,
Custance is as sweet as honey;
I her lamb and she my coney,
I mun be married a Sunday.

When we shall make our wedding feast,
When we shall make our wedding feast,
There shall be cheer for man and beast.
I mun be married a Sunday. 180
I mun be married a Sunday, &c.

Merrygreek. Lo, where she cometh! Some countenance to her make,
And ye shall hear me be plain with her for your sake.

SCENE IV

Merrygreek *and* Roister Doister. *Enter* Dame Custance

Dame Custance. What gauding and fooling is this afore my door?
Merrygreek. May not folks be honest, pray you, though they be poor?
Dame Custance. As that thing may be true, so rich folks may be fools.
Roister Doister. Her talk is as fine as she had learned in schools.
Merrygreek. Look partly toward her, and draw a little near.
Dame Custance. Get ye home, idle folks!
Merrygreek. Why, may not we be here?
Nay, and ye will haze, haze; otherwise, I tell you plain,
And ye will not haze, then give us our gear again.

1 gauding] sporting. 7 haze] have us.

Dame Custance. Indeed I have of yours much gay things, God save all.
Roister Doister. Speak gently to her, and let her take all. 10
Merrygreek. Ye are too tender-hearted; shall she make us daws?
Nay, dame, I will be plain with you in my friend's cause.
Roister Doister. Let all this pass, sweetheart, and accept my service!
Dame Custance. I will not be served with a fool, in no wise;
When I choose an husband, I hope to take a man.
Merrygreek. And where will ye find one which can do that he can?
Now this man toward you being so kind,
You not to make him an answer somewhat to his mind!
Dame Custance. I sent him a full answer by you, did I not?
Merrygreek. And I reported it.
Dame Custance. Nay, I must speak it again 20
Roister Doister. No, no! he told it all.
Merrygreek. Was I not meetly plain?
Roister Doister. Yes.
Merrygreek. But I would not tell all; for faith, if I had,
With you, Dame Custance, ere this hour it had been bad,
And not without cause, for this goodly personage
Meant no less than to join with you in marriage.
Dame Custance. Let him waste no more labour nor suit about me.
Merrygreek. Ye know not where your preferment lieth, I see,
He sending you such a token, ring and letter.
Dame Custance. Marry, here it is; ye never saw a better!
Merrygreek. Let us see your letter.

21 meetly] suitably.

Dame Custance. Hold, read it, if ye can. 30
And see what letter it is to win a woman!
Merrygreek. 'To mine own dear coney, bird, sweetheart, and pigsny,
Good Mistress Custance, present these by and by.'
Of this superscription do ye blame the style?
Dame Custance. With the rest as good stuff as ye read a great while!
Merrygreek. 'Sweet mistress, whereas I love you nothing at all,
Regarding your substance and riches chief of all,
For your personage, beauty, demeanour and wit
I commend me unto you never a whit.
Sorry to hear report of your good welfare. 40
For (as I hear say) such your conditions are
That ye be worthy favour of no living man;
To be abhorred of every honest man;
To be taken for a woman inclined to vice;
Nothing at all to virtue giving her due price.
Wherefore concerning marriage, ye are thought
Such a fine paragon, as ne'er honest man bought.
And now by these presents I do you advertise
That I am minded to marry you in no wise.
For your goods and substance, I could be content 50
To take you as ye are. If ye mind to be my wife,
Ye shall be assured for the time of my life
I will keep you right well from good raiment and fare;
Ye shall not be kept but in sorrow and care.
Ye shall in no wise live at your own liberty;
Do and say what ye lust, ye shall never please me;
But when ye are merry, I will be all sad,
When ye are sorry, I will be very glad;
When ye seek your heart's ease, I will be unkind;
At no time, in me shall ye much gentleness find. 60
But all things contrary to your will and mind
Shall be done: otherwise I will not be behind

32 coney] *see* I. iv. 25. pigsny] *see* I. iv. 42.

To speak. And as for all them that would do you wrong
I will so help and maintain, ye shall not live long.
Nor any foolish dolt shall cumber you but I.
I, whoe'er say nay, will stick by you till I die.
Thus good mistress Custance, the Lord you save and keep
From me Roister Doister, whether I wake or sleep.
Who favoureth you no less (ye may be bold)
Than this letter purporteth, which ye have unfold.' 70

Dame Custance. How by this letter of love? is it not fine?

Roister Doister. By the arms of Calais, it is none of mine!

Merrygreek. Fie, you are foul to blame! this is your own hand!

Dame Custance. Might not a woman be proud of such an husband?

Merrygreek. Ah, that ye would in a letter show such despite!

Roister Doister. Oh, I would I had him here, the which did it endite.

Merrygreek. Why, ye made it yourself, ye told me by this light.

Roister Doister. Yea, I meant I wrote it mine own self, yesternight.

Dame Custance. Iwis, sir, I would not have sent you such a mock.

Roister Doister. Ye may so take it, but I meant it not so, by Cock. 80

Merrygreek. Who can blame this woman to fume, and fret, and rage?
Tut, tut! yourself now have marred your own marriage.
Well, yet, mistress Custance, if ye can this remit,
This gentleman otherwise may your love requit.

72 By the arms of Calais] *this oath, used also by Skelton, is repeated in* IV. vii. 49.

Dame Custance. No! God be with you both, and seek no more to me. [*Exit.*

Roister Doister. Wough! she is gone for ever! I shall her no more see!

Merrygreek. What, weep? fie, for shame! and blubber? For manhood's sake,
Never let your foe so much pleasure of you take!
Rather play the man's part, and do love refrain.
If she despise you, e'en despise ye her again! 90

Roister Doister. By Goss, and for thy sake I defy her indeed!

Merrygreek. Yea, and perchance that way ye shall much sooner speed;
For one mad property these women have, in fey:
When ye will, they will not; will not ye, then will they.
Ah, foolish woman! Ah, most unlucky Custance!
Ah, unfortunate woman! Ah, peevish Custance!
Art thou to thine harms so obstinately bent
That thou canst not see where lieth thine high preferment?
Canst thou not lub dis man, which could lub dee so well?
Art thou so much thine own foe?

Roister Doister. Thou dost the truth tell. 100

Merrygreek. Well, I lament.

Roister Doister. So do I.

Merrygreek. Wherefore?

Roister Doister. For this thing
Because she is gone.

Merrygreek. I mourn for another thing.

Roister Doister. What is it, Merrygreek, wherefore thou dost grief take?

Merrygreek. That I am not a woman myself for your sake,
I would have you myself, and a straw for yond Gill!

91 By Goss] *an affected form of* By God. 105 Gill] wench.

And mock much of you, though it were against my will.
I would not, I warrant you, fall in such a rage
As so to refuse such a goodly personage.
Roister Doister. In faith, I heartily thank thee, Merrygreek.
Merrygreek. An I were a woman——
Roister Doister. Thou wouldest to me seek. 110
Merrygreek. For, though I say it, a goodly person ye be.
Roister Doister. No, no.
Merrygreek. Yes, a goodly man as e'er I did see.
Roister Doister. No, I am a poor homely man, as God made me.
Merrygreek. By the faith that I owe to God, sir, but ye be!
Would I might, for your sake, spend a thousand pound land.
Roister Doister. I dare say thou wouldest have me to thy husband.
Merrygreek. Yea; an I were the fairest lady in the shire,
And knew you as I know you, and see you now here—
Well, I say no more!
Roister Doister. Gramercies, with all my heart!
Merrygreek. But since that cannot be, will ye play a wise part? 120
Roister Doister. How should I?
Merrygreek. Refrain from Custance awhile now,
And I warrant her soon right glad to seek to you.
Ye shall see her anon come on her knees creeping,
And pray you to be good to her, salt tears weeping.
Roister Doister. But what an she come not?
Merrygreek. In faith, then, farewell she!
Or else if ye be wroth, ye may avenged be.
Roister Doister. By Cock's precious potstick, and e'en so I shall!

106 mock] see I. iv. 18.

I will utterly destroy her, and house and all!
But I would be avenged in the mean space,
On that vile scribbler, that did my wooing disgrace.

Merrygreek. 'Scribbler,' ko you? indeed, he is worthy no less. 131
I will call him to you, and ye bid me, doubtless.

Roister Doister. Yes, for although he had as many lives,
As a thousand widows, and a thousand wives,
As a thousand lions, and a thousand rats,
A thousand wolves, and a thousand cats,
A thousand bulls, and a thousand calves,
And a thousand legions divided in halves,
He shall never 'scape death on my sword's point—
Though I should be torn therefore joint by joint! 140

Merrygreek. Nay, if ye will kill him, I will not fetch him;
I will not in so much extremity set him.
He may yet amend, sir, and be an honest man.
Therefore pardon him, good soul, as much as ye can.

Roister Doister. Well, for thy sake, this once with his life he shall pass.
But I will hew him all to pieces, by the Mass!

Merrygreek. Nay, faith, ye shall promise that he shall no harm have,
Else I will not fetch him.

Roister Doister. I shall, so God me save!
But I may chide him a good?

Merrygreek. Yea, that do hardily.

Roister Doister. Go, then. 150

Merrygreek. I return, and bring him to you by-and-by.
[*Exit*.

SCENE V

Roister Doister

Roister Doister. What is a gentleman but his word and his promise?
I must now save this villain's life in any wise;

130 scribbler] Roister Doister *means* scrivener. 149 a good] in good earnest.

And yet at him already my hands do tickle,
I shall uneth hold them, they will be so fickle.
[*Enter* Merrygreek *and* Scrivener
But lo an Merrygreek have not brought him sens.
Merrygreek. Nay, I would I had of my purse paid forty pens!
Scrivener. So would I, too; but it needed not that stound.
Merrygreek. But the gentman had rather spent five thousand pound;
For it disgraced him at least five times so much.
Scrivener. He disgraced himself, his loutishness is such.
Roister Doister. How long they stand prating! Why comest thou not away? 11
Merrygreek. Come now to himself, and hark what he will say.
Scrivener. I am not afraid in his presence to appear.
Roister Doister. Art thou come, fellow?
Scrivener. How think you? am I not here?
Roister Doister. What hindrance hast thou done me, and what villainy?
Scrivener. It hath come of thyself, if thou hast had any.
Roister D. All the stock thou comest of, later or rather,
From thy first father's grandfather's father's father,
Nor all that shall come of thee, to the world's end,
Though to threescore generations they descend, 20
Can be able to make me a just recompense
For this trespass of thine and this one offence!
Scrivener. Wherein?
Roister Doister. Did not you make me a letter, brother?
Scrivener. Pay the like hire, I will make you such another.
Roister Doister. Nay, see and these whoreson Pharisees and Scribes
Do not get their living by polling and bribes!

4 uneth] with difficulty. 5 sens] since, already.
7 that stound] at that time. 17 rather] earlier.
26 polling] extortion.

If it were not for shame——

Scrivener. Nay, hold thy hands still!

Merrygreek. Why, did ye not promise that ye would not him spill?

Scrivener. Let him not spare me.

Roister Doister. Why, wilt thou strike me again?

Scrivener. Ye shall have as good as ye bring, of me; that is plain. 30

Merrygreek. I cannot blame him, sir, though your blows would him grieve.
For he knoweth present death to ensue of all ye give.

Roister Doister. Well, this man for once hath purchased thy pardon.

Scrivener. And what say ye to me? or else I will be gone.

Roister Doister. I say the letter thou madest me was not good.

Scrivener. Then did ye wrong copy it, of likelihood.

Roister Doister. Yes, out of thy copy word for word I wrote.

Scrivener. Then was it as ye prayed to have it, I wote,
But in reading and pointing there was made some fault.

Roister Doister. I wot not; but it made all my matter to halt. 40

Scrivener. How say you, is this mine original or no?

Roister Doister. The self same that I wrote out of, so mote I go.

Scrivener. Look you on your own fist, and I will look on this,
And let this man be judge whether I read amiss.
'To mine own dear cony, bird, sweetheart, and pigsny,
Good Mistress Custance, present these by-and-by.'
How now? doth not this superscription agree?

Roister Doister. Read that is within, and there ye shall the fault see.

28 spill] destroy. 42 wrote out of] copied.
43 fist] handwriting.

Scrivener. 'Sweet mistress, whereas I love you—nothing at all
Regarding your riches and substance, chief of all 50
For your personage, beauty, demeanour and wit—
I commend me unto you. Never a whit
Sorry to hear report of your good welfare;
For (as I hear say) such your conditions are
That ye be worthy favour; of no living man
To be abhorred; of every honest man
To be taken for a woman inclined to vice
Nothing at all; to virtue giving her due price.
Wherefore, concerning marriage, ye are thought
Such a fine paragon, as ne'er honest man bought. 60
And now by these presents I do you advertise
That I am minded to marry you—in no wise
For your goods and substance: I can be content
To take you as you are. If ye will be my wife,
Ye shall be assured for the time of my life
I will keep you right well. From good raiment and fare,
Ye shall not be kept; but in sorrow and care
Ye shall in no wise live; at your own liberty,
Do and say what ye lust: ye shall never please me
But when ye are merry; I will be all sad 70
When ye are sorry; I will be very glad
When ye seek your heart's ease; I will be unkind
At no time; in me shall ye much gentleness find.
But all things contrary to your will and mind
Shall be done otherwise; I will not be behind
To speak. And as for all they that would do you wrong
(I will so help and maintain ye), shall not live long.
Nor any foolish dolt shall cumber you; but I—
I, whoe'er say nay—will stick by you till I die.
Thus, good mistress Custance, the Lord you save and keep. 80
From me, Roister Doister, whether I wake or sleep,
Who favoureth you no less (ye may be bold)

Than this letter purporteth, which ye have unfold.'
Now, sir, what default can ye find in this letter?

Roister Doister. Of truth, in my mind, there cannot be a better.

Scrivener. Then was the fault in reading, and not in writing—
No, nor I dare say, in the form of enditing.
But who read this letter, that it sounded so naught?

Merrygreek. I read it, indeed.

Scrivener. Ye read it not as ye ought.

Roister Doister. Why, thou wretched villain! was all this same fault in thee? 90

Merrygreek. I knock your costard if ye offer to strike me!

Roister Doister. Strikest thou, indeed? and I offer but in jest?

Merrygreek. Yea, and rap you again except ye can sit in rest.
And I will no longer tarry here, me believe.

Roister Doister. What! wilt thou be angry, and I do thee forgive?
Fare thou well, scribbler. I cry thee mercy indeed!

Scrivener. Fare ye well, bibbler, and worthily may ye speed!

Roister Doister. If it were another but thou, it were a knave.

Merrygreek. Ye are another yourself, sir, the Lord us both save!
Albeit, in this matter I must your pardon crave. 100
Alas! would ye wish in me the wit that ye have?
But, as for my fault, I can quickly amend;
I will show Custance it was I that did offend.

Roister Doister. By so doing, her anger may be reformed.

Merrygreek. But, if by no entreaty she will be turned,
Then set light by her, and be as testy as she,
And do your force upon her with extremity.

91 costard] head. 104 reformed] appeased.

Roister Doister. Come on, therefore, let us go home, in sadness.

Merrygreek. That, if force shall need, all may be in a readiness,
And as for this letter, hardily let all go; 110
We will know where she refuse you for that or no.
[*Exeunt.*

ACT IV

SCENE I

Enter Sim Suresby

Suresby. Is there any man but I, Sim Suresby, alone,
That would have taken such an enterprise him upon,
In such an outrageous tempest as this was,
Such a dangerous gulf of the sea to pass?
I think verily Neptune's mighty godship
Was angry with some that was in our ship;
And, but for the honesty which in me he found,
I think for the others' sake we had been drowned.
But fie on that servant which for his master's wealth
Will stick for to hazard both his life and his health! 10
My master, Gawyn Goodluck, after me a day,
Because of the weather, thought best his ship to stay,
And now that I have the rough surges so well past,
God grant I may find all things safe here at last!
Then will I think all my travail well spent.
Now the first point wherefore my master hath me sent
Is to salute Dame Christian Custance, his wife
Espoused, whom he tendereth no less than his life.

111 where] whether. 9 wealth] welfare.

I must see how it is with her, well or wrong,
And whether for him she doth not now think long. 20
Then to other friends I have a message or tway;
And then so to return and meet him on the way.
Now will I go knock that I may dispatch with speed—
But lo, forth cometh herself, happily, indeed!

SCENE II

Sim Suresby. *Enter* Dame Custance

Dame Custance. I come to see if any more stirring be here.
But what stranger is this which doth to me appear?
Suresby. I will speak to her. Dame, the Lord you save and see!
Dame Custance. What! friend Sim Suresby? Forsooth, right welcome ye be!
How doth mine own Gawyn Goodluck? I pray thee tell?
Suresby. When he knoweth of your health, he will be perfect well.
Dame Custance. If he have perfect health, I am as I would be.
Suresby. Such news will please him well; this is as it should be.
Dame Custance. I think now long for him.
Suresby. And he as long for you.
Dame Custance. When will he be at home?
Suresby. His heart is here e'en now; 10
His body cometh after.
Dame Custance. I would see that fain.
Suresby. As fast as wind and sail can carry it amain—
But what two men are yond coming hitherward?
Dame Custance. Now, I shrew their best Christmas cheeks, both togetherward!

SCENE III

Dame Custance *and* Suresby. *Enter* Roister Doister *and* Merrygreek

Dame Custance. What mean these lewd fellows thus to trouble me still?
Sim Suresby here, perchance, shall thereof deem some ill,
And shall suspect in me some point of naughtiness,
An they come hitherward.
Suresby. What is their business?
Dame Custance. I have nought to them, nor they to me in sadness.
Suresby. Let us hearken them. Somewhat there is, I fear it.
Roister Doister. I will speak out aloud; best that she may hear it.
Merrygreek. Nay, alas, ye may so fear her out of her wit!
Roister Doister. By the cross of my sword, I will hurt her no whit!
Merrygreek. Will ye do no harm indeed? Shall I trust your word? 10
Roister Doister. By Roister Doister's faith, I will speak but in bord!
Suresby. Let us hearken them. Somewhat there is, I fear it.
Roister Doister. I will speak out aloud, I care not who hear it!
Sirs, see that my harness, my target, and my shield
Be made as bright now as when I was last in field,
As white as I should to war again to-morrow;
For sick shall I be but I work some folk sorrow.
Therefore see that all shine as bright as Saint George
Or as doth a key newly come from the smith's forge
I would have my sword and harness to shine so bright

5 in sadness] in sober earnest. 11 bord] jest.
14 harness] armour.

That I might therewith dim mine enemies' sight, 21
I would have it cast beams as fast, I tell you plain,
As doth the glittering grass after a shower of rain.
And see that, in case I should need to come to arming,
All things may be ready at a minute's warning!
For such chance may chance in an hour, do ye hear?

Merrygreek. As perchance shall not chance again in seven year.

Roister Doister. Now draw we near to her, and hear what shall be said.

Merrygreek. But I would not have you make her too much afraid.

Roister Doister. Well found, sweet wife, I trust, for all this your sour look! 30

Dame Custance. Wife! why call ye me wife?

Suresby. Wife! this gear goeth acrook!

Merrygreek. Nay, Mistress Custance, I warrant you, our letter
Is not as we read e'en now, but much better;
And where ye half stomached this gentleman afore
For this same letter, ye will love him now therefore.
Nor it is not this letter, though ye were a queen,
That should break marriage between you twain, I ween.

Dame Custance. I did not refuse him for the letter's sake.

Roister Doister. Then ye are content me for your husband to take?

Dame Custance. You for my husband to take? nothing less, truly! 40

Roister Doister. Yea, say so, sweet spouse, afore strangers hardily!

Merrygreek. And, though I have here his letter of love with me,
Yet his ring and tokens he sent keep safe with ye.

Dame Custance. A mischief take his tokens! and him, and thee too.
But what prate I with fools? have I nought else to do?

34 stomached] felt resentment against.

Come in with me, Sim Suresby, to take some repast.
Suresby. I must, ere I drink, by your leave, go in all haste
To a place or two, with earnest letters of his.
Dame Custance. Then come drink here with me.
Suresby. I thank you.
Dame Custance. Do not miss;
You shall have a token to your master with you. 50
Suresby. No tokens this time, gramercies! God be with you. [*Exit.*
Dame Custance. Surely this fellow misdeemeth some ill in me;
Which thing, but God help, will go near to spill me.
Roister Doister. Yea, farewell, fellow! And tell thy master, Goodluck,
That he cometh too late of this blossom to pluck!
Let him keep him there still, or at leastwise, make no haste;
As for his labour hither, he shall spend in waste:
His betters be in place now!
Merrygreek. [*Aside.*] As long as it will hold.
Dame Custance. I will be even with thee, thou beast, thou mayst be bold!
Roister Doister. Will ye have us then?
Dame Custance. I will never have thee! 60
Roister Doister. Then will I have you.
Dame Custance. No, the devil shall have thee!
I have gotten this hour more shame and harm by thee!
Than all thy life days thou canst do me honesty.
Merrygreek. Why now may ye see what it cometh to, in the end,
To make a deadly foe of your most loving friend!
And iwis, this letter, if ye would hear it now——
Dame Custance. I will hear none of it!
Merrygreek. In faith, would ravish you.
Dame Custance. He hath stained my name for ever, this is clear.

59 be bold] feel confident.

Roister Doister. I can make all as well in an hour—
Merrygreek. As ten year.
How say ye? will ye have him?
Dame Custance. No.
Merrygreek. Will ye take him? 70
Dame Custance. I defy him.
Merrygreek. At my word?
Dame Custance. A shame take him!
Waste no more wind, for it will never be.
Merrygreek. This one fault with twain shall be mended, ye shall see.
Gentle Mistress Custance now, good Mistress Custance,
Honey Mistress Custance now, sweet Mistress Custance,
Golden Mistress Custance now, white Mistress Custance,
Silken Mistress Custance now, fair Mistress Custance—
Dame Custance. Faith, rather than to marry with such a doltish lout,
I would match myself with a beggar, out of doubt!
Merrygreek. Then I can say no more. To speed we are not like, 80
Except ye rap out a rag of your rhetoric.
Dame Custance. Speak not of winning me; for it shall never be so.
Roister Doister. Yes, dame! I will have you, whether ye will or no.
I command you to love me! Wherefore should ye not?
Is not my love to you chafing and burning hot?
Merrygreek. To her! that is well said!
Roister Doister. Shall I so break my brain
To dote upon you, and ye not love us again?
Merrygreek. Well said yet!
Dame Custance. Go to, you goose!

76 white] dear; cf. I. i. 49.

Roister Doister. I say, Kit Custance,
In case ye will not haze, well, better yes, perchance!
Dame Custance. Avaunt, lozel! Pick thee hence!
Merrygreek. Well, sir, ye perceive, 90
For all your kind offer, she will not you receive.
Roister Doister. Then a straw for her! And a straw for her again!
She shall not be my wife, would she never so fain!
No, and though she would be at ten thousand pound cost!
Merrygreek. Lo, dame, ye may see what an husband ye have lost!
Dame Custance. Yea, no force; a jewel much better lost than found!
Merrygreek. Ah, ye will not believe how this doth my heart wound!
How should a marriage between you be toward,
If both parties draw back and become so froward?
Roister Doister. Nay, dame, I will fire thee out of thy house, 100
And destroy thee and all thine, and that by and by.
Merrygreek. Nay, for the passion of God, sir, do not so!
Roister Doister. Yes, except she will say yea to that she said no.
Dame Custance. And what! be there no officers, trow we, in town
To check idle loiterers bragging up and down?
Where be they by whom vagabonds should be re-prest,
That poor silly widows might live in peace and rest.
Shall I never rid thee out of my company?
I will call for help. What ho! come forth, True-penny!

89 haze] have us. 90 lozel] lout. 96 no force] it does not matter. 100 house] *as this does not rhyme with* by and by, *it has been suggested that Udall wrote* sty, *a contemptuous term for a dwelling.* 107 silly] helpless.

Enter Truepenny

Truepenny. Anon. What is your will, mistress? did ye call me? 110

Dame Custance. Yea; go run apace, and as fast as may be,

Pray Tristram Trusty, my most assured friend,

To be here by and by, that he may me defend.

Truepenny. That message so quickly shall be done, by God's grace,

That at my return ye shall say, I went apace. [*Exit.*

Dame Custance. Then shall we see, I trow, whether ye shall do me harm!

Roister Doister. Yes, in faith, Kit, I shall thee and thine so charm,

That all women incarnate by thee may beware.

Dame Custance. Nay, as for charming me, come hither if thou dare!

I shall clout thee till thou stink, both thee and thy train, 120

And coil thee mine own hands, and send thee home again.

Roister Doister. Yea, sayest thou me that, dame? Dost thou me threaten?

Go we, I will see whether I shall be beaten.

Merrygreek. Nay, for the pash of God, let me now treat peace,

For bloodshed will there be, in case this strife increase.

Ah, good Dame Custance, take better way with you!

Dame Custance. Let him do his worst!

Merrygreek. Yield in time.

Roister Doister. Come hence, thou!

[*Exeunt* Roister Doister *and* Merrygreek.

117 charm] overcome. 121 coil] beat. 124 for the pash] *apparently a short form of* for the passion; cf. l. 102, and IV. viii. 52, and V. v. 4.

SCENE IV

Dame Custance

Dame Custance. So, sirrah! If I should not with him take this way,
I should not be rid of him, I think, till doom's day.
I will call forth my folks, that, without any mocks,
If he come again, we may give him raps and knocks.
Madge Mumblecrust, come forth! and Tibet Talkapace!
Yea, and come forth, too, Mistress Annot Alyface!

Enter Tib. Talkapace, Ann. Alyface, *and* M. Mumblecrust

Ann. Alyface. I come.
Tib. Talkapace. And I am here.
M. Mumblecrust. And I am here too at length.
Dame Custance. Like warriors, if need be, ye must show your strength.
The man that this day hath thus beguiled you
Is Ralph Roister Doister, whom ye know well enow, 10
The most lout and dastard that ever on ground trod.
Tib. Talkapace. I see all folk mock him when he goeth abroad.
Dame Custance. What, pretty maid! will ye talk when I speak?
Tib. Talkapace. No, forsooth, good mistress.
Dame Custance. Will ye my tale break?
He threateneth to come hither with all his force to fight;
I charge you, if he come, on him with all your might!
M. Mumblecrust. I with my distaff will reach him one rap!
Tib. Talkapace. And I with my new broom will sweep him one swap,
And then with our great club I will reach him one rap!

Ann. Alyface. And I with our skimmer will fling him one flap! 20

Tib. Talkapace. Then Truepenny's firefork will him shrewdly fray,
And you with the spit may drive him quite away.

Dame Custance. Go, make all ready, that it may be e'en so.

Tib. Talkapace. For my part, I shrew them that last about it go!

[*Exeunt* Tib. *and* Ann.

SCENE V

Dame Custance

Dame Custance. Truepenny did promise me to run a great pace,
My friend Tristram Trusty to fetch into this place.
Indeed he dwelleth hence a good start, I confess;
But yet a quick messenger might twice since, as I guess,
Have gone and come again. Ah, yond I spy him now!

Enter Truepenny *and* Tristram Trusty

Truepenny. Ye are a slow goer, sir, I make God avow;
My mistress Custance will in me put all the blame.
Your legs be longer than mine; come apace, for shame!

Dame Custance. I can thee thank, Truepenny; thou hast done right well.

Truepenny. Mistress, since I went, no grass hath grown on my heel; 10
But Master Tristram Trusty here maketh no speed.

Dame Custance. That he came at all, I thank him in very deed,
For now have I need of the help of some wise man.

Trusty. Then may I be gone again, for none such I am.

3 start] distance.

Truepenny. Ye may be by your going; for no alderman
Can go, I dare say, a sadder pace than ye can.

Dame Custance. Truepenny, get thee in. Thou shalt among them know
How to use thyself, like a proper man, I trow.

Truepenny. I go. [*Exit*.

Dame Custance. Now, Tristram Trusty, I thank you right much;
For, at my first sending, to come ye never grutch. 20

Trusty. Dame Custance, God ye save! and, while my life shall last,
For my friend Goodluck's sake ye shall not send in wast.

Dame Custance. He shall give you thanks.

Trusty. I will do much for his sake.

Dame Custance. But, alack, I fear, great displeasure shall be take!

Trusty. Wherefore?

Dame Custance. For a foolish matter.

Trusty. What is your cause?

Dame Custance. I am ill accombred with a couple of daws.

Trusty. Nay, weep not, woman, but tell me what your cause is.
As concerning my friend is anything amiss?

Dame Custance. No, not on my part; but here was Sim Suresby—

Trusty. He was with me and told me so.

Dame Custance. And he stood by 30
While Ralph Roister Doister, with help of Merrygreek,
For promise of marriage did unto me seek.

Trusty. And had ye made any promise before them twain?

Dame Custance. No; I had rather be torn in pieces and slain!

16 sadder] more solemn. 26 accombred] encumbered. daws] dolts.

No man hath my faith and troth but Gawyn Goodluck,
And that before Suresby did I say, and there stuck,
But of certain letters there were such words spoken—

Trusty. He told me that too.

Dame Custance. And of a ring, and token,
That Suresby, I spied, did more than half suspect
That I my faith to Gawyn Goodluck did reject. 40

Trusty. But there was no such matter, Dame Custance, indeed?

Dame Custance. If ever my head thought it, God send me ill speed!
Wherefore I beseech you, with me to be a witness
That in all my life I never intended thing less,
And what a brainsick fool Ralph Roister Doister is
Yourself know well enough.

Trusty. Ye say full true, iwis!

Dame Custance. Because to be his wife I nor grant nor apply,
Hither will he come, he sweareth, by and by,
To kill both me and mine, and beat down my house flat.
Therefore I pray your aid.

Trusty. I warrant you that. 50

Dame Custance. Have I so many years lived a sober life,
And showed myself honest, maid, widow, and wife,
And now to be abused in such a vile sort?
Ye see how poor widows live, all void of comfort!

Trusty. I warrant him do you no harm nor wrong at all.

Dame Custance. No; but Matthew Merrygreek doth me most appal,
That he would join himself with such a wretched lout.

Trusty. He doth it for a jest; I know him out of doubt,
And here cometh Merrygreek.

Dame Custance. Then shall we hear his mind.

47 apply] take into consideration.

SCENE VI

Dame Custance *and* Trusty. *Enter* Merrygreek

Merrygreek. Custance and Trusty both, I do you here well find.

Dame Custance. Ah, Matthew Merrygreek, ye have used me well!

Merrygreek. Now for altogether ye must your answer tell:
Will ye have this man, woman? or else, will ye not?
Else will he come—never boar so brim nor toast so hot.

Trusty and Dame Custance. But why join ye with him?

Trusty. For mirth?

Dame Custance. Or else in sadness?

Merrygreek. The more fond of you both! hardily the matter guess.

Trusty. Lo, how say ye, dame?

Merrygreek. Why do ye think, Dame Custance,
That in this wooing I have meant aught but pastance?

Dame Custance. Much things ye spake, I wot, to maintain his dotage. 10

Merrygreek. But well might ye judge I spake it all in mockage.
For why, is Roister Doister a fit husband for you?

Trusty. I daresay ye never thought it.

Merrygreek. No; to God I vow!
And did not I know afore of the insurance
Between Gawyn Goodluck and Christian Custance?
And did not I for the nonce, by my conveyance,
Read his letter in a wrong sense for dalliance?
That, if you could have take it up at the first bound,
We should thereat such a sport and pastime have found,
That all the whole town should have been the merrier? 20

5 brim] furious. 6 in sadness] seriously.
7 fond] foolish. hardily] surely. 9 pastance] pastime.
14 insurance] contract. 16 conveyance] cunning.

Dame Custance. Ill ache your heads both! I was never wearier,
Nor never more vexed, since the first day I was born!
Trusty. But very well I wist he here did all in scorn.
Dame Custance. But I feared thereof to take dishonesty.
Merrygreek. This should both have made sport and showed your honesty;
And Goodluck, I dare swear, your wit therein would 'low.
Trusty. Yea, being no worse than we know it to be now.
Merrygreek. And nothing yet too late; for, when I come to him,
Hither will he repair with a sheep's look full grim,
By plain force and violence to drive you to yield. 30
Dame Custance. If ye two bid me, we will with him pitch a field,
I and my maids together.
Merrygreek. Let us see! be bold!
Dame Custance. Ye shall see women's war!
Trusty. That fight will I behold.
Merrygreek. If occasion serve, taking his part full brim,
I will strike at you, but the rap shall light on him,
When we first appear.
Dame Custance. Then will I run away
As though I were afeard.
Trusty. Do you that part well play;
And I will sue for peace.
Merrygreek. And I will set him on.
Then will he look as fierce as a Cotswold lion.
Trusty. But when goest thou for him?
Merrygreek. That do I very now. 40
Dame Custance. Ye shall find us here.
Merrygreek. Well, God have mercy on you! [*Exit.*
Trusty. There is no cause of fear. The least boy in the street——

24 dishonesty] dishonour. 26 'low] allow, approve.
34 brim] see l. 5. 39 Cotswold lion] sheep.

Dame Custance. Nay, the least girl I have will make him take his feet.
But hark! methink they make preparation.
Trusty. No force, it will be a good recreation.
Dame Custance. I will stand within, and step forth speedily,
And so make as though I ran away dreadfully.
[*Exeunt.*

SCENE VII

Enter Roister Doister, Doughty, Harpax, Merrygreek *and two drums with their ensigns*

Roister Doister. Now, sirs, keep your 'ray; and see your hearts be stout!
But where be these caitiffs? methink they dare not rout!
How sayest thou, Merrygreek? What doth Kit Custance say?
Merrygreek. I am loth to tell you.
Roister Doister. Tush, speak, man! yea or nay?
Merrygreek. Forsooth, sir, I have spoken for you all that I can.
But, if ye win her, ye must e'en play the man;
E'en to fight it out ye must a man's heart take.
Roister Doister. Yes, they shall know, and thou knowest, I have a stomacke.
Merrygreek. 'A stomach', quod you, yea, as good as e'er man had.
Roister Doister. I trow they shall find and feel that I am a lad. 10
Merrygreek. By this cross, I have seen you eat your meat as well

45 No force] doubtless. 47 dreadfully] in terror. S.D. *drums with their ensigns*] ? Drummers with their standards. *This has been transferred from the S.D. at the head of* Sc. viii. 1 'ray] array. 2 rout] stir. 8 a stomacke] bravery, *but taken by Merrygreek in its ordinary meaning.*

As any that e'er I have seen of or heard tell!
'A stomach', quod you? he that will that deny,
I know was never at dinner in your company!
Roister D. Nay, the stomach of a man it is that I mean!
Merrygreek. Nay, the stomach of a horse, or a dog, I ween.
Roister Doister. Nay, a man's stomach with a weapon, mean I.
Merrygreek. Ten men can scarce match you with a spoon in a pie.
Roister Doister. Nay, the stomach of a man to try in strife.
Merrygreek. I never saw your stomach cloyed yet in my life. 20
Roister Doister. Tush! I mean in strife or fighting to try.
Merrygreek. We shall see how ye will strike now, being angry.
Roister Doister. Have at thy pate, then! and save thy head if thou may!
Merrygreek. Nay, then, have at your pate again, by this day!
Roister Doister. Nay, thou mayst not strike at me again, in no wise.
Merrygreek. I cannot in fight make to you such warrantise.
But as for your foes here, let them the bargain 'by.
Roister Doister. Nay, as for they, shall every mother's child die.
And in this my fume a little thing might make me
To beat down house and all, and else the devil take me! 30
Merrygreek. If I were as ye be, by Gog's dear mother,
I would not leave one stone upon another,
Though she would redeem it with twenty thousand pounds.
Roister Doister. It shall be even so, by His lily wounds!

27 'by] aby, abide. 34 His lily] God's lovely.

Merrygreek. Be not at one with her upon any amends.
Roister Doister. No, though she make to me never so many friends,
Nor if all the world for her would undertake;
No, not God himself, neither, shall not her peace make!
On, therefore! March forward! Soft; stay awhile yet!
Merrygreek. On!
Roister Doister. Tarry!
Merrygreek. Forth!
Roister Doister. Back!
Merrygreek. On!
Roister Doister. Soft! Now forward set! 40

Enter Dame Custance

Dame Custance. What business have we here? Out! alas, alas! [*Exit.*
Roister Doister. Ha, ha, ha, ha, ha!
Didst thou see that, Merrygreek? how afraid she was?
Didst thou see how she fled apace out of my sight?
Ah, good sweet Custance! I pity her, by this light!
Merrygreek. That tender heart of yours will mar altogether.
Thus will ye be turned with wagging of a feather?
Roister Doister. On, sirs! keep your 'ray!
Merrygreek. On! Forth, while this gear is hot!
Roister Doister. Soft! The arms of Calais! I have one thing forgot.
Merrygreek. What lack we now?
Roister Doister. Retire! or else we be all slain! 50
Merrygreek. Back! for the pash of God! back, sirs! back again!
What is the great matter?
Roister Doister. This hasty forthgoing
Had almost brought us all to utter undoing!

48 'ray] array, order. 49 The arms of Calais] see III. iv. 72. 51 the pash of God] see IV. iii. 124.

It made me forget a thing most necessary.

Merrygreek. Well remembered of a captain, by Saint Mary!

Roister Doister. It is a thing must be had.

Merrygreek. Let us have it, then.

Roister Doister. But I wot not where, nor how.

Merrygreek. Then wot not I when. But what is it?

Roister Doister. Of a chief thing I am to seek.

Merrygreek. Tut! so will ye be, when ye have studied a week.
But tell me what it is.

Roister Doister. I lack yet an headpiece.

Merrygreek. The kitchen collocavit—the best hence to Greece, 61
Run, fetch it, Dobinet, and come at once withal,
And bring with thee my potgun, hanging by the wall! [*Exit* Doughty.
I have seen your head with it full many a time
Covered as safe as it had been with a skrine;
And I warrant it save your head from any stroke,
Except perchance to be amazed with the smoke;
I warrant your head therewith—except for the mist—
As safe as if it were fast locked up in a chist,
And lo, here our Dobinet cometh with it now! 70
[*Re-enter* Doughty.

Doughty. It will cover me to the shoulders well enow.

Merrygreek. Let me see it on.

Roister Doister. In faith, it doth meetly well.

Merrygreek. There can be no fitter thing. Now ye must us tell
What to do.

Roister Doister. Now forth in 'ray, sirs! and stop no more!

61 collocavit] *probably a Latinized form of* collock = a large pail. hence] from here. 63 potgun] pistol. 65 skrine] screen.

Merrygreek. Now Saint George to borrow! Drum, dub-a-dub afore!

Enter Trusty

Trusty. What mean you to do, sir? commit manslaughter?
Roister Doister. To kill forty such is a matter of laughter.
Trusty. And who is it, sir, whom ye intend thus to spill?
Roister Doister. Foolish Custance, here, forceth me against my will.
Trusty. And is there no mean your extreme wrath to slake? 80
She shall some amends unto your good maship make.
Roister Doister. I will none amends.
Trusty. Is her offence so sore?
Merrygreek. An he were a lout, she could have done no more.
She hath called him fool, and dressed him like a fool,
Mocked him like a fool, used him like a fool.
Trusty. Well, yet the sheriff, the justice, or constable,
Her misdemeanour to punish might be able.
Roister Doister. No, sir! I mine own self will in this present cause
Be sheriff, and justice, and whole judge of the laws,
This matter to amend, all officers be I shall— 90
Constable, bailiff, sergeant—
Merrygreek. And hangman and all.
Trusty. Yet a noble courage, and the heart of a man,
Should more honour win by bearing with a woman.
Therefore take the law, and let her answer thereto.
Roister Doister. Merrygreek, the best way were even so to do.
What honour should it be with a woman to fight?
Merrygreek. And what then! will ye thus forgo and lose your right?

75 to borrow] be our surety. 84 dressed] treated.

Roister Doister. Nay, I will take the law on her withouten grace.

Trusty. Or, if your maship could pardon this one trespace,
I pray you forgive her.

Roister Doister. Hoh!

Merrygreek. Tush! tush, sir, do not! 100
Be good, master, to her.

Roister Doister. Hoh!

Merrygreek. Tush, I say, do not!
And what! shall your people here return straight home?

Trusty. Yea; levy the camp, sirs, and hence again, each one!

Roister Doister. But be still in readiness if I hap to call;
I cannot tell what sudden chance may befall.

Merrygreek. Do not off your harness, sirs, I you advise,
At the least for this fortnight, in no manner wise;
Perchance in an hour when all ye think least,
Our master's appetite to fight will be best.
But soft! Ere ye go, have one at Custance house!

Roister Doister. Soft, what wilt thou do?

Merrygreek. Once discharge my harquebouse;
And, for my heart's ease, have once more with my potgun. 112

Roister Doister. Hold thy hands! else is all our purpose clean fordone.

Merrygreek. An it cost me my life!

Roister Doister. I say thou shalt not!

Merrygreek. By the matte, but I will! Have once more with hail shot!
I will have some pennyworth. I will not lose all.

100 Hoh!] an exclamation by heralds to stop a fight.
106 harness] armour. 115 By the matte] *probably a perversion of* by the Mass.

SCENE VIII

Merrygreek, Roister Doister, Doughty, Harpax, *and drums as before. Enter* Dame Custance

Dame Custance. What caitiffs are those that so shake my house wall?
Merrygreek. Ah, sirrah! now, Custance, if ye had so much wit,
I would see you ask pardon, and yourselves submit.
Dame Custance. Have I still this ado with a couple of fools?
Merrygreek. Hear ye what she saith?
Dame Custance. Maidens come forth with your tools!

Enter Ann. Alyface, Tib. Talkapace, M. Mumblecrust, *and* Truepenny

Roister Doister. In a ray!
Merrygreek. Dubbadub, sirrah!
Roister Doister. In a ray!
They come suddenly on us.
Merrygreek. Dubbadub!
Roister Doister. In a ray!
That ever I was born, we are taken tardy!
Merrygreek. Now, sirs, quit ourselves like tall men and hardy.
Dame Custance. On afore, Truepenny! Hold thine own, Annot! 10
On toward them, Tibet! for 'scape us they cannot.
Come forth, Madge Mumblecrust! to stand fast togither.
Merrygreek. God send us a fair day!
Roister Doister. See, they march on hither.
Tib. Talkapace. But, mistress!
Dame Custance. What sayest thou?
Tib. Talkapace. Shall I go fetch our goose?
Dame Custance. What to do?

Tib. Talkapace. To yonder captain I will turn her loose:
An she gape and hiss at him, as she doth at me,
I durst jeopard my hand she will make him flee.
Dame Custance. On! Forward!
Roister Doister. They come!
Merrygreek. Stand!
Roister Doister. Hold!
Merrygreek. Keep!
Roister Doister. There!
Merrygreek. Strike!
Roister Doister. Take heed.
Dame Custance. Well said, Truepenny!
Truepenny. Ah, whoresons!
Dame Custance. Well done, indeed.
Merrygreek. Hold thine own, Harpax! Down with them, Dobinet! 20
Dame Custance. Now, Madge! There, Annot! Now, stick them, Tibet!
Tib. Talkapace. All my chief quarrel is to this same little knave
That beguiled me last day. Nothing shall him save.
Doughty. Down with this little quean that hath at me such spite!
Save you from her, master; it is a very sprite!
Dame Custance. I myself will Mounsire Grand Captain undertake!
Roister Doister. They win ground.
Merrygreek. Save yourself, sir, for God's sake!
Roister Doister. Out alas! I am slain! help!
Merrygreek. Save yourself!
Roister Doister. Alas!
Merrygreek. Nay, then, have at you, mistress!
Roister Doister. Thou hittest me, alas!
Merrygreek. I will strike at Custance here.
Roister Doister. Thou hittest me!
Merrygreek. So I will! 30
Nay, mistress Custance.

Roister Doister. Alas, thou hittest me still! Hold!
Merrygreek. Save yourself, sir.
Roister Doister. Help! out! alas, I am slain!
Merrygreek. Truce! hold your hands! truce for a pissing-while or twain!
Nay, how say you, Custance. For saving of your life,
Will ye yield, and grant to be this gentman's wife?
Dame Custance. Ye told me he loved me. Call ye this love?
Merrygreek. He loved awhile, even like a turtledove.
Dame Custance. Gay love, God save it, so soon hot, so soon cold!
Merrygreek. I am sorry for you. He could love you yet, so he could.
Roister Doister. Nay, by Cock's precious, she shall be none of mine. 40
Merrygreek. Why so?
Roister Doister. Come away. By the matte, she is mankine!
I durst adventure the loss of my right hand
If she did not slay her other husband:
And see, if she prepare not again to fight!
Merrygreek. What then? Saint George to borrow, our ladies' knight!
Roister Doister. Slay else whom she will, by Gog, she shall not slay me!
Merrygreek. How then?
Roister Doister. Rather than to be slain, I will flee.
Dame Custance. To it again, my knightesses! down with them all!
Roister Doister. Away, away, away! She will else kill us all!
Merrygreek. Nay, stick to it, like an hardy man and a tall. 50

40 by Cock's precious] see III. iv. 127. 41 By the matte] see IV. vii. 115. mankine] mankind, masculine. 45 to borrow] be our defender!

Roister Doister. Oh, bones! thou hittest me! Away, or else die we shall!

Merrygreek. Away, for the pash of our sweet Lord Jesus Christ.

Dame Custance. Away, lout and lubber! or I shall be thy priest.

[*Exeunt* Merrygreek, Roister Doister, *and his men.*

So this field is ours, we have driven them all away.

Tib. Talkapace. Thanks to God, mistress, ye have had a fair day!

Dame Custance. Well, now go ye in, and make yourself some good cheer.

All. We go.

Trusty. Ah, sir, what a field we have had here!

Dame Custance. Friend Tristram, I pray you, be a witness with me.

Trusty. Dame Custance, I shall depose for your honesty,
And now fare ye well, except something else ye wold. 60

Dame Custance. Not now; but when I need to send, I will be bold.
I thank you for these pains. [*Exit.*] And now I will get me in.
Now Roister Doister will no more wooing begin!

[*Exit.*

ACT V

SCENE I

Enter Gawyn Goodluck *and* Sim Suresby

Goodluck. Sim Suresby, my trusty man, now advise thee well,
And see that no false surmises thou me tell:
Was there such ado about Custance, of a truth?

53 be thy priest] perform the last office for you, kill you.

Suresby. To report that I heard and saw, to me is ruth,
But both my duty and name and property
Warneth me to you to show fidelity.
It may be well enough, and I wish it so to be;
She may herself discharge, and try her honesty,
Yet their claim to her, methought, was very large,
For with letters, rings and tokens they did her charge:
Which when I heard and saw, I would none to you bring. 11

Goodluck. No, by Saint Marie! I allow thee in that thing!
Ah, sirrah, now I see truth in the proverb old:
All things that shineth is not by and by pure gold.
If any do live a woman of honesty,
I would have sworn Christian Custance had been she.

Suresby. Sir, though I to you be a servant true and just,
Yet do not ye therefore your faithful spouse mistrust;
But examine the matter, and if ye shall it find
To be all well, be not ye for my words unkind. 20

Goodluck. I shall do that is right, and as I see cause why.
But here cometh Custance forth; we shall know by and by.

SCENE II

Goodluck *and* Suresby. *Enter* Dame Custance

Dame Custance. I come forth to see and hearken for news good,
For about this hour is the time, of likelihood,
That Gawyn Goodluck, by the sayings of Suresby,
Would be at home. And lo, yond I see him, I!

5 property] character. 8 try] make proof of.
12 allow] approve. 22 by and by] immediately.

What! Gawyn Goodluck, the only hope of my life!
Welcome home! and kiss me, your true espoused wife!

Goodluck. Nay, soft, Dame Custance! I must first, by your licence,
See whether all things be clear in your conscience.
I hear of your doings to me very strange.

Dame Custance. What, fear ye that my faith towards you should change? 10

Goodluck. I must needs mistrust ye be elsewhere entangled,
For I hear that certain men with you have wrangled
About the promise of marriage by you to them made.

Dame Custance. Could any man's report your mind therein persuade?

Goodluck. Well, ye must therein declare yourself to stand clear,
Else I and you, Dame Custance, may not join this year.

Dame Custance. Then would I were dead, and fair laid in my grave!
Ah, Suresby! is this the honesty that ye have
To hurt me with your report, not knowing the thing?

Suresby. If ye be honest, my words can hurt you nothing; 20
But what I heard and saw, I might not but report.

Dame Custance. Ah, Lord, help poor widows, destitute of comfort!
Truly, most dear spouse, nought was done but for pastance.

Goodluck. But such kind of sporting is homely dalliance.

Dame Custance. If ye knew the truth, ye would take all in good part.

Goodluck. By your leave, I am not half well skilled in that art.

Dame Custance. It was none but Roister Doister, that foolish mome.

24 homely] uncomely. 27 mome] dolt.

Goodluck. Yea, Custance, 'Better', they say, 'a bad 'scuse than none.'
Dame Custance. Why, Tristram Trusty, sir, your true and faithful friend,
Was privy both to the beginning and the end. 30
Let him be the judge, and for me testify.
Goodluck. I will the more credit that he shall verify.
And because I will the truth know e'en as it is,
I will to him myself, and know all without miss.
Come on, Sim Suresby, that before my friend thou may
Avouch the same words which thou didst to me say.
[*Exeunt* Goodluck *and* Suresby.

SCENE III

Dame Custance

Dame Custance. O Lord! how necessary it is now of days,
That each body live uprightly all manner ways;
For let never so little a gap be open,
And be sure of this—the worst shall be spoken!
How innocent stand I in this for deed or thought!
And yet see what mistrust towards me it hath wrought!
But thou, Lord, knowest all folks' thoughts and eke intents,
And thou art the deliverer of all innocents.
Thou didst help the advoutress that she might be amended;
Much more, then, help, Lord, that never ill intended!
Thou didst help Susanna, wrongfully accused, 11
And no less dost thou see, Lord, how I am now abused.
Thou didst help Hester, when she should have died,
Help also, good Lord, that my truth may be tried!

9 advoutress] adulteress.

Yet if Gawyn Goodluck with Tristram Trusty speak,
I trust of ill report the force shall be but weak.
And lo! yond they come, sadly talking together.
I will abide, and not shrink for their coming hither.

SCENE IV

Dame Custance. *Enter* Goodluck, Trusty, *and* Suresby

Goodluck. And was it none other than ye to me report?
Trusty. No; and here were ye wished to have seen the sport.
Goodluck. Would I had, rather than half of that in my purse!
Suresby. And I do much rejoice the matter was no worse.
And, like as to open it I was to you faithful,
So of Dame Custance' honest truth I am joyful;
For God forfend that I should hurt her by false report.
Goodluck. Well, I will no longer hold her in discomfort.
Dame Custance. Now come they hitherward. I trust all shall be well.
Goodluck. Sweet Custance, neither heart can think nor tongue tell 10
How much I joy in your constant fidelity.
Come now, kiss me, the pearl of perfect honesty!
Dame Custance. God let me no longer to continue in life
Than I shall towards you continue a true wife!
Goodluck. Well, now to make you for this some part of amends,
I shall desire first you, and then such of our friends
As shall to you seem best, to sup at home with me,
Where at your fought field we shall laugh and merry be.
Suresby. And mistress, I beseech you, take with me no grief;
I did a true man's part, not wishing you reprief. 20

19 grief] grudge.

Dame Custance. Though hasty reports through surmises growing
May of poor innocents be utter overthrowing,
Yet, because to thy master thou hast a true heart,
And I know mine own truth, I forgive thee for my part.
Goodluck. Go we all to my house, and of this gear no more!
Go prepare all things, Sim Suresby; hence, run afore!
Suresby. I go. [*Exit.*
Goodluck. But who cometh yond? Matthew Merrygreek?
Dame Custance. Roister Doister's champion; I shrew his best cheek!
Trusty. Roister Doister self, your wooer, is with him, too.
Surely some thing there is with us they have to do. 30

SCENE V

Goodluck, Trusty, *and* Dame Custance. *Enter* Merrygreek *and* Roister Doister

Merrygreek. Yond I see Gawyn Goodluck, to whom lieth my message.
I will first salute him after his long voyage,
And then make all thing well concerning your behalf.
Roister Doister. Yea, for the pash of God!
Merrygreek. Hence out of sight, ye calf,
Till I have spoke with them, and then I will you fet.
Roister Doister. In God's name. [*Exit* Roister Doister.
Merrygreek. What, Master Gawyn Goodluck, well met!
And from your long voyage I bid you right welcome home.
Goodluck. I thank you.
Merrygreek. I come to you from an honest mome.

28 I shrew . . . cheek] see IV. ii. 14. 4 pash of God] see IV. iii. 124.

Goodluck. Who is that?
Merrygreek. Roister Doister, that doughty kite.
Dame Custance. Fie! I can scarcely abide ye should his name recite. 10
Merrygreek. Ye must take him to favour, and pardon all past,
He heareth of your return, and is full ill aghast.
Goodluck. I am right well content he have with us some cheer.
Dame Custance. Fie upon him, beast! Then will not I be there.
Goodluck. Why, Custance! do ye hate him more than ye love me?
Dame Custance. But for your mind, sir, where he were would I not be!
Trusty. He would make us all laugh.
Merrygreek. Ye ne'er had better sport.
Goodluck. I pray you, sweet Custance, let him to us resort.
Dame Custance. To your will I assent.
Merrygreek. Why, such a fool it is
As no man for good pastime would forgo or miss. 20
Goodluck. Fetch him to go with us.
Merrygreek. He will be a glad man. [*Exit.*
Trusty. We must, to make us mirth, maintain him all we can.
And lo, yond he cometh, and Merrygreek with him!
Dame Custance. At his first entrance ye shall see I will him trim!
But first let us hearken the gentleman's wise talk.
Trusty. I pray you, mark, if ever ye saw crane so stalk.

SCENE VI

Dame Custance, Goodluck, *and* Trusty. *Enter* Roister Doister *and* Merrygreek

Roister Doister. May I then be bold?
Merrygreek. I warrant you, on my word.

They say they shall be sick but ye be at their board.
Roister Doister. They were not angry, then?
Merrygreek. Yes, at first, and made strange;
But when I said your anger to favour should change,
And therewith had commended you accordingly,
They were all in love with your maship by and by,
And cried you mercy that they had done you wrong.
Roister Doister. For why no man, woman, nor child can hate me long?
Merrygreek. 'We fear', quod they, 'he will be avenged one day;
Then for a penny give all our lives we may!' 10
Roister Doister. Said they so indeed?
Merrygreek. Did they? Yea, even with one voice.
'He will forgive all,' quod I. Oh, how they did rejoice!
Roister Doister. Ha, ha, ha!
Merrygreek. 'Go fetch him', say they, 'while he is in good mood,
For, have his anger who lust, we will not, by the rood!'
Roister Doister. I pray God that it be all true that thou hast me told
And that she fight no more.
Merrygreek. I warrant you, be bold.
To them, and salute them!
Roister Doister. Sirs, I greet you all well.
All. Your mastership is welcome!
Dame Custance. Saving my quarrel!
For, sure, I will put you up into the Exchequer—
Merrygreek. Why so? better nay. Wherefore?
Dame Custance. For an usurer. 20
Roister Doister. I am no usurer, good mistress, by His arms!
Merrygreek. When took he gain of money to any man's harms?
Dame Custance. Yes, a foul usurer he is, ye shall see else—

Roister Doister. Didst not thou promise she would pick no more quarrels?
Dame Custance. He will lend no blows but he have in recompense
Fifteen for one: which is too much, of conscience!
Roister Doister. Ah, dame, by the ancient law of arms, a man
Hath no honour to foil his hands on a woman.
Dame Custance. And, where other usurers take their gains yearly,
This man is angry but he have his by and by. 30
Goodluck. Sir, do not for her sake bear me your displeasure.
Merrygreek. Well, he shall with you talk thereof more at leisure.
Upon your good usage, he will now shake your hand.
Roister Doister. And much heartily welcome from a strange land.
Merrygreek. Be not afeard, Gawyn, to let him shake your fist!
Goodluck. Oh, the most honest gentleman that e'er I wist!
I beseech your maship to take pain to sup with us!
Merrygreek. He shall not say you nay; and I too, by Jesus!
Because ye shall be friends, and let all quarrels pass.
Roister Doister. I will be as good friends with them as ere I was. 40
Merrygreek. Then let me fetch your choir that we may have a song.
Roister Doister. Go. [*Exit* Merrygreek.
Goodluck. I have heard no melody all this year long.

Re-enter Merrygreek *with* Doughty *and* Harpax

Merrygreek. Come on, sirs, quickly!
Roister Doister. Sing on, sirs, for my friends' sake.
Doughty. Call ye these your friends?

28 foil] foul.

Roister Doister. Sing on, and no mo words make!
[*Here they sing.*

Goodluck. The Lord preserve our most noble Queen of renown,
And her virtues reward with the heavenly crown.

Dame Custance. The Lord strengthen her most excellent Majesty,
Long to reign over us in all prosperity.

Trusty. That her godly proceedings the faith to defend
He may 'stablish and maintain through to the end.

Merrygreek. God grant her, as she doth, the Gospel to protect, 51
Learning and virtue to advance, and vice to correct.

Roister Doister. God grant her loving subjects both the mind and grace,
Her most godly proceedings worthily to embrace.

Harpax. Her Highness' most worthy counsellors God prosper
With honour and love of all men to minister.

All. God grant the nobility her to serve and love,
With all the whole commonty, as doth them behove.

AMEN

58 commonty] commonalty.

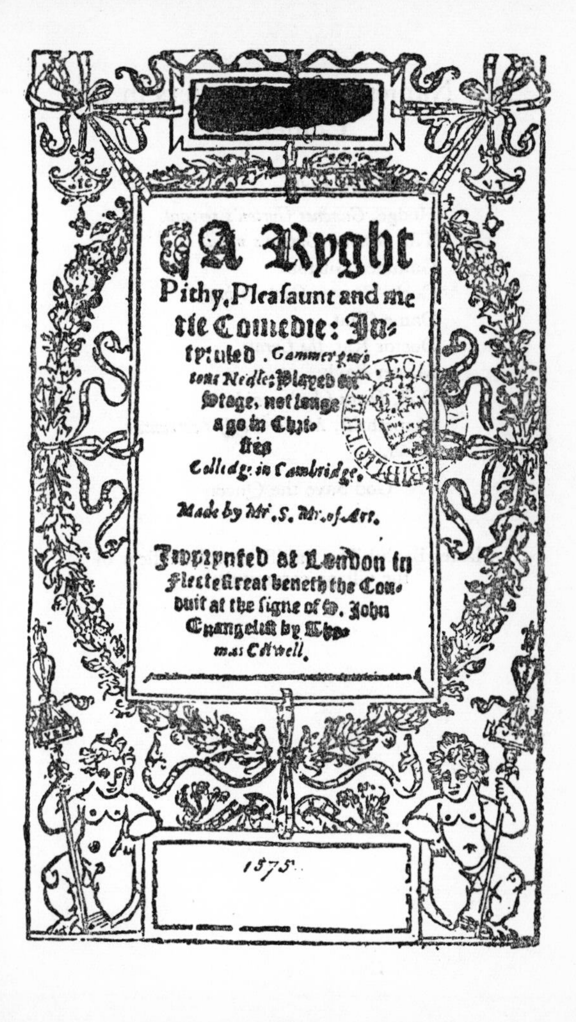

A Ryght
Pithy, Pleasaunt and me
rie Comedie: In-
tytuled Gammer gur-
tons Nedle: Played on
Stage, not longe
ago in Chri-
stes
Colledge in Cambridge.

Made by Mr. S. Mr. of Art.

Imprynted at London in
Fleetestreat beneth the Conduit at the signe of S. John
Evangelist by Tho-
mas Colwell.

1575

The Names of the Speakers in this Comedy

Diccon, *the Bedlam.*
Hodge, *Gammer Gurton's servant.*
Tib, *Gammer Gurton's maid.*
Gammer Gurton.
Cock, *Gammer Gurton's boy.*
Dame Chat.
Doctor Rat, *the Curate.*
Master Bayly.
Doll, *Dame Chat's maid.*
Scapethrift, *Master Bayly's servant.*
Mutes.

God Save the Queen

Master Bayly] The Bailiff, or chief officer of the village community.

GAMMER GURTON'S NEEDLE

THE PROLOGUE

As Gammer Gurton with many a wide stitch
Sat piecing and patching of Hodge her man's brich,
By chance or misfortune, as she her gear tost,
In Hodge' leather breeches her needle she lost.
When Diccon the Bedlam had heard by report
That good Gammer Gurton was robbed in this sort,
He quietly persuaded with her in that stound
Dame Chat, her dear gossip, this needle had found;
Yet knew she no more of this matter, alas!
Than knoweth Tom, our clerk, what the priest saith at mass. 10
Hereof there ensued so fearful a fray,
Mas Doctor was sent for, these gossips to stay,
Because he was curate, and esteemed full wise;
Who found that he sought not, by Diccon's device.
When all things were tumbled and clean out of fashion,
Whether it were by fortune, or some other constellation,
Suddenly the neele Hodge found by the pricking,
And drew it out of his buttock, where he felt it sticking.
Their hearts then at rest with perfect security, 19
With a pot of good ale they struck up their *plaudite*.

7 stound] crisis. 12 Mas] Master. 13 curate] parish priest, vicar. 17 neele] needle; so *passim*. 20 *plaudite*] signal for applause.

ACT I. SCENE I

Diccon

Diccon. Many a mile have I walked, divers and sundry ways,
And many a good man's house have I been at in my days;
Many a gossip's cup in my time have I tasted,
And many a broach and spit have I both turned and basted;
Many a piece of bacon have I had out of their balks,
In running over the country, with long and weary walks;
Yet came my foot never within those door cheeks,
To seek flesh or fish, garlick, onions, or leeks,
That ever I saw a sort in such a plight
As here within this house appeareth to my sight. 10
There is howling and scowling, all cast in a dump,
With whewling and puling, as though they had lost a trump.
Sighing and sobbing, they weep and they wail;
I marvel in my mind what the devil they ail.
The old trot sits groaning, with alas! and alas!
And Tib wrings her hands, and takes on in worse case.
With poor Cock, their boy, they be driven in such fits,
I fear me the folks be not well in their wits.
Ask them what they ail, or who brought them in this stay,
They answer not at all, but 'alack!' and 'welaway!' 20
When I saw it booted not, out at doors I hied me,
And caught a slip of bacon, when I saw that none spied me,
Which I intend not far hence, unless my purpose fail,
Shall serve for a shoeing-horn to draw on two pots of ale.

4 broach] spit. 5 balks] beams from which bacon was hung. 9 sort] set of people. 15 trot] crone.

SCENE II

Diccon, Hodge

Hodge. See! So cham arrayed with dabbling in the dirt!
She that set me to ditching, ich would she had the squirt!
Was never poor soul that such a life had.
Gog's bones! This vilthy glay has drest me too bad!
God's soul! See how this stuff tears!
Ich were better to be a bearward and set to keep bears!
By the Mass, here is a gash, a shameful hole indeed!
An one stitch tear further, a man may thrust in his head.
Diccon. By my father's soul, Hodge, if I should now be sworn,
I cannot choose but say thy breech is foul betorn, 10
But the next remedy in such a case and hap
Is to planch on a piece as broad as thy cap.
Hodge. Gog's soul, man, 'tis not yet two days fully ended
Since my dame Gurton, cham sure, these breeches amended;
But cham made such a drudge to trudge at every need
Chwold rend it though it were stitched with sturdy packthread.
Diccon. Hodge, let thy breeches go, and speak and tell me soon
What devil aileth Gammer Gurton and Tib her maid to frown.
Hodge. Tush, man, th'art deceived: 'tis their daily look;

1–2 cham . . . ich] *the conventional stage rustic forms for* I am *and* I; cf. *Roister Doister*, I. iii. 99–100. 4 glay] clay; *a pseudo-dialectical form.* 12 planch] clap.

They cower so over the coals, their eyes be bleared with smoke. 20

Diccon. Nay, by the Mass, I perfectly perceived, as I came hither,
That either Tib and her dame hath been by the ears together,
Or else as great a matter, as thou shalt shortly see.

Hodge. Now, ich beseech our Lord they never better agree!

Diccon. By Gog's soul, there they sit as still as stones in the street,
As though they had been taken with fairies, or else with some ill sprite.

Hodge. Gog's heart! I durst have laid my cap to a crown
Chwould learn of some prancome as soon as ich came to town.

Diccon. Why, Hodge, art thou inspired? Or didst thou thereof hear?

Hodge. Nay, but ich saw such a wonder as ich saw not this seven year. 30
Tom Tankard's cow, by Gog's bones! She set me up her sail,
And flinging about his half acre, fisking with her tail,
As though there had been in her arse a swarm of bees;
And chad not cried 'tphrowh, whore,' she'd leapt out of his leas.

Diccon. Why, Hodge, lies the cunning in Tom Tankard's cow's tail?

Hodge. Well, ich chave heard some say such tokens do not fail.
But canst thou not tell, in faith, Diccon, why she frowns, or whereat?
Hath no man stolen her ducks or hens, or gelded Gib, her cat?

Diccon. What devil can I tell, man? I could not have one word!

28 prancome] prank. 32 fisking] whisking.

They gave no more heed to my talk than thou wouldst to a lord. 40

Hodge. Ich cannot still but muse, what marvellous thing it is.
Chill in and know myself what matters are amiss.
[*Exit.*

Diccon. Then farewell, Hodge, awhile, since thou dost inward haste,
For I will into the good wife Chat's, to feel how the ale doth taste. [*Exit.*

SCENE III

Hodge *and* Tib

Hodge. Cham aghast; by the Mass, ich wot not what to do.
Chad need bless me well before ich go them to.
Perchance some felon sprite may haunt our house indeed;
And then chwere but a noddy to venture where cha no need.

Tib. Cham worse than mad, by the Mass, to be at this stay!
Cham chid, cham blamed, and beaten, all t'hours on the day;
Lamed and hunger-starved, pricked up all in jags,
Having no patch to hide my back, save a few rotten rags!

Hodge. I say, Tib—if thou be Tib, as I trow sure thou be—
What devil make ado is this, between our dame and thee? 10

Tib. Gog's bread, Hodge, thou had a good turn thou wert not here this while!
It had been better for some of us to have been hence a mile;

7 jags] tatters.

My gammer is so out of course and frantic all at ones,
That Cock, our boy, and I, poor wench, have felt it on our bones.

Hodge. What is the matter—say on, Tib—whereat she taketh so on?

Tib. She is undone, she saith, alas! Her joy and life is gone!
If she hear not of some comfort, she is, faith! but dead;
Shall never come within her lips one inch of meat nor bread.

Hodge. By'r Lady, cham not very glad to see her in this dump.
Chold a noble her stool hath fallen, and she hath broke her rump. 20

Tib. Nay, and that were the worst, we would not greatly care
For bursting of her huckle bone, or breaking of her chair;
But greater, greater, is her grief, as, Hodge, we shall all feel!

Hodge. Gog's wounds, Tib! My gammer has never lost her neele?

Tib. Her neele!

Hodge. Her neele!

Tib. Her neele!
By him that made me, it is true, Hodge, I tell thee.

Hodge. Gog's sacrament, I would she had lost t'heart out of her belly!
The Devil, or else his dame, they ought her, sure, a shame!
How a murrion came this chance, say, Tib! unto our dame?

Tib. My gammer sat her down on her pess, and bade me reach thy breeches, 30

20 Chold] I hold, wager. 28 ought] owed, had in store. 30 pess] hassock.

And by and by (a vengeance in it!) or she had take
  two stitches
To clap a clout upon thine arse, by chance aside she
  leers,
And Gib, our cat, in the milk-pan she spied over
  head and ears.
'Ah, whore! Out, thief!' She cried aloud, and swapt
  the breeches down.
Up went her staff, and out leapt Gib at doors into
  the town,
And since that time was never wight could set their
  eyes upon it.
Gog's malison chave, Cock and I, bid twenty times
  light on it.

Hodge. And is not then my breeches sewed up, to-
  morrow that I should wear?

Tib. No, in faith, Hodge, thy breeches lie for all this
  never the near.

Hodge. Now a vengeance light on all the sort, that
  better should have kept it, 40
The cat, the house, and Tib, our maid, that better
  should have swept it!
See where she cometh crawling! Come on, in twenty
  devils' way!
Ye have made a fair day's work, have you not?
  Pray you, say!

SCENE IV

Gammer, Hodge, Tib, *and* Cock.

Gammer. Alas, Hodge, alas! I may well curse and ban
This day, that ever I saw it, with Gib and the milk-
  pan;
For these and ill luck together, as knoweth Cock,
  my boy,

31 by and by . . . or] immediately . . . before. 32 leers] looks obliquely. 34 swapt] threw. 37 Gog's malison] God's curse. 39 near] nearer, readier.

Have stuck away my dear neele, and robbed me of my joy,
My fair long straight neele, that was mine only treasure;
The first day of my sorrow is, and last end of my pleasure!

Hodge. Might ha kept it when ye had it! But fools will be fools still.
Lose that is vast in your hands ye need not but ye will.

Gammer. Go hie thee, Tib, and run thou, whore, to th'end here of the town!
Didst carry out dust in thy lap; seek where thou pourest it down, 10
And as thou sawest me roking in the ashes where I mourned,
So see in all the heap of dust thou leave no straw unturned.

Tib. That chall, Gammer, swith and tite, and soon be here again!

Gammer. Tib, stoop and look down to the ground to it, and take some pain. [*Exit* Tib.

Hodge. Here is a pretty matter, to see this gear how it goes;
By Gog's soul, I think you would lose your arse an it were loose!
Your neele lost, it is pity you should lack care and endless sorrow.
Gog's death! How shall my breeches be sewed? Shall I go thus to-morrow?

Gammer. Ah Hodge, Hodge! if that ich could find my neele, by the reed,
Chould sew thy breeches, ich promise thee, with full good double threed, 20
And set a patch on either knee should last this months twain.

11 roking] *variant of* rucking = crouching. 13 swith and tite] quickly and promptly. 19 reed] *a variant of* rood = crucifix.

Now God and good Saint Sithe I pray to send it home again!

Hodge. Whereto served your hands and eyes, but this your neele to keep?
What devil had you else to do? Ye kept, ich wot, no sheep!
Cham fain abroad to dig and delve, in water, mire, and clay,
Sossing and possing in the dirt still from day to day.
A hundred things that be abroad, cham set to see them weele,
And four of you sit idle at home, and cannot keep a neele!

Gammer. My neele! Alas! Ich lost it, Hodge, what time ich me up hasted
To save the milk set up for thee, which Gib, our cat, hath wasted. 30

Hodge. The Devil he burst both Gib and Tib, with all the rest!
Cham always sure of the worst end, who ever have the best!
Where ha you been fidging abroad, since you your neele lost?

Gammer. Within the house, and at the door, sitting by this same post,
Where I was looking a long hour, before these folks came here;
But welaway, all was in vain, my neele is never the near!

Hodge. Set me a candle, let me seek, and grope wherever it be.
Gog's heart, ye be so foolish, ich think, you know it not when you it see!

Gammer. Come hither, Cock; what, Cock, I say!

Cock. How, Gammer?

Gammer. Go, hie thee soon,

22 Saint Sithe] St. Osyth. 26 Sossing and possing] splashing and tramping. 33 fidging] restlessly moving.

And grope behind the old brass pan, which thing when thou hast done, 40
There shalt thou find an old shoe, wherein if thou look well,
Thou shalt find lying an inch of a white tallow candell.
Light it, and bring it tite away.

Cock. That shall be done anon.

Gammer. Nay, tarry, Hodge, till thou hast light, and then we'll seek each one.

Hodge. Come away, ye whoreson boy, are ye asleep? Ye must have a crier!

Cock. Ich cannot get the candle light: here is almost no fire.

Hodge. Chill hold thee a penny chill make thee come, if that ich may catch thine ears!
Art deaf, thou whoreson boy? Cock, I say; why canst not hear 's?

Gammer. Beat him not, Hodge, but help the boy, and come you two together. [*Exeunt.*

SCENE V

Gammer, Tib, *and* Cock

Gammer. How now, Tib? quick, let 's hear what news thou hast brought hether!

Tib. Chave tost and tumbled yonder heap over and over again,
And winnowed it through my fingers, as men would winnow grain;
Not so much as a hen's turd but in pieces I tare it,
Or whatsoever clod or clay I found, I did not spare it,
Looking within and eke without, to find your neele, alas!
But all in vain and without help! Your neele is where it was.

43 tite] see l. 13.

Gammer. Alas my neele! We shall never meet! Adieu, adieu, for aye!

Tib. Not so, Gammer, we might it find, if we knew where it lay.

Cock. Gog's cross, Gammer, if ye will laugh, look in but at the door, 10
And see how Hodge lieth tumbling and tossing amidst the flour,
Raking there some fire to find among the ashes dead,
Where there is not one spark so big as a pin's head;
At last in a dark corner two sparks he thought he sees,
Which were indeed nought else but Gib our cat's two eyes.
'Puff!' quoth Hodge, thinking thereby to have fire without doubt;
With that Gib shut her two eyes, and so the fire was out;
And by and by them opened, even as they were before;
With that the sparks appeared, even as they had done of yore; 19
And even as Hodge blew the fire (as he did think),
Gib, as she felt the blast, straightway began to wink;
Till Hodge fell of swearing, as came best to his turn,
The fire was sure bewitched, and therefore would not burn.
At last Gib up the stairs, among the old posts and pins,
And Hodge he hied him after, till broke were both his shins;
Cursing and swearing oaths were never of his making,
That Gib would fire the house if that she were not taken.

Gammer. See, here is all the thought that the foolish urchin taketh!
And Tib, methink, at his elbow almost as merry maketh.

This is all the wit ye have, when others make their moan. 30
Come down, Hodge, where art thou? and let the cat alone!

Hodge [*from within the house*]. Gog's heart, help and come up! Gib in her tail hath fire,
And is like to burn all, if she get a little higher!
Come down, quoth you? Nay, then you might count me a patch.
The house cometh down on your heads, if it take once the thatch.

Gammer. It is the cat's eyes, fool, that shineth in the dark.

Hodge. Hath the cat, do you think, in every eye a spark?

Gammer. No, but they shine as like fire as ever man see.

Hodge. By the Mass, an she burn all, yoush bear the blame for me!

Gammer. Come down and help to seek here our neele, that it were found. 40
Down, Tib, on the knees, I say! Down, Cock, to the ground!
To God I make avow, and so to good Saint Anne,
A candle shall they have apiece, get it where I can,
If I may my neele find in one place or in other.

Hodge [*entering*]. Now a vengeance on Gib light, on Gib and Gib's mother,
And all the generation of cats both far and near!
Look on this ground, whoreson, thinkst thou the neele is here?

Cock. By my troth, Gammer, methought your neele here I saw,
But when my fingers touched it, I felt it was a straw.

Tib. See, Hodge, what's this? may it not be within it?

Hodge. Break it, fool, with thy hand, and see an thou canst find it. 51

34 patch] fool. 39 youshl] you shall.

Tib. Nay, break it you, Hodge, according to your word.

Hodge. Gog's sides! fie! it stinks; it is a cat's turd!
It were well done to make thee eat it, by the Mass!

Gammer. This matter amendeth not; my neele is still where it was.
Our candle is at an end, let us all in quite,
And come another time, when we have more light.
[*Exeunt.*

ACT II

First a Song

Back and side go bare, go bare,
Both foot and hand go cold;
But belly, God send thee good ale enough,
Whether it be new or old.
I cannot eat but little meat,
My stomach is not good;
But sure I think that I can drink
With him that wears a hood.
Though I go bare, take ye no care,
I am nothing a-cold; 10
I stuff my skin so full within
Of jolly good ale and old.
Back and side go bare, go bare, &c.

I love no roast but a nut brown toast
And a crab laid in the fire.
A little bread shall do me stead:
Much bread I not desire.
No frost nor snow, no wind, I trow,
Can hurt me if I wold;
I am so wrapped, and throughly lapped 20
Of jolly good ale and old.
Back and side go bare, &c.

15 crab] crab-apple.

And Tib my wife, that as her life
Loveth well good ale to seek,
Full oft drinks she till ye may see
The tears run down her cheek;
Then doth she troll to me the bowl
Even as a malt-worm should;
And saith, sweetheart, I took my part
Of this jolly good ale and old. 30
Back and side go bare, &c.

Now let them drink till they nod and wink,
Even as good fellows should do;
They shall not miss to have the bliss
Good ale doth bring men to;
And all poor souls that have scoured bowls,
Or have them lustly trolled,
God save the lives of them and their wives,
Whether they be young or old.
Back and side go bare, &c. 40

SCENE I

Enter Diccon

Diccon. Well done, by Gog's malt! Well sung and well said!
Come on, mother Chat, as thou art true maid,
One fresh pot of ale let 's see, to make an end
Against this cold weather my naked arms to defend!
This gear it warms the soul! Now, wind, blow on the worst!
And let us drink and swill till that our bellies burst!
Now were he a wise man by cunning could define
Which way my journey lieth, or where Diccon will dine!
But one good turn I have: be it by night or day,
South, east, north or west, I am never out of my way!
[*Enter* Hodge.

28 malt-worm] a lover of malt, a toper.

Hodge. Chym goodly rewarded, cham I not, do you think? 11
Chad a goodly dinner for all my sweat and swink!
Neither butter, cheese, milk, onions, flesh, nor fish,
Save this poor piece of barley bread: 'tis a pleasant costly dish!
Diccon. Hail, fellow Hodge, and well to fare with thy meat, if thou have any:
But by thy words, as I them smelled, thy daintrels be not many.
Hodge. Daintrels, Diccon? Gog's soul, man, save this piece of dry horsebread,
Cha bit no bit this livelong day, no crumb come in my head:
My guts they yawl-crawl, and all my belly rumbleth;
The puddings cannot lie still, each one over other tumbleth. 20
By Gog's heart, cham so vexed, and in my belly penn'd,
Chould one piece were at the spitalhouse, another at the castle end!
Diccon. Why, Hodge, was there none at home thy dinner for to set?
Hodge. Gog's bread, Diccon, ich came too late, was nothing there to get!
Gib (a foul fiend might on her light!) licked the milk-pan so clean,
See, Diccon, 'twas not so well washed this seven year, as ich ween!
A pestilence light on all ill luck! Chad thought, yet for all this
Of a morsel of bacon behind the door at worst should not miss:
But when ich sought a slip to cut, as ich was wont to do,

12 swink] toil. 16 daintrels] dainties. 20 puddings] entrails. 21 penn'd] *apparently dialectical form of* pined = tormented.

Gog's soul, Diccon! Gib, our cat, had eat the bacon too! 30

[*Which bacon Diccon stole, as is declared before.*

Diccon. Ill luck, quoth he! Marry, swear it, Hodge! This day, the truth to tell,
Thou rose not on thy right side, or else blessed thee not well.
Thy milk slopped up! Thy bacon filched! That was too bad luck, Hodge!

Hodge. Nay, nay, there was a fouler fault, my gammer ga me the dodge;
Seest not how cham rent and torn, my heels, my knees, and my breech?
Chad thought, as ich sat by the fire, help here and there a stitch:
But there ich was poopt indeed.

Diccon. Why, Hodge?

Hodge. Boots not, man, to tell.
Cham so dressed amongst a sort of fools, chad better be in hell.
My gammer (cham ashamed to say), by God, served me not weel.

Diccon. How so, Hodge?

Hodge. Has she not gone, trowest now, and lost her neele? 40

Diccon. Her eel, Hodge? Who fished of late? That was a dainty dish!

Hodge. Tush, tush, her neele, her neele, her neele, man! 'Tis neither flesh nor fish;
A little thing with an hole in the end, as bright as any siller,
Small, long, sharp at the point, and straight as any pillar.

Diccon. I know not what a devil thou mean'st, thou bring'st me more in doubt.

Hodge. Know'st not with what Tom Tailor's man sits broaching through a clout?

37 poopt] deceived. 46 broaching] piercing.

A neele, a neele, a neele! My gammer's neele is gone.

Diccon. Her neele, Hodge? Now I smell thee! That was a chance alone!

By the Mass, thou hast a shameful loss, an it were but for thy breeches.

Hodge. Gog's soul, man, chould give a crown chad it but three stitches. 50

Diccon. How sayest thou, Hodge? What should he have, again thy needle got?

Hodge. By'm vather's soul, an chad it, chould give him a new grot.

Diccon. Canst thou keep counsel in this case?

Hodge. Else chwould my tongue were out.

Diccon. Do thou but then by my advice, and I will fetch it without doubt.

Hodge. Chill run, chill ride, chill dig, chill delve, chill toil, chill trudge, shalt see;

Chill hold, chill draw, chill pull, chill pinch, chill kneel on my bare knee;

Chill scrape, chill scratch, chill sift, chill seek, chill bow, chill bend, chill sweat,

Chill stoop, chill stir, chill cap, chill kneel, chill creep on hands and feet;

Chill be thy bondman, Diccon, ich swear by sun and moon.

An channot somewhat to stop this gap, cham utterly undone! 60

[*Pointing behind to his torn breeches.*

Diccon. Why, is there any special cause thou takest hereat such sorrow?

Hodge. Kirstian Clack, Tom Simpson's maid, by the Mass, comes hither to-morrow,

Cham not able to say, between us what may hap;

She smiled on me the last Sunday, when ich put off my cap.

Diccon. Well, Hodge, this is a matter of weight, and must be kept close,

58 cap] take off my cap. 65 close] secret.

It might else turn to both our costs, as the world now goes.
Shalt swear to be no blab, Hodge?

Hodge. Chill, Diccon.

Diccon. Then go to,
Lay thine hand here; say after me as thou shall hear me do.
Hast no book?

Hodge. Cha no book, I!

Diccon. Then needs must force us both
Upon my breech to lay thine hand, and there to take thine oath. 70

Hodge. I, Hodge, breechless
Swear to Diccon, rechless,
By the cross that I shall kiss,
To keep his counsel close,
And always me to dispose
To work that his pleasure is.

[*Here he kisseth* Diccon's *breech.*

Diccon. Now, Hodge, see thou take heed,
And do as I thee bid;
For so I judge it meet;
This needle again to win, 80
There is no shift therein
But conjure up a spreet.

Hodge. What, the great devil, Diccon, I say?

Diccon. Yea, in good faith, that is the way,
Fetched with some pretty charm.

Hodge. Soft, Diccon, be not too hasty yet,
By the Mass, for ich begin to sweat!
Cham afraid of some harm.

Diccon [*drawing a circle*]. Come hither, then, and stir thee nat
One inch out of this circle plat, 90
But stand as I thee teach.

Hodge. And shall ich be here safe from their claws?

Diccon. The master devil with his long paws
Here to thee cannot reach.

Now will I settle me to this gear.
Hodge. I say, Diccon, hear me, hear!
Go softly to this matter!
Diccon. What devil, man! Art afraid of nought?
Hodge. Canst not tarry a little thought
Till ich make a curtsy of water? 100
Diccon. Stand still to it; why shouldest thou fear him?
Hodge. Gog's sides, Diccon, methink ich hear him!
And tarry, chal mar all!
Diccon. The matter is no worse than I told it.
Hodge. By the Mass, cham able no longer to hold it!
Too bad! ich must beray the hall!
Diccon. Stand to it, Hodge! Stir not, you whoreson!
What devil, be thine arse-strings bursten?
Thyself awhile but stay,
The devil, I smell him, will be here anon. 110
Hodge. Hold him fast, Diccon, cham gone! Cham gone!
Chill not be at that fray! [*Exit* Hodge.

SCENE II

Diccon

Diccon. Fie, shitten knave, and out upon thee!
Above all other louts, fie on thee!
Is not here a cleanly prank?
But thy matter was no better,
Nor thy presence here no sweeter,
To fly I can thee thank.

Here is a matter worthy glosing,
Of Gammer Gurton's needle losing,
And a foul piece of wark!
A man I think might make a play, 10
And need no word to this they say,
Being but half a clark.

106 beray] befoul.

Soft, let me alone! I will take the charge
This matter further to enlarge
Within a time short.
If ye will mark my toys, and note,
I will give ye leave to cut my throat
If I make not good sport.

Dame Chat, I say, where be ye? Within?
Chat. [*Speaking from inside her house.*] Who have we there maketh such a din? 20
Diccon. Here is a good fellow, maketh no great danger.
Chat. What, Diccon? Come near, ye be no stranger.
We be fast set at trump, man, hard by the fire;
Thou shalt set on the king, if thou come a little nigher.
Diccon. Nay, nay, there is no tarrying; I must be gone again.
But first for you in counsel I have a word or twain.
Chat. [*To her maid.*] Come hither, Doll! Doll, sit down and play this game,
And as thou sawest me do, see thou do even the same.
There is five trumps beside the queen, the hindmost thou shalt find her.
Take heed of Sim Glover's wife, she hath an eye behind her! [*Comes out of her house.* 30
Now, Diccon, say your will.
Diccon. Nay, soft a little yet;
I would not tell it my sister, the matter is so great.
There I will have you swear by our dear Lady of Boulogne,
Saint Dunstan, and Saint Donnyke, with the three kings of Cologne,
That ye shall keep it secret.
Chat. Gog's bread! That will I do!
As secret as mine own thought, by God and the devil too!

23 trump] a game of cards. 34 Donnyke] Dominic. the three . . . Cologne] the three Magi.

Diccon. Here is Gammer Gurton, your neighbour, a sad and heavy wight:
Her goodly fair red cock at home was stole this last night.
Chat. Gog's soul! Her cock with the yellow legs, that nightly crowed so just?
Diccon. That cock is stolen.
Chat. What, was he fetched out of the hen's rust? 40
Diccon. I cannot tell where the devil he was kept, under key or lock;
But Tib hath tickled in Gammer's ear, that you should steal the cock.
Chat. Have I, strong whore? by bread and salt!—
Diccon. What, soft, I say, be still!
Say not one word for all this gear.
Chat. By the Mass, that I will!
I will have the young whore by the head, and the old trot by the throat.
Diccon. Not one word, Dame Chat, I say; not one word, for my coat!
Chat. Shall such a beggar's brawl as that, thinkest thou, make me a thief?
The pox light on her whore's sides, a pestilence and a mischief!
Come out, thou hungry needy bitch! O that my nails be short!
Diccon. Gog's bread, woman, hold your peace! This gear will else pass sport! 50
I would not for an hundred pound this matter should be known,
That I am author of this tale, or have abroad it blown!
Did ye not swear ye would be ruled, before the tale I told?
I said ye must all secret keep, and ye said sure ye wold.

37 heavy] sorrowful. 39 just] regularly. 40 rust] roost. 47 brawl] brat.

Chat. Would you suffer, yourself, Diccon, such a sort to revile you,
With slanderous words to blot your name, and so to defile you?
Diccon. No, Goodwife Chat, I would be loth such drabs should blot my name;
But yet ye must so order all that Diccon bear no blame.
Chat. Go to, then, what is your rede? Say on your mind, ye shall me rule herein.
Diccon. Godamercy to Dame Chat! In faith thou must the gear begin. 60
It is twenty pound to a goose turd, my gammer will not tarry,
But hitherward she comes as fast as her legs can her carry,
To brawl with you about her cock; for well I heard Tib say
The cock was roasted in your house to breakfast yesterday;
And when ye had the carcase eaten, the feathers ye out flung,
And Doll, your maid, the legs she hid a foot deep in the dung.
Chat. Oh, gracious God! My heart it bursts!
Diccon. Well, rule yourself a space;
And Gammer Gurton, when she cometh anon into this place,
Then to the quean, let 's see, tell her your mind and spare not.
So shall Diccon blameless be; and then, go to, I care not! 70
Chat. Then, whore, beware her throat! I can abide no longer.
In faith, old witch, it shall be seen which of us two be stronger!
And, Diccon, but at your request I would not stay one hour.

59 rede] advice.

Diccon. Well, keep it till she be here, and then out let it pour!
In the meanwhile get you in, and make no words of this.
More of this matter within this hour to hear you shall not miss,
Because I knew you are my friend, hide it I could not, doubtless.
Ye know your harm, see ye be wise about your own business!
So fare ye well.

Chat. Nay, soft, Diccon, and drink! What, Doll, I say!
Bring here a cup of the best ale; let's see, come quickly away! [*Exit.* 80

SCENE III

Diccon [*To the audience.*

Diccon. Ye see, masters, that one end tapped of this my short devise!
Now must we broach th'other too, before the smoke arise;
And by the time they have awhile run, I trust ye need not crave it.
But look, what lieth in both their hearts, ye are like, sure, to have it.

Enter Hodge

Hodge. Yea, Gog's soul, art alive yet? What, Diccon, dare ich come?

Diccon. A man is well hied to trust to thee; I will say nothing but mum;
But an ye come any nearer, I pray you see all be sweet!

Hodge. Tush, man, is Gammer's neele found? That chould gladly weet.

6 is well hied] speeds well. 8 weet] know.

Diccon. She may thank thee it is not found, for if thou had kept thy standing,
The devil he would have fetched it out, even, Hodge, at thy commanding. 10
Hodge. Gog's heart, and could he tell nothing where the neele might be found?
Diccon. Ye foolish dolt, ye were to seek, ere we had got our ground;
Therefore his tale so doubtful was that I could not perceive it.
Hodge. Then ich see well something was said, chope one day yet to have it.
But Diccon, Diccon, did not the devil cry 'ho, ho, ho'?
Diccon. If thou hadst tarried where thou stoodst, thou wouldest have said so!
Hodge. Durst swear of a book, chard him roar, straight after ich was gone.
But tell me, Diccon, what said the knave? Let me hear it anon.
Diccon. The whoreson talked to me, I know not well of what.
One while his tongue it ran and paltered of a cat, 20
Another while he stammered still upon a Rat;
Last of all, there was nothing but every word, Chat, Chat;
But this I well perceived before I would him rid,
Between Chat, and the Rat, and the cat, the needle is hid.
Now whether Gib, our cat, have eat it in her maw,
Or Doctor Rat, our curate, have found it in the straw,
Or this Dame Chat, your neighbour, have stolen it, God he knoweth!
But by the morrow at this time, we shall learn how the matter goeth.
Hodge. Canst not learn to-night, man? Seest not what is here? [*Pointing behind to his torn breeches.*

14 chope] I hope. 17 chard] I heard.

Diccon. 'Tis not possible to make it sooner appear. 30
Hodge. Alas, Diccon, then chave no shift, but—lest ich tarry too long—
Hie me to Sim Glover's shop, there to seek for a thong,
Therewith this breech to tache and tie as ich may.
Diccon. To-morrow, Hodge, if we chance to meet, shalt see what I will say. [*Exit* Hodge.

SCENE IV

Diccon

Diccon. Now this gear must forward go, for here my gammer cometh.
[*To the audience*] Be still awhile and say nothing; make here a little roomth.

Enter Gammer

Gammer. Good Lord, shall never be my luck my neele again to spie?
Alas, the while! 'tis past my help, where 'tis still it must lie!
Diccon. Now, Jesus! Gammer Gurton, what driveth you to this sadness?
I fear me, by my conscience, you will sure fall to madness.
Gammer. Who is that? What, Diccon? cham lost, man! fie, fie!
Diccon. Marry, fie on them that be worthy! But what should be your trouble?
Gammer. Alas! The more ich think on it, my sorrow it waxeth double.
My goodly tossing spurrier's neele chave lost ich wot not where. 10
Diccon. Your neele? When?

33 tache] fasten. 2 roomth] room. 10 tossing] that moves quickly to and fro. spurrier's] spur-maker's.

Gammer. My neele, alas! Ich might full ill it spare,
As God himself he knoweth, ne'er one beside chave.
Diccon. If this be all, good Gammer, I warrant you all is save.
Gammer. Why, know you any tidings which way my neele is gone?
Diccon. Yea, that I do doubtless, as ye shall hear anon.
A see a thing this matter toucheth, within these twenty hours,
Even at this gate, before my face, by a neighbour of yours.
She stooped me down, and up she took a needle or a pin.
I durst be sworn it was even yours, by all my mother's kin.
Gammer. It was my neele, Diccon, ich wot; for here, even by this post, 20
Ich sat, what time as ich upstart, and so my neele it lost.
Who was it, lief son? Speak, ich pray thee, and quickly tell me that!
Diccon. A subtle quean as any in this town, your neighbour here, Dame Chat.
Gammer. Dame Chat, Diccon? Let me be gone, chill thither in post haste.
Diccon. Take my council yet or ye go, for fear ye walk in waste.
It is a murrain crafty drab, and froward to be pleased;
An ye take not the better way, our needle yet ye lese it:
For when she took it up, even here before your doors,
'What, soft, Dame Chat,' quoth I, 'that same is none of yours.'
'Avaunt,' quoth she, 'Sir knave! What pratest thou of that I find? 30
I would thou hast kissed me I wot where;' she meant, I know, behind;

22 lief] dear. 26 murrain] plaguy. 27 lese] lose.

And home she went as brag as it had been a body-louse,
And I after, as bold as it had been the goodman of the house.
But there an ye had heard her, how she began to scold!
The tongue it went on pattens, by him that Judas sold!
Each other word, I was a knave, and you a whore of whores,
Because I spake in your behalf, and said the neele was yours.

Gammer. Gog's bread, and thinks that callet thus to keep my neele me fro'?

Diccon. Let her alone, an she minds none other but even to dress you so.

Gammer. By the Mass, chill rather spend the coat that is on my back! 40
Thinks the false quean by such a slight that chill my neele lack?

Diccon. Sleep not your gear, I counsel you, but of this take good heed:
Let not be known I told you of it, how well soever ye speed.

Gammer. Chill in, Diccon, a clean apron to take and set before me;
An ich may my neele once see, chill, sure, remember thee! [*Exit* Gammer.

SCENE V

Diccon

Diccon. Here will the sport begin; if these two once may meet,
Their cheer, durst lay money, will prove scarcely sweet.

32 brag] brisk. 42 Sleep not] neglect not.

My gammer, sure, intends to be upon her bones
With staves, or with clubs, or else with cobble stones.
Dame Chat, on the other side, if she be far behind
I am right far deceived; she is given to it of kind.
He that may tarry by it awhile, and that but short,
I warrant him, trust to it, he shall see all the sport.
Into the town will I, my friends to visit there,
And hither straight again to see th'end of this gear.
In the meantime, fellows, pipe up; your fiddles, I say, take them, 11
And let your friends hear such mirth as ye can make them. [*Exit.*

ACT III

SCENE I

Enter Hodge

Hodge. Sim Glover, yet gramercy! Cham meetly well sped now,
Th'art even as good a fellow as ever kissed a cow!
Here is a thong indeed, by the Mass, though ich speak it;
Tom Tankard's great bald curtal, I think, could not break it!
And when he spied my needle to be so straight and hard,
Hays lent me here his nawl, to set the gib forward,
As for my gammer's neele, the flying fiend go weet!
Chill not now go to the door again with it to meet.
Chould make shift good enough an chad a candle's end;
The chief hole in my breech with these two chill amend. 10

4 bald curtal] piebald horse with docked tail. 6 Hays] he has. nawl] awl, *wrongly formed from* an awl. set . . . forward] hasten matters on.

SCENE II

Hodge. *Enter* Gammer

Gammer. Now Hodge, mayst now be glad, cha news to tell thee;
Ich know who has my neele; ich trust soon shalt it see.
Hodge. The devil thou does! Hast heard, Gammer, indeed, or dost but jest?
Gammer. 'Tis as true as steel, Hodge.
Hodge. Why, knowest well where didst lese 't?
Gammer. Ich know who found it, and took it up! Shalt see or it be long.
Hodge. God's mother dear! If that be true, farewell both nawl and thong!
But who has it, Gammer, say on; chould fain hear it disclosed.
Gammer. That false vixen, that same Dame Chat, that counts herself so honest.
Hodge. Who told you so?
Gammer. That same did Diccon the bedlam, which saw it done.
Hodge. Diccon? It is a vengeable knave, Gammer, 'tis a bonable whoreson, 10
Can do more things than that, else cham deceived evil:
By the Mass, ich saw him of late call up a great black devil!
O, the knave cried 'Ho, ho!', he roared and he thundered,
An ye'ad been here, cham sure y'ould murrainly ha wondered.
Gammer. Was not thou afraid, Hodge, to see him in this place?
Hodge. No, and chad come to me, chould have laid him on the face,
Chould have, promised him!

10 bonable] abominable. 14 ye'ad] ye had. murrainly] see II. iv. 26.

Gammer. But, Hodge, had he no horns to push?
Hodge. As long as your two arms. Saw ye never Friar Rush
Painted on a cloth, with a sidelong cow's tail,
And crooked cloven feet, and many a hooked nail? 20
For all the world, if I should judge, chould reckon him his brother.
Look, even what face Friar Rush had, the devil had such another.
Gammer. Now Jesus mercy, Hodge! Did Diccon in him bring?
Hodge. Nay, Gammer, hear me speak, chill tell you a greater thing;
The devil (when Diccon had him, ich heard him wondrous weel)
Said plainly here before us, that Dame Chat had your neele.
Gammer. Then let us go, and ask her wherefore she minds to keep it;
Seeing we know so much, 'twere a madness now to sleep it.
Hodge. Go to her, Gammer; see ye not where she stands in her doors?
Bid her give you the neele, 'tis none of hers but yours. 30
[*They approach Dame Chat's house.*

SCENE III

Gammer *and* Hodge. Dame Chat *inside her house.*

Gammer. Dame Chat, chould pray thee fair, let me have that is mine!
Chill not this twenty years take one fart that is thine;
Therefore give me mine own, and let me live beside thee.

18 Friar Rush] *a prose 'History of Friar Rush', an evil spirit disguised as a friar, of medieval German origin, appeared in 1568.* 28 sleep] see II. iv. 42.

Chat. Why art thou crept from home hither, to mine own doors to chide me?
Hence, doting drab, avaunt, or I shall set thee further!
Intends thou and that knave me in my house to murther?
Gammer. Tush, gape not so on me, woman! Shalt not yet eat me!
Nor all the friends thou hast in this shall not entreat me!
Mine own goods I will have, and ask thee no by-leave,
What, woman! Poor folks must have right, though the thing you aggrieve. 10
Chat. Give thee thy right, and hang thee up, with all thy beggar's brood!
What, wilt thou make me a thief, and say I stole thy good?
Gammer. Chill say nothing, ich warrant thee, but that ich can prove it well.
Thou fetched my good even from my door, cham able this to tell!
Chat. Did I, old witch, steal oft was thine? How should that thing be known?
Gammer. Ich can no tell; but up thou tookst it as though it had been thine own,
Chat. Marry, fie on thee, thou old gib, with all my very heart!
Gammer. Nay, fie on thee, thou ramp, thou rig, with all that take thy part!
Chat. A vengeance on those lips that layeth such things to my charge!
Gammer. A vengeance on those callet's hips, whose conscience is so large! 20
Chat. Come out, hog!
Gammer. Come out, hog, and let have me right!
Chat [*coming out*]. Thou arrant witch!

15 oft] aught. 18 ramp . . . rig] old hag . . . anton.
20 callet's] drab's.

Gammer. Thou bawdy bitch, chill make thee curse this night!
Chat. A bag and a wallet!
Gammer. A cart for a callet!
Chat. Why, weenest thou thus to prevail?
I hold thee a groat, I shall patch thy coat!
Gammer. Thou wert as good kiss my tail!
Thou slut, thou cut, thou rakes, thou jakes! Will not shame make thee hide thee?
Chat. Thou scald, thou bald, thou rotten, thou glutton! I will no longer chide thee,
But I will teach thee to keep home.
Gammer. Wilt thou, drunken beast?
Hodge. Stick to her, Gammer! Take her by the head, chill warrant you this feast!
Smite, I say, Gammer! Bite, I say, Gammer! I trow ye will be keen!
Where be your nails? Claw her by the jaws, pull me out both her eyne. 30
Gog's bones, Gammer, hold up your head!
Chat. I trow, drab, I shall dress thee.
Tarry, thou knave, I hold thee a groat I shall make these hands bless thee!
Take thou this, old whore, for amends, and learn thy tongue well to tame,
And say thou met at this bickering, not thy fellow but thy dame!
Hodge. Where is the strong-stewed whore? Chill gear a whore's mark!
Stand out one's way, that ich kill none in the dark!
Up, Gammer, an ye be alive! Chill fight now for us both.
Come no near me, thou scald callet! To kill thee ich were loth.

23 wallet] *probably with reference to the special meaning of* a beggar's bag. cart for a callet] *with reference to the whipping of lewd women at the cart-tail.* 25 cut] drab. 32 bless] drub. 35 gear] give her.

Chat. Art here again, thou hoddy peak? What, Doll! Bring me out my spite.
Hodge. Chill broach thee with this, by'm father's soul, chill conjure that foul sprite! 40
[*To* Cock *within the Gammer's house.*
Let door stand, Cock! Why comes, indeed? Keep door, thou whoreson boy!
Chat. Stand to it, thou dastard, for thine ears, ise teach thee, a sluttish toy!
Hodge. Gog's wounds, whore, chill make thee avaunt! Take heed, Cock, pull in the latch!
Chat. I'faith, sir Loose-breech, had ye tarried, ye should have found your match!
Gammer. Now 'ware thy throat, losel, thouse pay for all!
Hodge. Well said, Gammer, by my soul.
House her, souse her, bounce her, trounce her, pull out her throat-bowl!
Chat. Comest behind me, thou withered witch? An I get once on foot
Thouse pay for all, thou old tarleather! I'll teach thee what 'longs to't!
Take thee this to make up thy mouth, till time thou come by more!
Hodge. Up, Gammer, stand on your feet; where is the old whore? 50
Faith, would chad her by the face, chould crack her callet crown!
Gammer. Ah, Hodge, Hodge, where was thy help, when vixen had me down?
Hodge. By the Mass, Gammer, but for my staff Chat had gone nigh to spill you!
Ich think the harlot had not cared, an chad not come, to kill you.
But shall we lose our neele thus?
Gammer. No, Hodge, chware loth do so,

39 hoddy peak] blockhead. 45 losel] scoundrel. 46 throat-bowl] Adam's apple. 48 tarleather] a strip of raw sheep-skin, *here used as a term of abuse.*

Thinkest thou chill take that at her hand? No, Hodge, ich tell thee no!

Hodge. Chould yet this fray were well take up, and our neele at home.
'Twill be my chance else some to kill, wherever it be or whom!

Gammer. We have a parson, Hodge, thou knows, a man esteemèd wise,
Mast Doctor Rat; chill for him send, and let me hear his advise. 60
He will her shrive for all this gear, and give her penance strait;
Wese have our neele, else Dame Chat comes ne'er within heaven gate.

Hodge. Yea, marry, Gammer, that ich think best; will you now for him send?
The sooner Doctor Rat be here, the sooner wese ha an end,
And hear, Gammer! Diccon's devil, as ich remember well,
Of cat, and Chat, and Doctor Rat, a felonous tale did tell.
Chold you forty pound, that is the way your neele to get again.

Gammer. Chill ha him straight! Call out the boy, wese make him take the pain.

Hodge. What, Cock, I say! Come out! What devil! Canst not hear?

Enter Cock

Cock. How now, Hodge? How does Gammer, is yet the weather clear? 70
What would chave me to do?

Gammer. Come hither, Cock, anon!
Hence swith to Doctor Rat, hie thee that thou were gone,

60 Mast] Master. 62 Wese] we shall. 66 felonous] evil. 72 swith] see I. iv. 13.

And pray him come speak with me, cham not well at ease.
Shalt have him at his chamber, or else at Mother Bee's;
Else seek him at Hob Filcher's shop, for as chard it reported,
There is the best ale in all the town, and now is most resorted.

Cock. And shall ich bring him with me, Gammer?

Gammer. Yea, by and by, good Cock.

Cock. Shalt see that shall be here anon, else let me have on the dock.

Hodge. Now, Gammer, shall we two go in, and tarry for his coming?
What devil, woman! Pluck up your heart, and leave off all this gluming. 80
Though she were stronger at the first, as ich think ye did find her,
Yet there ye drest the drunken sow, what time ye came behind her.

Gammer. Nay, nay, cham sure she lost not all, for, set th'end to the beginning,
And ich doubt not but she will make small boast of her winning. [*Exeunt.*

SCENE IV

Enter Tib, Hodge, *and* Gammer

Tib. See, Gammer, Gammer, Gib, our cat, cham afraid what she aileth;
She stands me gasping behind the door, as though her wind her faileth:
Now let ich doubt what Gib should mean, that now she doth so dote.

Hodge. Hold hither! I chould twenty pound, your neele is in her throat.

78 dock] buttock.

Grope her, ich say, methinks ich feel it; does not prick your hand?

Gammer. Ich can feel nothing.

Hodge. No, ich know there 's not within this land
A murrainer cat then Gib is, betwixt the Thames and Tyne;
Shase as much wit in her head almost as chave in mine!

Tib. Faith, shase eaten something, that will not easily down;
Whether she got it at home, or abroad in the town 10
Ich cannot tell.

Gammer. Alas, ich fear it be some crooked pin!
And then farewell Gib! She is undone, and lost all save the skin!

Hodge. 'Tis your neele, woman, I say! Gog's soul! give me a knife,
And chill have it out of her maw, or else chall lose my life!

Gammer. What! Nay, Hodge, fie! Kill not our cat, 'tis all the cats we ha now.

Hodge. By the Mass, Dame Chat hays me so moved, ich care not what I kill, ma God avow!
Go to, then, Tib, to this gear! Hold up her tail and take her!
Chill see what devil is in her guts! Chill take the pains to rake her!

Gammer. Rake a cat, Hodge! What wouldst thou do?

Hodge. What, thinkest that cham not able?
Did not Tom Tankard rake his curtal toore day standing in the stable? [*Enter* Cock. 20

Gammer. Soft! Be content, let 's hear what news Cock bringeth from Mast Rat.

Cock. Gammer, chave been there as you bade, you wot well about what.
'Twill not be long before he come, ich durst swear of a book.

16 ma] I make. 20 toore] t'other.

He bids you see ye be at home, and there for him to look.

Gammer. Where didst thou find him, boy? Was he not where I told thee?

Cock. Yes, yes, even at Hob Filcher's house, by him that bought and sold me!
A cup of ale had in his hand, and a crab lay in the fire;
Chad much ado to go and come, all was so full of mire.
And, Gammer, one thing I can tell, Hob Filcher's nawl was lost,
And Doctor Rat found it again, hard beside the door post. 30
I chould a penny can say something your neele again to set.

Gammer. Cham glad to hear so much, Cock, then trust he will not let
To help us herein best he can; therefore till time he come
Let us go in; if there be aught to get thou shalt have some.

ACT IV

SCENE I

Enter Doctor Rat

D. Rat. A man were better twenty times be a bandog and bark,
Than here among such a sort be parish priest or clark,
Where he shall never be at rest one pissing-while a day,
But he must trudge about the town, this way and that way;
Here to a drab, there to a thief, his shoes to tear and rent,

27 crab] crab-apple. 32 let] fail.

And that which is worst of all, at every knave's commandment!
I had not sit the space to drink two pots of ale,
But Gammer Gurton's sorry boy was straightway at my tail,
And she was sick, and I must come, to do I wot not what!
If once her finger's end but ache, trudge! Call for Doctor Rat! 10
And when I come not at their call, I only thereby lose;
For I am sure to lack therefore a tithe pig or a goose.
I warrant you, when truth is known, and told they have their tale,
The matter whereabout I come is not worth a half-penny worth of ale;
Yet must I talk so sage and smooth, as though I were a gloser
Else, ere the year come at an end, I shall be sure the loser. [*Enter* Gammer.
What work ye, Gammer Gurton? How? Here is your friend Mast Rat.

Gammer. Ah, good Mast Doctor! Cha troubled, cha troubled you, chwot well that!

D. Rat. How do ye, woman? Be ye lusty, or be ye not well at ease?

Gammer. By gis, Master, cham not sick, but yet chave a disease. 20
Chad a foul turn now of late, chill tell it you, by gigs!

D. Rat. Hath your brown cow cast her calf, or your sandy sow her pigs?

Gammer. No, but chad been as good they had as this, ich wot weel.

D. Rat. What is the matter?

Gammer. Alas, alas! Cha lost my good neele!
My neele, I say, and wot ye what, a drab came by and spied it,

15 gloser] glozer, flatterer. 20 chave a disease] am ill at ease. 21 by gigs] *apparently a corruption of* by gis = by Jesus.

And when I asked her for the same, the filth flatly denied it.

D. Rat. What was she that?

Gammer. A dame, ich warrant you! She began to scold and brawl—

Alas, alas! Come hither, Hodge! This wretch can tell you all.

SCENE II

Doctor Rat *and* Gammer. *Enter* Hodge

Hodge. Good morrow, Gaffer Vicar!

D. Rat. Come on, fellow, let us hear!

Thy dame hath said to me, thou knowest of all this gear;

Let 's see what thou canst say.

Hodge. By'm fay, sir, that ye shall.

What matter so ever there was done, ich can tell your maship all:

My Gammer Gurton here, see now,
sat her down at this door, see now;
And, as she began to stir her, see now,
her neele fell to the floor, see now;
And while her staff she took, see now,
at Gib her cat to fling, see now, 10
Her neele was lost in the floor, see now.
Is not this a wondrous thing, see now?
Then came the quean Dame Chat, see now,
to ask for her black cup, see now:
And even here at this gate, see now,
she took that neele up, see now:
My Gammer then she yede, see now,
her neele again to bring, see now,
And was caught by the head, see now.
Is not this a wondrous thing, see now? 20

17 yede] went.

She tare my Gammer's coat, see now,
and scratched her by the face, see now;
Chad thought shad stopped her throat, see now.
Is not this a wondrous case, see now?
When ich saw this, ich was wroth, see now,
and start between them twain, see now;
Else ich durst take a book oath, see now,
my gammer had been slain, see now.

Gammer. This is even the whole matter, as Hodge has plainly told;
And chould fain be quiet for my part, that chould. 30
But help us, good Master, beseech ye that ye do:
Else shall we both be beaten and lose our neele too.

D. Rat. What would ye have me to do? Tell me, that I were gone;
I will do the best that I can, to set you both at one.
But be ye sure Dame Chat hath this your neele found?

Enter Diccon.

Gammer. Here comes the man that see her take it up off the ground.
Ask him yourself, Master Rat, if ye believe not me:
And help me to my neele, for God's sake and Saint Charity!

D. Rat. Come near, Diccon, and let us hear what thou can express.
Wilt thou be sworn thou seest Dame Chat this woman's neele have? 40

Diccon. Nay, by St. Benit, will I not, then might ye think me rave!

Gammer. Why, didst not thou tell me so even here? Canst thou for shame deny it?

Diccon. Aye, marry, Gammer; but I said I would not abide by it.

D. Rat. Will you say a thing, and not stick to it to try it?

Diccon. 'Stick to it', quoth you, Master Rat? Marry, sir, I defy it!

Nay, there is many an honest man, when he such blasts hath blown
In his friend's ears, he would be loth the same by him were known.
If such a toy be used oft among the honesty,
It may beseem a simple man of your and my degree.

D. Rat. Then we be never the nearer, for all that you can tell! 50

Diccon. Yea, marry, sir, if ye will do by mine advice and counsel.
If Mother Chat see all us here, she knoweth how the matter goes;
Therefore I rede you three go hence, and within keep close,
And I will into Dame Chat's house, and so the matter use,
That ere you could go twice to church I warrant you hear news.
She shall look well about her, but, I durst lay a pledge,
Ye shall of Gammer's neele have shortly better knowledge.

Gammer. Now, gentle Diccon, do so, and, good sir, let us trudge.

D. Rat. By the Mass, I may not tarry so long to be your judge.

Diccon. 'Tis but a little while, man; what! take so much pain! 60
If I hear no news of it, I will come sooner again.

Hodge. Tarry so much, good Master Doctor, of your gentleness!

D. Rat. Then let us hie us inward, and, Diccon, speed thy business. [*Exeunt.*

48 the honesty] 'the quality'. 53 rede] advise.

SCENE III

Diccon

Diccon. [*To the audience.*] Now, sirs, do you no more, but keep my counsel just,
And Doctor Rat shall thus catch some good, I trust.
But Mother Chat, my gossip, talk first withal I must:
For she must be chief captain to lay the Rat in the dust. [*Enter* Dame Chat.
Good even, Dame Chat, in faith, and well met in this place!

Chat. Good even, my friend Diccon; whither walk ye this pace?

Diccon. By my truth, even to you, to learn how the world goeth.
Heard ye no more of the other matter? Say me, now, by your troth!

Chat. O yes, Diccon, here the old whore, and Hodge, that great knave—
But, in faith, I would thou hadst seen—O Lord, I dressed them brave! 10
She bare me two or three souses behind in the nape of the neck,
Till I made her old weasand to answer again, 'Keck!'
And Hodge, that dirty dastard, that at her elbow stands—
If one pair of legs had not been worth two pair of hands,
He had had his beard shaven if my nails would have served,
And not without a cause, for the knave it well deserved.

Diccon. By the Mass, I can thee thank, wench, thou didst so well acquit thee!

11 souses] thumps. 12 weasand] windpipe.

Chat. An thadst seen him, Diccon, it would have made thee beshit thee
For laughter. The whoreson dolt at last caught up a club,
As though he would have slain the master devil Beelzebub. 20
But I set him soon inward.

Diccon. O Lord, there is the thing
That Hodge is so offended! That makes him start and fling!

Chat. Why? Makes the knave any moiling, as ye have seen or heard?

Diccon. Even now I saw him last, like a madman he fared,
And sware by heaven and hell he would awreak his sorrow,
And leave you never a hen alive, by eight of the clock to-morrow;
Therefore mark what I say, and my words see that ye trust.
Your hens be as good as dead, if ye leave them on the rust.

Chat. The knave dare as well go hang himself, as go upon my ground.

Diccon. Well, yet take heed I say, I must tell you my tale round. 30
Have you not about your house, behind your furnace or lead
A hole where a crafty knave may creep in for need?

Chat. Yes, by the Mass, a hole broke down, even within these two days.

Diccon. Hodge he intends this same night to slip in there aways.

Chat. O Christ! That I were sure of it! In faith he should have his meed!

18 thadst] thou hadst. 22 fling] rush about.
23 moiling] worry, ado. 28 rust] roost. 31 furnace] oven. lead] brewing-cauldron.

Diccon. Watch well, for the knave will be there as sure as is your creed.
I would spend myself a shilling to have him swingèd well.
Chat. I am as glad as a woman can be of this thing to hear tell.
By Gog's bones, when he cometh, now that I know the matter,
He shall sure at the first skip to leap in scalding water, 40
With a worse turn besides; when he will, let him come.
Diccon. I tell you as my sister; you know what meaneth 'mum'! [*Exit* Dame Chat.

SCENE IV

Diccon

Diccon. Now lack I but my doctor to play his part again.
And lo where he cometh towards, peradventure to his pain! [*Enter* Doctor Rat.
D. Rat. What good news, Diccon, fellow? Is Mother Chat at home?
Diccon. She is, sir, and she is not, but it please her to whom;
Yet did I take her tardy, as subtle as she was.
D. Rat. The thing that thou wentst for, hast thou brought it to pass?
Diccon. I have done that I have done, be it worse, be it better,
And Dame Chat at her wits end I have almost set her.
D. Rat. Why, hast thou spied the neele? Quickly, I pray thee, tell!
Diccon. I have spied it, in faith, sir, I handled myself so well; 10
And yet the crafty quean had almost take my trump.
But ere all came to an end, I set her in a dump.
D. Rat. How so, I pray thee, Diccon?

Diccon. Marry, sir, will ye hear?
She was clapped down on the backside, by Cock's mother dear,
And there she sat sewing a halter or a band,
With no other thing save Gammer's needle in her hand.
As soon as any knock, if the filth be in doubt,
She needs but once puff, and her candle is out:
Now I, sir, knowing of every door the pin,
Came nicely, and said no word, till time I was within; 20
And there I saw the neele, even with these two eyes;
Whoever say the contrary, I will swear he lies.

D. Rat. O Diccon, that I was not there then in thy stead!

Diccon. Well, if ye will be ordered, and do by my rede,
I will bring you to a place, as the house stands,
Where ye shall take the drab with the neele in her hands.

D. Rat. For God's sake do so, Diccon, and I will 'gage my gown
To give thee a full pot of the best ale in the town.

Diccon. Follow me but a little, and mark what I will say;
Lay down your gown beside you; go to, come on your way! 30
See ye not what is here? A hole wherein ye may creep
Into the house, and suddenly unawares among them leap;
There shall ye find the bitchfox and the neele together.
Do as I bid you, man, come on your ways hither!

D. Rat. Art thou sure, Diccon, the swill-tub stands not hereabout?

Diccon. I was within myself, man, even now, there is no doubt.

20 nicely] cautiously.

Go softly, make no noise; give me your foot, Sir John.
Here will I wait upon you, till you come out anon.

D. Rat. Help, Diccon! Out, alas! I shall be slain among them!

Diccon. If they give you not the needle, tell them that ye will hang them. 40
'Ware that! How, my wenches! Have ye caught the Fox
That used to make revel among your hens and Cocks?
Save his life yet for his order, though he sustain some pain.
Gog's bread! I am afraid they will beat out his brain.
[*Exit.*

D. Rat. Woe worth the hour that I came here!
And woe worth him that wrought this gear!
A sort of drabs and queans have me blessed—
Was ever creature half so evil dressed?
Whoever it wrought, and first did invent it
He shall, I warrant him, ere long repent it! 50
I will spend all I have without my skin
But he shall be brought to the plight I am in!
Master Bayly, I trow, an he be worth his ears,
Will snaffle these murderers and all that them bears.
I will surely neither bite nor sup
Till I fetch him hither, this matter to take up.
[*Exit.*

ACT V

SCENE I

Enter Doctor Rat, Master Bayly, *and* Scapethrift

Bayly. I can perceive none other, I speak it from my heart,
But either ye are in all the fault, or else in the greatest part.

37 Sir John] 'Sir' *here used in addressing a clergyman.*
47 blessed] drubbed. 54 bears] supports.

D. Rat. If it be counted his fault, besides all his grieves,
When a poor man is spoiled and beaten among thieves,
Then I confess my fault herein, at this season;
But I hope you will not judge so much against reason.

Bayly. And, methinks, by your own tale, of all that ye name,
If any played the thief, you were the very same.
The women they did nothing, as your words make probation,
But stoutly withstood your forcible invasion. 10
If that a thief at your window to enter should begin,
Would you hold forth your hand and help to pull him in?
Or you would keep him out? I pray you answer me.

D. Rat. Marry, keep him out, and a good cause why!
But I am no thief, sir, but an honest learned clark.

Bayly. Yea, but who knoweth that, when he meets you in the dark?
I am sure your learning shines not out at your nose!
Was it any marvel though the poor woman arose
And start up, being afraid of that was in her purse?
Methink you may be glad that your luck was no worse. 20

D. Rat. Is not this evil enough, I pray you, as you think? [*Showing his broken head.*

Bayly. Yea, but a man in the dark, if chances do wink,
As soon he smites his father as any other man,
Because for lack of light discern him he ne can.
Might it not have been your luck with a spit to have been slain?

D. Rat. I think I am little better, my scalp is cloven to the brain.
If there be all the remedy, I know who bears the knocks.

3 grieves] griefs. 22 if chances do wink] if luck is blind.

Bayly. By my troth, and well worthy besides to kiss the stocks!
To come in on the back side, when ye might go about!
I know none such, unless they long to have their brains knocked out. 30

D. Rat. Well, will you be so good, sir, as talk with Dame Chat,
And know what she intended? I ask no more but that.

Bayly. [*To* Scapethrift.] Let her be called, fellow, because of Master Doctor,
I warrant in this case she will be her own proctor;
She will tell her own tale in metre or in prose,
And bid you seek your remedy, and so go wipe your nose.

SCENE II

Master Bayly *and* Doctor Rat. *Enter* Scapethrift *with* Dame Chat

Bayly. Dame Chat, Master Doctor upon you here complained
That you and your maids should him much misorder,
And taketh many an oath, that no word he feigned,
Laying to your charge, how you thought him to murder;
And on his part again, that same man saith furder
He never offended you in word nor intent.
To hear you answer hereto, we have now for you sent.

Chat. That I would have murdered him? Fie on him, wretch,
And evil mought he thee for it, our Lord I beseech.
I will swear on all the books that opens and shuts, 10
He faineth this tale out of his own guts;
For this seven weeks with me I am sure he sat not down.
Nay, ye have other minions, in the other end of the town,

9 evil . . . thee] ill may he thrive.

Where ye were liker to catch such a blow,
Than anywhere else, as far as I know!

Bayly. Belike, then, Master Doctor, yon stripe there ye got not!

D. Rat. Think you I am so mad that where I was beat I wot not?
Will ye believe this quean, before she hath tried it?
It is not the first deed she hath done, and afterwards denied it.

Chat. What, man, will you say I broke your head? 20

D. Rat. How canst thou prove the contrary?

Chat. Nay, how provest thou that I did the dead?

D. Rat. Too plainly, by St. Mary,
This proof I trow may serve, though I no word spoke!
[*Showing his broken head.*

Chat. Because thy head is broken, was it I that it broke?
I saw thee, Rat, I tell thee, not once within this fortnight.

D. Rat. No, marry, thou sawest me not, for why thou hadst no light;
But I felt thee for all the dark, beshrew thy smooth cheeks!
And thou groped me, this will declare any day this six weeks. [*Showing his head.*

Bayly. Answer me to this, Mast Rat: when caught you this harm of yours? 30

D. Rat. A while ago, sir, God he knoweth, within less than these two hours.

Bayly. Dame Chat, was there none with you (confess, i'faith) about that season?
What, woman? Let it be what it will, 'tis neither felony nor treason.

Chat. Yea, by my faith, Master Bayly, there was a knave not far
Who caught one good fillip on the brow with a door-bar,

22 dead] *variant of* deed. 29 groped] seized.

And well was he worthy, as it seemed to me;
But what is that to this man, since this was not he?

Bayly. Who was it then? Let's hear!

D. Rat. Alas, sir, ask you that?
Is it not made plain enough by the own mouth of Dame Chat?
The time agreeth, my head is broken, her tongue cannot lie, 40
Only upon a bare nay she saith it was not I.

Chat. No, marry, was it not indeed! Ye shall hear by this one thing:
This afternoon a friend of mine for goodwill gave me warning,
And bade me well look to my roost, and all my capons' pens,
For if I took not better heed, a knave would have my hens.
Then I, to save my goods, took so much pains as him to watch;
And as good fortune served me, it was my chance him for to catch.
What strokes he bare away, or other what was his gains,
I wot not, but sure I am he had something for his pains!

Bayly. Yet tells thou not who it was.

Chat. Who it was? A false thief, 50
That came like a false fox my pullain to kill and mischief!

Bayly. But knowest thou not his name?

Chat. I know it; but what than?
It was that crafty cullion, Hodge, my Gammer Gurton's man.

Bayly. Call me the knave hither, he shall sure kiss the stocks.
I shall teach him a lesson for filching hens or cocks!

51 pullain] poultry. 53 cullion] rascal.

D. Rat. I marvel, Master Bayly, so bleared be your eyes;
An egg is not so full of meat, as she is full of lies:
When she hath played this prank, to excuse all this gear,
She layeth the fault in such a one, as I know was not there.

Chat. Was he not there? Look on his pate, that shall be his witness! 60

D. Rat. I would my head were half so whole; I would seek no redress!

[*Enter* Gammer Gurton.

Bayly. God bless you, Gammer Gurton!

Gammer. God dild you, master mine!

Bayly. Thou hast a knave within thy house—Hodge, a servant of thine;
They tell me that busy knave is such a filching one,
That hen, pig, goose or capon, thy neighbour can have none.

Gammer. By God, cham much amoved, to hear any such report!
Hodge was not wont, ich trow, to 'have him in that sort.

Chat. A thievisher knave is not alive, more filching, nor more false;
Many a truer man than he has hanged up by the halse;
And thou, his dame—of all his theft thou art the sole receiver; 70
For Hodge to catch, and thou to keep, I never knew none better!

Gammer. Sir-reverence of your masterdom, an you were out adoor,

62 God dild] *a corruption of* God yield = God reward! 67 'have] behave. 69 halse] neck. 72 Sir-reverence] With all respect to.

Chould be so bold, for all her brags, to call her arrant whore;
An ich knew Hodge as bad as tow, ich wish me endless sorrow
And chould not take the pains to hang him up before to-morrow!

Chat. What have I stolen from thee or thine, thou ill-favoured old trot?

Gammer. A great deal more, by God's blest, than chever by thee got!
That thou knowest well, I need not say it.

Bayly. Stop there, I say,
And tell me here, I pray you, this matter by the way,
How chance Hodge is not here? Him would I fain have had. 80

Gammer. Alas, sir, he'll be here anon; ha be handled too bad.

Chat. Master Bayly, sir, ye be not such a fool, well I know,
But ye perceive by this lingering there is a pad in the straw.

[*Thinking that* Hodge's *head was broke, and that* Gammer *would not let him come before them.*

Gammer. Chill show you his face, ich warrant thee; lo, now where he is!

[*Enter* Hodge.

Bayly. Come on, fellow, it is told me thou art a shrew, iwis:
Thy neighbour's hens thou takest, and playest the two-legged fox;
Their chickens and their capons too, and now and then their cocks.

Hodge. Ich defy them all that dare it say, cham as true as the best!

74 tow] thou, i.e. Dame Chat. 77 chever] I(ch) ever. 83 a pad in the straw] a toad in the straw, *proverbial for a hidden mischief.*

Bayly. Wert not thou take within this hour in Dame Chat's hens' nest?

Hodge. Take there? No, master; chould not do't for a house full of gold! 90

Chat. Thou or the devil in thy coat—swear this I dare be bold.

D. Rat. Swear me no swearing, quean, the devil he give thee sorrow!
All is not worth a gnat thou canst swear till to-morrow:
Where is the harm he hath? Show it, by God's bread!
Ye beat him with a witness, but the stripes light on my head!

Hodge. Beat me? Gog's blessed body, chould first, ich trow, have burst thee!
Ich think an chad my hands loose, callet, chould have crust thee!

Chat. Thou shitten knave, I trow thou knowest the full weight of my fist;
I am fouly deceived unless thy head and my door-bar kist.

Hodge. Hold thy chat, whore, thou criest so loud, can no man else be hard. 100

Chat. Well, knave, and I had thee alone, I would surely rap thy costard!

Bayly. Sir, answer me to this: is thy head whole or broken?

Hodge. Yea, Master Bayly, blest be every good token,
Is my head whole! Ich warrant you, 'tis neither scurvy nor scald!
What, you foul beast, does think 'tis either piled or bald?
Nay, ich thank God, chill not for all that thou mayst spend
That chad one scab on my narse as broad as thy finger's end.

Bayly. Come nearer here!

105 piled] hairless. 107 narse] cf. III. i. 6.

Hodge. Yes, that I dare.
Bayly. By our Lady, here is no harm,
Hodge's head is whole enough, for all Dame Chat's charm.
Chat. By Gog's blest, however the thing he cloaks or smoulders, 110
I know the blows he bare away, either with head or shoulders.
Camest thou not, knave, within this hour, creeping into my pens,
And there was caught within my house groping among my hens?
Hodge. A plague both on the hens and thee! A cart, whore, a cart!
Chould I were hanged as high as a tree an chwere as false as thou art!
Give my gammer again her washical thou stole away in thy lap!
Gammer. Yea, Master Bayly, there is a thing you know not on, mayhap;
This drab she keeps away my good, the devil he might her snare!
Ich pray you that ich might have a right action on her.
Chat. Have I thy good, old filth, or any such old sows? 120
I am as true, I would thou knew, as skin between thy brows!
Gammer. Many a truer hath been hanged, though you escape the danger!
Chat. Thou shalt answer, by God's pity, for this thy foul slander!
Bayly. Why, what can ye charge her withal? To say so ye do not well.
Gammer. Marry, a vengeance to her heart! That whore has stolen my neele!

110 smoulders] smothers up. 114 A cart] *see* III. iii. 23. 116 washical] what shall I call it.

Chat. Thy needle, old witch? How so? It were alms thy soul to knock!
So didst thou say the other day that I had stolen thy cock,
And roasted him to my breakfast, which shall not be forgotten;
The devil pull out thy lying tongue and teeth that be so rotten!

Gammer. Give me my neele! As for my cock, chould be very loth 130
That chould hear tell he should hang on thy false faith and troth.

Bayly. Your talk is such, I can scarce learn who should be most in fault.

Gammer. Yet shall be find no other wight, save she, by bread and salt!

Bayly. Keep ye content awhile, see that your tongues ye hold.
Methinks you should remember this is no place to scold.
How knowest thou, Gammer Gurton, Dame Chat thy needle had?

Gammer. To name you, sir, the party, chould not be very glad.

Bayly. Yea, but we must needs hear it, and therefore say it boldly.

Gammer. Such one as told the tale full soberly and coldly,
Even he that looked on—will swear on a book—
What time this drunken gossip my fair long neele uptook, 141
Diccon, master, the Bedlam, cham very sure ye know him.

Bayly. A false knave, by God's pity! Ye were but a fool to trow him.
I durst adventure well the price of my best cape,
That when the end is known, all will turn to a jape.

Told he not you that besides she stole your cock that tide?

Gammer. No, master, no indeed; for then he should have lied.

My cock is, I thank Christ, safe and well a-fine.

Chat. Yea, but that ragged colt, that whore, that Tib of thine,

Said plainly thy cock was stolen, and in my house was eaten. 150

That lying cut is lost that she is not swinged and beaten,

And yet for all my good name, it were a small amends!

I pick not this gear, hearest thou, out of my finger's ends;

But he that heard it told me, who thou of late didst name,

Diccon, whom all men knows, it was the very same.

Bayly. This is the case: you lost your needle about the doors,

And she answers again, she has no cock of yours;

Thus in your talk and action, from that you do intend,

She is whole five mile wide, from that she doth defend.

Will you say she hath your cock?

Gammer. No, marry, sir, that chill not, 160

Bayly. Will you confess her neele?

Chat. Will I? No sir, will I not.

Bayly. Then there lieth all the matter.

Gammer. Soft, master, by the way!

Ye know she could do little, an she could not say nay.

Bayly. Yea, but he that made one lie about your cock stealing,

Will not stick to make another, what time lies be in dealing.

I ween the end will prove this brawl did first arise

Upon no other ground but only Diccon's lies.

148 a-fine] in the end. 151 cut] see III. iii. 25

Chat. Though some be lies, as you belike have espied them,
Yet other some be true, by proof I have well tried them.
Bayly. What other thing beside this, Dame Chat?
Chat. Marry, sir, even this. 170
The tale I told before, the self same tale it was his;
He gave me, like a friend, warning against my loss,
Else had my hens be stolen each one, by God's cross!
He told me Hodge would come, and in he came indeed,
But as the matter chanced, with greater haste than speed.
This truth was said, and true was found, as truly I report.
Bayly. If Doctor Rat be not deceived, it was of another sort.
D. Rat. By God's mother, thou and he be a couple of subtle foxes!
Between you and Hodge, I bear away the boxes.
Did not Diccon appoint the place, where thou shouldst stand to meet him? 180
Chat. Yes, by the Mass, and if he came, bade me not stick to speet him.
D. Rat. God's sacrament! The villain knave hath dressed us round about!
He is the cause of all this brawl, that dirty shitten lout!
When Gammer Gurton here complained, and made a rueful moan,
I heard him swear that you had gotten her needle that was gone;
And this to try, he further said, he was full loth; howbeit
He was content with small ado to bring me where to see it.
And where ye sat, he said full certain, if I would follow his rede,

179 boxes] blows. 181 speet] spit, stab at.

Into your house a privy way he would me guide and lead,
And where ye had it in your hands, sewing about a clout, 190
And set me in the back hole, thereby to find you out:
And whilst I sought a quietness, creeping upon my knees,
I found the weight of your door bar for my reward and fees.
Such is the luck that some men gets, while they begin to mell
In setting at one such as were out, minding to make all well.

Hodge. Was not well blest, Gammer, to scape that stour? And chad been there,
Then chad been dressed, belike, as ill, by the Mass, as Gaffer Vicar.

Bayly. Marry, sir, here is a sport alone; I looked for such an end.
If Diccon had not played the knave, this had been soon amend.
My Gammer here he made a fool, and dressed her as she was; 200
And Goodwife Chat he set to school, till both parts cried alas!
And Doctor Rat was not behind, whilst Chat his crown did pare.
I would the knave had been stark blind, if Hodge had not his share.

Hodge. Cham meetly well sped already amongs, cham dressed like a colt!
An chad not had the better wit, chad been made a dolt.

Bayly. [*To* Scapethrift.] Sir knave, make haste Diccon were here, fetch him, wherever he be!

[*Exit* Scapethrift.

196 stour] to-do. 197 dressed] served out.
204 amongs] all this while.

Chat. Fie on the villain, fie, fie! that makes us thus agree!

Gammer. Fie on him, knave, with all my heart! Now fie! and fie again!

D. Rat. Now 'fie on him!' may I best say, whom he hath almost slain.

[*Re-enter* Scapethrift *with* Diccon.

Bayly. Lo where he cometh at hand, belike he was not fare! 210

Diccon, here be two or three thy company cannot spare.

Diccon. God bless you, an you may be blest, so many all at once.

Chat. Come knave, it were a good deed to geld thee, by Cock's bones!

Seest not thy handiwork? Sir Rat, can ye forbear him?

Diccon. A vengeance on those hands light, for my hands came not near him.

The whoreson priest hath lift the pot in some of these alewives' chairs

That his head would not serve him, belike, to come down the stairs.

Bayly. Nay, soft! Thou mayest not play the knave, and have this language too!

If thou thy tongue bridle a while, the better mayest thou do.

Confess the truth, as I shall ask, and cease awhile to fable; 220

And for thy fault I promise thee thy handling shall be reasonable.

Hast thou not made a lie or two, to set these two by the ears?

Diccon. What if I have? Five hundred such have I seen within these seven years:

I am sorry for nothing else but that I see not the sport

Which was between them when they met, as they themselves report.

Bayly. The greatest thing—Master Rat, ye see how he is drest!

Diccon. What devil need he be groping so deep, in Goodwife Chat's hens' nest?

Bayly. Yea, but it was thy drift to bring him into the briars.

Diccon. God's bread! Hath not such an old fool wit to save his ears?

He showeth himself herein, ye see, so very a cox, 230
The cat was not so madly allured by the fox
To run into the snares was set for him, doubtless;
For he leapt in for mice, and this Sir John for madness.

D. Rat. Well, an ye shift no better, ye losel, lither, and lazy,
I will go near for this to make ye leap at a daisy.
In the king's name, Master Bayly, I charge you set him fast.

Diccon. What, fast at cards, or fast on sleep? It is the thing I did last.

D. Rat. Nay, fast in fetters, false varlet, according to thy deeds.

Bayly. Master Doctor, there is no remedy, I must entreat you needs
Some other kind of punishment.

D. Rat. Nay by all hallows 240
His punishment, if I may judge, shall be naught else but the gallows.

Bayly. That were too sore, a spiritual man to be so extreme!

D. Rat. Is he worthy any better, sir? How do ye judge and deem?

Bayly. I grant him worthy punishment, but in no wise so great.

230 cox] cokes, fool. 234 lither] sluggard. 235 leap at a daisy] be hanged. 236 In the king's name] *see Introduction.* 239 needs] necessarily.

Gammer. It is a shame, ich tell you plain, for such false knaves entreat!
He has almost undone us all—that is as true as steel—
And yet for all this great ado cham never the ne'er my neele!
Bayly. Canst thou not say anything to that, Diccon, with least or most?
Diccon. Yea, marry, sir, this much I can say well, the needle is lost.
Bayly. Nay, canst not thou tell which way that needle may be found? 250
Diccon. No, by my fay, sir, though I might have an hundred pound.
Hodge. Thou liar, lickdish, didst not say the neele would be gitten?
Diccon. No, Hodge, by the same token, you were that time beshitten
For fear of Hobgoblin—you wot well what I mean;
As long as it is since, I fear me yet ye be scarce clean.
Bayly. Well, Master Rat, you must both learn and teach us to forgive.
Since Diccon hath confession made, and is so clean shrive,
If ye to me consent, to amend this heavy chance,
I will enjoin him here some open kind of penance,
Of this condition (where ye know my fee is twenty pence): 260
For the bloodshed, I am agreed with you here to dispense;
Ye shall go quit, so that ye grant the matter now to run
To end with mirth among us all, even as it was begun.
Chat. Say yea, Master Vicar, and he shall sure confess to be your debtor,
And all we that be here present, will love you much the better.

D. Rat. My part is the worst; but since you all hereon agree,
Go even to, Master Bayly! Let it be so for me!

Bayly. How sayest thou, Diccon? Art content this shall on me depend?

Diccon. Go to, Master Bayly, say on your mind, I know ye are my friend.

Bayly. Then mark ye well: To recompense this thy former action— 270
Because thou hast offended all, to make them satisfaction,
Before their faces here kneel down, and, as I shall thee teach—
For thou shalt take an oath of Hodge's leather breech:
First, for Master Doctor, upon pain of his curse,
Where he will pay for all, thou never draw thy purse;
And when ye meet at one pot he shall have the first pull,
And thou shalt never offer him the cup but it be full.
To Goodwife Chat thou shalt be sworn, even on the same wise,
If she refuse thy money once, never to offer it twice.
Thou shalt be bound by the same, here as thou dost take it, 280
When thou mayest drink of free cost, thou never forsake it.
For Gammer Gurton's sake, again sworn shalt thou be,
To help her to her needle again if it do lie in thee;
And likewise be bound, by the virtue of that,
To be of good abearing to Gib her great cat.
Last of all, for Hodge the oath to scan,
Thou shalt never take him for fine gentleman.

Hodge. Come, on, fellow Diccon, chall be even with thee now!

Bayly. Thou wilt not stick to do this, Diccon, I trow?

Diccon. Now, by my father's skin! My hand down I lay it! 290

Look, as I have promised, I will not denay it.
But, Hodge, take good heed now, thou do not beshite me! [*And gave him a good blow on the buttock.*

Hodge. Gog's heart! Thou false villain, dost thou bite me?

Bayly. What, Hodge, doth he hurt thee ere ever he begin?

Hodge. He thrust me into the buttock with a bodkin or a pin!
I say, Gammer! Gammer!

Gammer. How now Hodge, how now?

Hodge. God's malt, Gammer Gurton!

Gammer. Thou art mad, ich trow!

Hodge. Will you see the devil, Gammer?

Gammer. The devil, son! God bless us!

Hodge. Chould ich were hanged, Gammer——

Gammer. Marry, see, ye might dress us——

Hodge. Chave it, by the Mass, Gammer!

Gammer. What? Not my neele, Hodge? 300

Hodge. Your neele, Gammer! Your neele!

Gammer. No, fie, dost but dodge!

Hodge. Cha found your neele, Gammer, here in my hand be it!

Gammer. For all the loves on earth, Hodge, let me see it!

Hodge. Soft, Gammer!

Gammer. Good Hodge!

Hodge. Soft, ich say; tarry awhile!

Gammer. Nay, sweet Hodge, say truth, and do not me beguile!

Hodge. Cham sure on it, ich warrant you; it goes no more astray.

Gammer. Hodge, when I speak so fair; wilt still say me nay?

Hodge. Go near the light, Gammer, this—well, in faith, good luck!—
Chwas almost undone, 'twas so far in my buttock!

Gammer. 'Tis mine owne dear neele, Hodge, sickerly I wot! 310

Hodge. Cham I not a good son, Gammer, cham I not?
Gammer. Christ's blessing light on thee, hast made me for ever!
Hodge. Ich knew that ich must find it, else chould a had it never!
Chat. By my troth, gossip Gurton, I am even as glad
As though I mine own self as good a turn had!
Bayly. And I, by my conscience, to see it so come forth,
Rejoice so much at it as three needles be worth.
D. Rat. I am no whit sorry to see you so rejoice.
Diccon. Nor I much the gladder for all this noise;
Yet say 'Gramercy, Diccon,' for springing of the game. 320
Gammer. Gramercy, Diccon, twenty times! O how glad cham!
If that chould do so much, your Masterdom to come hether, [*To* Master Bayly.
Master Rat, Goodwife Chat, and Diccon together,
Cha but one halfpenny, as far as ich know it,
And chill not rest this night till ich bestow it.
If ever ye love me, let us go in and drink.
Bayly. I am content, if the rest think as I think.
Master Rat, it shall be best for you if we so do;
Then shall you warm you and dress yourself too.
Diccon. [*To the audience.*] Soft, sirs, take us with you, the company shall be the more! 330
As proud comes behind, they say, as any goes before!
But now, my good masters, since we must be gone,
And leave you behind us here all alone;
Since at our last ending thus merry we be,
For Gammer Gurton's needle's sake, let us have a *plaudite*!

FINIS.

Imprinted at London
in Fleet Street beneath the Conduit,
at the sign of S. John Evangelist, by
Thomas Colwell
1575

SVPPOSES:

A Comedie written in the Italian tongue by Ariosto, and Englished by George Gascoygne of Grayes Inne Esquire, and there presented.

The names of the Actors.

Balia, the Nurse.
Polynesta, the yong woman.
Cleander, the Doctor, suter to Polynesta.
Pasyphilo, the Parasite.
Carion, the Doctors man.
Dulypo, fayned seruant and louer of Polynesta.
Erostrato, fayned master and suter to Polynesta.
Dalio & Crapyno: } seruantes to fayned Erostrato.
Scenæse, a gentleman stranger.
Paquetto & Petrucio } his seruantes.
Damon, father to Polynesta.
Neuola, and two other his seruants.
Psyteria, an olde hag in his house.
Phylogano, a Scycilian gentleman, father to Erostrato.
Lytio, his seruant.
Ferrarese, an Inkeper of Ferrara.

The Comedie presented in Ferrara.

The Names of the Actors

Balia, *the Nurse.*
Polynesta, *the Young Woman.*
Cleander, *the Doctor, suitor to* Polynesta.
Pasiphilo, *the Parasite.*
Carion, *the Doctor's man.*
Dulippo, *feigned servant and lover of* Polynesta.
Erostrato, *feigned master and suitor to* Polynesta.
Dalio & Crapino } *servants to feigned* Erostrato.
A Siennese, *a gentleman stranger.*
Paquetto & Petrucio } *his servants.*
Damon, *father to* Polynesta.
Nevola, *and two other his servants.*
Psiteria, *an old hag in his house.*
Philogano, *a Sicilian gentleman, father to* Erostrato.
Litio, *his servant.*
A Ferrarese, *an Innkeeper of* Ferrara.

The Comedy presented as it were in Ferrara.

the Doctor] the Doctor of Laws.

THE PROLOGUE OR ARGUMENT

I suppose you are assembled here, supposing to reap the fruit of my travails: and to be plain, I mean presently to present you with a Comedy called Supposes: the very name whereof may peradventure drive into every of your heads a sundry suppose, to suppose the meaning of our supposes. Some percase will suppose we mean to occupy your ears with sophistical handling of subtle suppositions. Some other will suppose we go about to decipher unto you some quaint conceits, which hitherto have been only supposed as it were in shadows: and some I see smiling as though they supposed we would trouble you with the vain suppose of some wanton suppose. But understand, this our suppose is nothing else but a mistaking or imagination of one thing for another. For you shall see the master supposed for the servant, the servant for the master: the freeman for a slave, and the bondslave for a freeman: the stranger for a well-known friend, and the familiar for a stranger. But what? I suppose that even already you suppose me very fond, that have so simply disclosed unto you the subtleties of these our supposes: where otherwise indeed I suppose you should have heard almost the last of our supposes, before you could have supposed any of them aright. Let this then suffice.

2 presently] immediately. 6 percase] perhaps. 11 shadows] pictures. 20 fond] foolish.

SUPPOSES

ACT I

SCENE I

Enter Balia, *the nurse, and* Polynesta, *the young woman*

Balia. Here is nobody; come forth, Polynesta, let us look about, to be sure lest any man hear our talk: for I think within the house the tables, the planks, the beds, the portals, yea and the cupboards themselves have ears.

Polynesta. You might as well have said, the windows and the doors: do you not see how they hearken?

Balia. Well you jest fair, but I would advise you take heed, I have bidden you a thousand times beware: you will be spied one day talking with Dulippo. 11

Polynesta. And why should I not talk with Dulippo, as well as with any other, I pray you?

Balia. I have given you a wherefore for this why many times: but go to, follow your own advice till you overwhelm us all with sudden mishap.

Polynesta. A great mishap I promise you: marry, God's blessing on their heart that set such a brooch on my cap. 19

Balia. Well, look well about you. A man would think it were enough for you secretly to rejoice that by my help you have passed so many pleasant nights together: and yet by my troth I do it more than half against my will, for I would rather you had settled your fancy in some noble family; yea and it is no small grief unto me, that (rejecting the suits of so many nobles and gentlemen) you have chosen for your darling a poor servant of your father's, by whom shame and infamy is the best dower you can look for to attain. 30

4 portals] partitions.

Polynesta. And, I pray you, whom may I thank but gentle nurse? that continually praising him, what for his personage, his courtesy, and above all, the extreme passions of his mind, in fine you would never cease till I accepted him, delighted in him, and at length desired him with no less affection than he erst desired me.

Balia. I cannot deny but at the beginning I did recommend him unto you (as indeed I may say that for myself I have a pitiful heart) seeing the depth of his unbridled affection, and that continually he never ceased to fill mine ears with lamentable complaints.

Polynesta. Nay, rather that he filled your purse with bribes and rewards, nurse. 43

Balia. Well, you may judge of nurse as you list. Indeed, I have thought it always a deed of charity to help the miserable young men, whose tender youth consumeth with the furious flames of love. But be you sure if I had thought you would have passed to the terms you now stand in, pity nor pension, penny nor paternoster should ever have made nurse once to open her mouth in the cause. 51

Polynesta. No, of honesty, I pray you, who first brought him into my chamber? Who first taught him the way to my bed but you? Fie! nurse, fie! Never speak of it, for shame, you will make me tell a wise tale anon.

Balia. And have I these thanks for my good will? Why then I see well I shall be counted the cause of all mishap. 59

Polynesta. Nay, rather the author of my good hap (gentle nurse) for I would thou knowest I love not Dulippo, nor any of so mean estate, but have bestowed my love more worthily than thou deemest: but I will say no more at this time.

Balia. Then I am glad you have changed your mind yet.

49 pension] payment. 55–6 tell a wise tale] say what I should be sorry for.

Polynesta. Nay, I neither have changed, nor will change it.

Balia. Then I understand you not, how said you?

Polynesta. Marry, I say that I love not Dulippo, nor any such as he, and yet I neither have changed nor will change my mind. 72

Balia. I cannot tell. You love to lie with Dulippo very well: this gear is Greek to me: either it hangs not well together, or I am very dull of understanding: speak plain, I pray you.

Polynesta. I can speak no plainer, I have sworn to the contrary.

Balia. How? Make you so dainty to tell it nurse, lest she should reveal it? You have trusted me as far as may be (I may show to you) in things that touch your honour if they were known: and make you strange to tell me this? I am sure it is but a trifle in comparison of those things whereof heretofore you have made me privy.

Polynesta. Well, it is of greater importance than you think, nurse: yet would I tell it you under condition and promise that you shall not tell it again, nor give any sign or token to be suspected that you know it.

Balia. I promise you of my honesty, say on. 90

Polynesta. Well, hear you me then: this young man whom you have always taken for Dulippo, is a noble-born Sicilian, his right name Erostrato, son to Philogano, one of the worthiest men in that country.

Balia. How, Erostrato? Is it not our neighbour, which——?

Polynesta. Hold thy talking, nurse, and hearken to me, that I may explain the whole case unto thee. The man whom to this day you have supposed to be Dulippo, is (as I say) Erostrato, a gentleman that came from Sicilia to study in this city; and even at his first arrival met me in the street, fell enamoured of me, and of such vehement force were the passions he

The first suppose and ground of all the supposes.

suffered, that immediately he cast aside both long gown and books, and determined on me only to apply his study. And to the end he might the more commodiously both see me and talk with me, he exchanged both name, habit, clothes and credit with his servant Dulippo (whom only he brought with him out of Sicilia). And so with the turning of a hand, of Erostrato a gentleman he became Dulippo a serving man, and soon after sought service of my father, and obtained it.

Balia. Are you sure of this? 114

Polynesta. Yea, out of doubt. On the other side Dulippo took upon him the name of Erostrato his master, the habit, the credit, books, and all things needful to a student, and in short space profited very much, and is now esteemed as you see.

Balia. Are there no other Sicilians here: nor none that pass this way, which may discover them? 121

Polynesta. Very few that pass this way, and few or none that tarry here any time.

Balia. This hath been a strange adventure: but I pray you how hang these things together? That the student whom you say to be the servant, and not the master, is become an earnest suitor to you, and requireth you of your father in marriage? 128

Polynesta. That is a policy devised between them, to put Doctor Dotipole out of conceit: the old dotard, he that so instantly doth lie upon my father for me. But look where he comes, as God help me it is he; out upon him, what a lusky younker is this! Yet I had rather be a nun a thousand times, than be cumbered with such a coistrel.

Balia. Daughter, you have reason, but let us go in before he come any nearer. 137

[Polynesta *goeth in, and* Balia *stayeth a little while after, speaking a word or two to the doctor, and then departeth.*

131 instantly doth lie upon] is insistently urgent to.
133 lusky] slothful. 135 coistrel] varlet.

SCENE II

Balia, *nurse. Enter* Cleander, *doctor, and* Pasiphilo, *parasite*

Cleander. Were these dames here, or did mine eyes dazzle?

Pasiphilo. Nay, for here were Polynesta and her nurse.

Cleander. Was my Polynesta here? alas, I knew her not.

Balia. [*Aside.*] He must have better eyesight that should marry your Polynesta, or else he may chance to oversee the best point in his tables sometimes.

Pasiphilo. Sir, it is no marvel, the air is very misty to-day: I myself knew her better by her apparel than by her face. 12

Cleander. In good faith, and I thank God I have mine eyesight good and perfect, little worse than when I was but twenty years old.

Pasiphilo. How can it be otherwise? You are but young.

Cleander. I am fifty years old.

Pasiphilo. [*Aside.*] He tells ten less than he is.

Cleander. What sayst thou of ten less? 20

Pasiphilo. I say I would have thought you ten less; you look like one of six and thirty, or seven and thirty at the most.

Cleander. I am no less than I tell.

Pasiphilo. You are like enough to live fifty more: show me your hand.

Cleander. Why, is Pasiphilo a chiromancer?

Pasiphilo. What is not Pasiphilo? I pray you show me it a little.

Cleander. Here it is. 30

Pasiphilo. O how straight and infract is this line of life? You will live to the years of Melchisedech.

Cleander. Thou wouldst say, Methusalem.

Pasiphilo. Why, is it not all one?

Cleander. I perceive you are no very good Bibler, Pasiphilo.

Pasiphilo. Yes, sir, an excellent good bibbler, specially in a bottle. Oh, what a mount of Venus here is! but this light serveth not very well, I will behold it another day, when the air is clearer, and tell you somewhat, peradventure to your contentation. 41

Cleander. You shall do me great pleasure: but tell me, I pray thee, Pasiphilo, whom dost thou think Polynesta liketh better, Erostrato or me?

Pasiphilo. Why, you, out of doubt. She is a gentlewoman of a noble mind, and maketh greater account of the reputation she shall have in marrying your worship, than that poor scholar, whose birth and parentage God knoweth, and very few else.

Cleander. Yet he taketh it upon him bravely in this country. 51

Pasiphilo. Yea, where no man knoweth the contrary: but let him brave it, boast his birth, and do what he can, the virtue and knowledge that is within this body of yours, is worth more than all the country he came from.

Cleander. It becometh not a man to praise himself: but indeed I may say (and say truly) that my knowledge hath stood me in better stead at a pinch than could all the goods in the world. I came out of Otranto when the Turks won it, and first I came to Padua, after hither, where by reading, counselling, and pleading, within twenty years I have gathered and gained as good as ten thousand ducats. 63

Pasiphilo. Yea, marry, this is the right knowledge: Philosophy, Poetry, Logic, and all the rest, are but pickling sciences in comparison to this.

Cleander. But pickling indeed, whereof we have a verse:

The trade of law doth fill the boistrous bags;
They swim in silk, when others roist in rags. 70

61 after] afterwards. reading] lecturing. 66 pickling] trifling. 69 boistrous] bulky. 70 roist] bluster.

Pasiphilo. O excellent verse! who made it? Virgil?

Cleander. Virgil? tush, it is written in one of our glosses.

Pasiphilo. Sure, whosoever wrote it, the moral is excellent, and worthy to be written in letters of gold. But to the purpose: I think you shall never recover the wealth that you lost at Otranto.

Cleander. I think I have doubled it, or rather made it four times as much: but, indeed, I lost mine only son there, a child of five years old.

Another suppose.

Pasiphilo. O great pity! 81

Cleander. Yea, I had rather have lost all the goods in the world.

Pasiphilo. Alas, alas: by God, and grafts of such a stock are very geason in these days.

Cleander. I know not whether he were slain, or the Turks took him and kept him as a bondslave.

Pasiphilo. Alas, I could weep for compassion, but there is no remedy but patience; you shall get many by this young damsel with the grace of God. 90

Cleander. Yea, if I get her.

Pasiphilo. Get her? Why doubt you of that?

Cleander. Why? Her father holds me off with delays, so that I must needs doubt.

Pasiphilo. Content yourself, sir, he is a wise man, and desirous to place his daughter well: he will not be too rash in his determination, he will think well of the matter. And let him think; for the longer he thinketh, the more good of you shall he think: whose wealth? whose virtue? whose skill? or whose estimation can he compare to yours in this city? 101

Cleander. And hast thou not told him that I would make his daughter a dower of two thousand ducats?

Pasiphilo. Why, even now, I came but from thence since.

Cleander. What said he?

85 geason] rare. 106 since] just now.

Pasiphilo. Nothing, but that Erostrato had proffered the like.

Cleander. Erostrato? How can he make any dower, and his father yet alive? 111

Pasiphilo. Think you I did not tell him so? Yes, I warrant you, I forgot nothing that may further your cause: and doubt you not, Erostrato shall never have her unless it be in a dream.

Cleander. Well, gentle Pasiphilo, go thy ways and tell Damon I require nothing but his daughter. I will none of his goods: I shall enrich her of mine own; and if this dower of two thousand ducats seem not sufficient, I will make it five hundred more, yea a thousand, or whatsoever he will demand rather than fail. Go to, Pasiphilo, show thyself friendly in working this feat for me. Spare for no cost; since I have gone thus far, I will be loth to be out-bidden. Go!

Pasiphilo. Where shall I come to you again?

Cleander. At my house.

Pasiphilo. When?

Cleander. When thou wilt.

Pasiphilo. Shall I come at dinner time?

Cleander. I would bid thee to dinner, but it is a Saint's even which I have ever fasted. 131

Pasiphilo. [*Aside*.] Fast till thou famish!

Cleander. Hark!

Pasiphilo. [*Aside*.] He speaketh of a dead man's fast.

Cleander. Thou hearest me not.

Pasiphilo. [*Aside*.] Nor thou understandest me not.

Cleander. I dare say thou art angry I bid thee not to dinner: but come if thou wilt, thou shalt take such as thou findest.

Pasiphilo. What? think you I know not where to dine? 141

Cleander. Yes, Pasiphilo, thou art not to seek.

Pasiphilo. No, be you sure, there are enough will pray me.

Cleander. That I know well enough, Pasiphilo, but

thou canst not be better welcome in any place than to me; I will tarry for thee.

Pasiphilo. Well, since you will needs, I will come.

Cleander. Despatch then, and bring no news but good. 150

Pasiphilo. [*Aside.*] Better than my reward, by the rood. [*Exit* Cleander.

SCENE III

Pasiphilo

Pasiphilo. O miserable, covetous wretch, he findeth an excuse by St. Nicholas' fast, because I should not dine with him, as though I should dine at his own dish. He maketh goodly feasts I promise you, it is no wonder though he think me bound unto him for my fare; for over and besides that his provision is as scant as may be, yet there is great difference between his diet and mine. I never so much as sip of the wine that he tasteth, I feed at the board's end with brown bread. Marry! I reach always to his own dish, for there are no more but that only on the table. Yet he thinks that for one such dinner I am bound to do him all the service that I can, and thinks me sufficiently rewarded for all my travail with one such festival promotion. And yet peradventure some men think I have great gains under him: but I may say and swear, that this dozen year I have not gained so much in value as the points at my hose (which are but three with codpiece, point and all). He thinks that I may feed upon his favour and fair words; but if I could not otherwise provide for one, Pasiphilo were in a wise case. Pasiphilo hath more pastures to pass in than one, I warrant you: I am of household with this scholar Erostrato (his rival), as well as with Domine Cleander, now with the one, and then with the other, according as I see their caters

25 caters] buyers of provisions.

provide good cheer at the market. And I find the means so to handle the matter, that I am welcome to both. If the one see me talk with the other, I make him believe it is to hearken news in the furtherance of his cause: and thus I become a broker on both sides. Well, let them both apply the matter as well as they can, for indeed I will travail for none of them both: yet will I seem to work wonders on each hand. But is not this one of Damon's servants that cometh forth? It is: of him I shall understand where his master is. [*Enter* Dulippo.] Whither goeth this jolly gallant?

Dulippo. I come to seek somebody that may accompany my master at dinner; he is alone, and would fain have good company. 40

Pasiphilo. Seek no farther, you could never have found one better than me.

Dulippo. I have no commission to bring so many.

Pasiphilo. How many? I will come alone.

Dulippo. How canst thou come alone, that hast continually a legion of ravening wolves within thee?

Pasiphilo. Thou doest (as servants commonly do) hate all that love to visit their masters.

Dulippo. And why?

Pasiphilo. Because they have too many teeth, as you think. 51

Dulippo. Nay, because they have too many tongues.

Pasiphilo. Tongues? I pray you what did my tongue ever hurt you?

Dulippo. I speak but merrily with you, Pasiphilo. Go in, my master is ready to dine.

Pasiphilo. What? Dineth he so early?

Dulippo. He that riseth early, dineth early.

Pasiphilo. I would I were his man. Master doctor never dineth till noon, and how delicately then, God knoweth. I will be bold to go in, for I count myself bidden. [Pasiphilo *goeth within.* 62

Dulippo. You were best so. Hard hap had I when

I first began this unfortunate enterprise; for I supposed the readiest medicine to my miserable affects had been to change name, clothes, and credit with my servant, and to place myself in Damon's service: thinking that as shivering cold by glowing fire, thirst by drink, hunger by pleasant repasts, and a thousand such-like passions find remedy by their contraries, so my restless desire might have found quiet by continual contemplation. But alas, I find that only love is unsatiable. For as the fly playeth with the flame till at last she is cause of her own decay, so the lover that thinketh with kissing and colling to content his unbridled appetite, is commonly seen the only cause of his own consumption. Two years are now past since (under the colour of Damon's service) I have been a sworn servant to Cupid: of whom I have received as much favour and grace as ever man found in his service. I have free liberty at all times to behold my desired, to talk with her, to embrace her, yea (be it spoken in secret) to lie with her. I reap the fruits of my desire: yet as my joys abound, even so my pains increase. I fare like the covetous man, that having all the world at will, is never yet content: the more I have, the more I desire. Alas, what wretched estate have I brought myself unto, if in the end of all my far fetches, she be given by her father to this old doting doctor, this buzzard, this bribing villain, that by so many means seeketh to obtain her at her father's hands? I know she loveth me best of all others, but what may that prevail when perforce she shall be constrained to marry another? Alas, the pleasant taste of my sugared joys doth yet remain so perfect in my remembrance, that the least sop of sorrow seemeth more sour than gall in my mouth. If I had never known delight, with better contentation might I have

65 affects] feelings. 75 colling] cuddling. 89 far fetches] far-reaching stratagems. 90 buzzard] an inferior kind of hawk; *hence*, a dolt.

passed these dreadful dolours. And if this old Mumpsimus (whom the pox consume!) should win her, then may I say, 'Farewell the pleasant talk, the kind embracings, yea, farewell the sight of my Polynesta'; for he like a jealous wretch will pen her up, that I think the birds of the air shall not win the sight of her. I hoped to have cast a block in his way, by the means that my servant (who is supposed to be Erostrato, and with my habit and credit is well esteemed) should proffer himself a suitor, at the least to countervail the doctor's proffers. But my master, knowing the wealth of the one, and doubting the state of the other, is determined to be fed no longer with fair words, but to accept the doctor (whom he right well knoweth) for his son-in-law. Well, my servant promised me yesterday to devise yet again some new conspiracy to drive master doctor out of conceit, and to lay a snare that the fox himself might be caught in: what it is, I know not, nor I saw him not since he went about it. I will go see if he be within, that at least if he help me not, he may yet prolong my life for this once. But here cometh his lackey! 120

Here must Crapino *be coming in with a basket and a stick in his hand*

SCENE IV

Dulippo *and* Crapino

Dulippo. Ho, Jack Pack, where is Erostrato?

Crapino. Erostrato? Marry, he is in his skin.

Dulippo. Ah, whoreson boy, I say, how shall I find Erostrato?

Crapino. Find him? How mean you, by the week or by the year?

99 Mumpsimus] fogey. 5 Find] *here used in the sense of* board.

Dulippo. You crack-halter! If I catch you by the ears, I shall make you answer me directly.

Crapino. Indeed?

Dulippo. Tarry me a little. 10

Crapino. In faith, sir, I have no leisure.

Dulippo. Shall we try who can run fastest?

Crapino. Your legs be longer than mine, you should have given me the advantage.

Dulippo. Go to, tell me where is Erostrato?

Crapino. I left him in the street, where he gave me this casket (this basket I would have said) and bade me bear it to Dalio, and return to him at the Duke's palace. 19

Dulippo. If thou see him, tell him I must needs speak with him immediately: or abide awhile, I will go seek him myself, rather than be suspected by going to his house.

[Crapino *departeth, and* Dulippo *also: after* Dulippo *cometh in again seeking* Erostrato.

ACT II. SCENE I

Dulippo

Dulippo. I think if I had as many eyes as Argus, I could not have sought a man more narrowly in every street and every by-lane. There are not many gentlemen, scholars nor merchants in the city of Ferrara, but I have met with them, except him: peradventure he is come home another way. But look where he cometh at the last! [*Enter* Erostrato.

Erostrato. In good time have I spied my good master.

Dulippo. For the love of God call me Dulippo (not master); maintain the credit that thou hast hitherto kept, and let me alone. 11

Erostrato. Yet, sir, let me sometimes do my duty unto you, especially where nobody heareth.

Dulippo. Yea, but so long the parrot useth to cry 'knap' in sport, that at the last she calleth her master 'knave' in earnest: so long you will use to call me master, that at the last we shall be heard. What news?

Erostrato. Good.

Dulippo. Indeed?

Erostrato. Yea, excellent, we have as good as won the wager. 21

Dulippo. Oh, how happy were I if this were true!

Erostrato. Hear you me. Yesternight in the evening I walked out, and found Pasiphilo, and with small entreating I had him home to supper, where by such means as I used, he became my great friend, and told me the whole order of our adversary's determination: yea, and what Damon doth intend to do also, and hath promised me that from time to time what he can espy he will bring me word of it. 30

Dulippo. I cannot tell whether you know him or no; he is not to trust unto, a very flattering and a lying knave.

Erostrato. I know him very well, he cannot deceive me: and this that he hath told me I know must needs be true.

Dulippo. And what was it in effect?

Erostrato. That Damon had purposed to give his daughter in marriage to this doctor, upon the dower that he hath proffered. 40

Another suppose.

Dulippo. Are these your good news? your excellent news?

Erostrato. Stay awhile, you will understand me before you hear me.

Dulippo. Well, say on.

Erostrato. I answered to that, I was ready to make her the like dower.

Dulippo. Well said.

15 knap] rogue. cf. *Roister Doister*, III. iii. 84.

Erostrato. Abide, you hear not the worst yet.

Dulippo. O God, is there any worse behind? 50

Erostrato. Worse? Why what assurance could you suppose that I might make without some special consent from Philogano my father?

Dulippo. Nay, you can tell, you are better scholar than I.

Erostrato. Indeed, you have lost your time: for the books that you toss nowadays treat of small science.

Dulippo. Leave thy jesting, and proceed. 58

Erostrato. I said further, that I received letters lately from my father, whereby I understood that he would be here very shortly to perform all that I had proffered: therefore I required him to request Damon on my behalf, that he would stay his promise to the doctor for a fortnight or more.

Dulippo. This is somewhat yet, for by this means I shall be sure to linger and live in hope one fortnight longer: but, at the fortnight's end when Philogano cometh not, how shall I then do? Yea, and though he came, how may I any way hope of his consent, when he shall see that to follow this amorous enterprise I have set aside all study, all remembrance of my duty, and all dread of shame. Alas, alas, I may go hang myself. 73

Erostrato. Comfort yourself, man, and trust in me: there is a salve for every sore, and doubt you not, to this mischief we shall find a remedy.

Dulippo. O friend, revive me, that hitherto since I first attempted this matter have been continually dying.

Erostrato. Well, hearken awhile then. This morning I took my horse and rode into the fields to solace myself, and as I passed the ford beyond St. Anthony's gate, I met at the foot of the hill a gentleman riding with two or three men: and as methought by his habit and his looks, he should be none of the wisest. He saluted me, and I him: I asked him from whence he

57 toss] turn over.

came, and whither he would? He answered that he had come from Venice, then from Padua, now was going to Ferrara, and so to his country, which is Sienna. As soon as I knew him to be a Siennese, suddenly lifting up mine eyes (as it were with an admiration) I said unto him, 'Are you a Siennese, and come to Ferrara?' 'Why not?' said he. Quoth I (half and more with a trembling voice) 'Know you the danger that should ensue if you be known in Ferrara to be a Siennese?' He, more than half amazed, desired me earnestly to tell him what I meant.

Dulippo. I understand not whereto this tendeth.

Erostrato. I believe you: but hearken to me.

Dulippo. Go to then. 99

Erostrato. I answered him in this sort: 'Gentleman, because I have heretofore found very courteous entertainment in your country (being a student there), I account myself as it were bound to a Siennese: and therefore if I knew of any mishap towards any of that country, God forbid but I should disclose it. And I marvel that you knew not of the injury that your countrymen offered this other day to the ambassadors of Count Hercules.'

Dulippo. What tales he telleth me! What appertain these to me? 110

Erostrato. If you will hearken awhile, you shall find them no tales, but that they appertain to you more than you think for.

Dulippo. Forth!

Erostrato. I told him further, these ambassadors of Count Hercules had divers mules, wagons, and charettes, laden with divers costly jewels, gorgeous furniture, and other things which they carried as presents (passing that way) to the king of Naples: the which were not only stayed in Sienna by the officers whom you call customers, but searched, ransacked,

91 admiration] astonishment. 121 customers] custom-house officers.

tossed and turned, and in the end exacted for tribute, as if they had been the goods of a mean merchant.

Dulippo. Whither the devil will he? Is it possible that this gear appertain anything to my cause? I find neither head nor foot in it.

Erostrato. O how impatient you are! I pray you stay awhile.

Dulippo. Go to yet awhile then. 129

Erostrato. I proceeded, that upon these causes the Duke sent his Chancellor to declare the case unto the Senate there, of whom he had the most uncourteous answer that ever was heard: whereupon he was so enraged with all of that country, that for revenge he had sworn to spoil as many of them as ever should come to Ferrara, and to send them home in their doublet and their hose.

Dulippo. And I pray thee how couldest thou upon the sudden devise or imagine such a lie? and to what purpose? 140

Erostrato. You shall hear by and by a thing as fit for our purpose as any could have happened.

Dulippo. I would fain hear you conclude.

Erostrato. You would fain leap over the stile before you come at the hedge: I would you had heard me, and seen the gestures that I enforced to make him believe this.

Dulippo. I believe you, for I know you can counterfeit well. 149

Erostrato. Further, I said, the Duke had charged upon great penalties that the innholders and victuallers should bring word daily of as many Siennese as came to their houses. The gentleman being (as I guessed at the first) a man of small sapientia, when he heard these news, would have turned his horse another way.

Dulippo. By likelihood he was not very wise when he would believe that of his country, which, if it had been true, every man must needs have known it.

Erostrato. Why not? When he had not been in his

country for a month past, and I told him this had happened within these seven days. 161

Dulippo. Belike he was of small experience.

Erostrato. I think, of as little as may be, but best of all for our purpose; and good adventure it was that I met with such an one. Now hearken, I pray you.

Dulippo. Make an end, I pray thee.

Erostrato. He, as I say, when he heard these words, would have turned the bridle: and I, feigning a countenance as though I were somewhat pensive and careful for him, paused a while, and after with a great sigh said to him: 'Gentleman, for the courtesy that (as I said) I have found in your country, and because your affairs shall be the better dispatched, I will find the means to lodge you in my house, and you shall say to every man, that you are a Sicilian of Cathanea, your name Philogano, father to me that am indeed of that country and city, called here Erostrato. And I (to pleasure you) will (during your abode here) do you reverence as you were my father.' 179

Dulippo. Out upon me, what a gross-headed fool am I! Now I perceive whereto this tale tendeth.

Erostrato. Well, and how like you of it?

Dulippo. Indifferently, but one thing I doubt.

Erostrato. What is that?

Dulippo. Marry! that when he hath been here two or three days, he shall hear of every man that there is no such thing between the Duke and the town of Sienna. 188

Erostrato. As for that, let me alone. I do entertain and will entertain him so well that within these two or three days I will disclose unto him all the whole matter, and doubt not but to bring him in for performance of as much as I have promised to Damon; for what hurt can it be to him, when he shall bind a strange name and not his own?

Dulippo. What, think you he will be entreated to

183 Indifferently] Moderately.

stand bound for a dower of two thousand ducats by the year?

Erostrato. Yea, why not (if it were ten thousand) as long as he is not indeed the man that is bound? 200

Dulippo. Well, if it be so, what shall we be the nearer to our purpose?

Erostrato. Why! when we have done as much as we can, how can we do any more?

Dulippo. And where have you left him?

Erostrato. At the inn, because of his horses: he and his men shall lie in my house.

Dulippo. Why brought you him not with you?

Erostrato. I thought better to use your advice first.

Dulippo. Well, go take him home, make him all the cheer you can, spare for no cost, I will allow it. 211

Erostrato. Content, look where he cometh.

Dulippo. Is this he? Go meet him. By my troth, he looks even like a good soul. He that fisheth for him might be sure to catch a cod's head. I will rest here awhile to decipher him.

[Erostrato *espieth the* Siennese *and goeth towards him:* Dulippo *standeth aside.*

SCENE II

Erostrato. *Enter the* Siennese, *with* Paquetto *and* Petrucio, *his servants*

Siennese. He that travelleth in this world passeth by many perils.

Paquetto. You say true, sir. If the boat had been a little more laden this morning at the ferry, we had been all drowned, for I think there are none of us that could have swum.

Another suppose.

Siennese. I speak not of that.

Paquetto. Oh, you mean the foul way that we had since we came from this Padua. I promise you I was

211 allow] approve.

afraid, twice or thrice, that your mule would have lain fast in the mire. 11

Siennese. Jesu, what a blockhead thou art, I speak of the peril we are in presently since we came into this city.

Paquetto. A great peril, I promise you, that we were no sooner arrived, but you found a friend that brought you from the inn and lodged you in his own house.

Siennese. Yea, marry! God reward the gentle young man that we met, for else we had been in a wise case by this time. But have done with these tales, and take you heed, and you also, sirrah, take heed that none of you say we be Siennese, and remember that you call me Philogano of Cathanea.

A doltish suppose.

Paquetto. Sure, I shall never remember these outlandish words; I could well remember Haccanea.

Siennese. I say Cathanea, and not Haccanea, with a vengeance!

Paquetto. Let another name it then when need is, for I shall never remember it.

Siennese. Then hold thy peace, and take heed thou name not Sienna. 31

Paquetto. How say you, if I feign myself dumb, as I did once in the house of Crisobolus?

Siennese. Do as thou thinkest best. But look where cometh the gentleman whom we are so much bound unto.

Erostrato. Welcome, my dear father Philogano.

Siennese. Gramercy, my good son Erostrato.

Erostrato. That is well said; be mindful of your tongue, for these Ferrarese be as crafty as the devil of hell. 41

Siennese. No, no, be you sure we will do as you have bidden us.

Erostrato. For if you should name Sienna they would spoil you immediately, and turn you out of the town, with more shame than I would should befall you for a thousand crowns.

Siennese. I warrant you, I was giving them warning as I came to you, and I doubt not but they will take good heed. 50

Erostrato. Yea, and trust not the servants of my household too far, for they are Ferrarese all, and never knew my father, nor came never in Sicilia. This is my house, will it please you to go in? I will follow.

[*They go in.* Dulippo *tarrieth and espieth the* Doctor *coming in with his man.*

SCENE III

Dulippo *alone*

Dulippo. This gear hath had no evil beginning, if it continue so and fall to happy end. But is not this the silly Doctor with the side bonnet, the doting fool, that dare presume to become a suitor to such a peerless paragon? O how covetousness doth blind the common sort of men! Damon, more desirous of the dower than mindful of his gentle and gallant daughter, hath determined to make him his son-in-law, who for his age may be his father-in-law: and hath greater respect to the abundance of goods than to his own natural child. He beareth well in mind to fill his own purse, but he little remembreth that his daughter's purse shall be continually empty, unless Master Doctor fill it with double duck eggs. Alas! I jest and have no joy. I will stand here aside and laugh a little at this lobcock. 15

[Dulippo *espieth the* Doctor *and his man coming.*

SCENE IV

Dulippo. *Enter* Carion, *the doctor's man, and* Cleander

Carion. Master, what the devil mean you to go seek guests at this time of the day? The Mayor's officers

15 lobcock] lubber.

have dined ere this time, which are always the last in the market.

Cleander. I come to seek Pasiphilo, to the end he may dine with me.

Carion. As though six mouths, and the cat for the seventh, be not sufficient to eat an harlotry shotterel, a pennyworth of cheese, and half a score spurlings: this is all the dainties you have dressed for you and your family. 11

Cleander. Ah, greedy gut, art thou afeard thou shalt want?

Carion. I am afeard indeed; it is not the first time I have found it so.

Dulippo. [*Aside*.] Shall I make some sport with this gallant? What shall I say to him?

Cleander. Thou art afeard belike that he will eat thee and the rest.

Carion. Nay, rather that he will eat your mule, both hair and hide. 21

Cleander. Hair and hide? And why not flesh and all?

Carion. Because she hath none. If she had any flesh, I think you had eaten her yourself by this time.

Cleander. She may thank you, then, for your good attendance.

Carion. Nay, she may thank you for your small allowance.

Dulippo. [*Aside*.] In faith now let me alone. 30

Cleander. Hold thy peace, drunken knave, and espy me Pasiphilo.

Dulippo. [*Aside*.] Since I can do no better, I will set such a stance between him and Pasiphilo that all this town shall not make them friends.

Carion. Could you not have sent to seek him, but you must come yourself? Surely you come for some other purpose, for if you would have had Pasiphilo to

8 harlotry shotterel] wretched pike of the first year. 9 spurlings] smelts. 34 stance] distance.

dinner, I warrant you he would have tarried here an hour since. 40

Cleander. Hold thy peace, here is one of Damon's servants, of him I shall understand where he is. Good fellow, art thou not one of Damon's servants?

Another suppose.

Dulippo. Yes sir, at your commandment.

Cleander. Gramercy, tell me then, hath Pasiphilo been there this day or no?

Dulippo. Yes sir, and I think he be there still, ha, ha, ha!

Cleander. What laughest thou? 50

Dulippo. At a thing that every man may not laugh at.

Cleander. What?

Dulippo. Talk that Pasiphilo had with my master this day.

Cleander. What talk I pray thee?

Dulippo. I may not tell it.

Cleander. Doth it concern me?

Dulippo. Nay, I will say nothing.

Cleander. Tell me.

Dulippo. I can say no more. 60

Cleander. I would but know if it concern me, I pray thee tell me.

Dulippo. I would tell you, if I were sure you would not tell it again.

Cleander. Believe me, I will keep it close. Carion, give us leave a little, go aside!

Dulippo. If my master should know that it came by me, I were better die a thousand deaths.

Cleander. He shall never know it, say on.

Dulippo. Yea, but what assurance shall I have? 70

Cleander. I lay thee my faith and honesty in pawn.

Dulippo. A pretty pawn, the fulkers will not lend you a farthing on it.

Cleander. Yea, but amongst honest men it is more worth than gold.

72 fulkers] pawnbrokers.

Dulippo. Yea, marry, sir, but where be they? But will you needs have me tell it unto you?

Cleander. Yea, I pray thee, if it anything appertain to me. 79

Dulippo. Yes, it is of you, and I would gladly tell it you, because I would not have such a man of worship so scorned by a villain ribald.

Cleander. I pray thee tell me then.

Dulippo. I will tell you so that you will swear never to tell it to Pasiphilo, to my master, nor to any other body.

Carion. [*Aside.*] Surely it is some toy devised to get some money of him.

Cleander. I think I have a book here. 89

Carion. [*Aside.*] If he knew him as well as I, he would never go about it, for he may as soon get one of his teeth from his jaws with a pair of pinchers, as a penny out of his purse with such a conceit.

Cleander. Here is a letter will serve the turn: I swear to thee by the contents hereof never to disclose it to any man.

Dulippo. I will tell you, I am sorry to see how Pasiphilo doth abuse you, persuading you that always he laboureth for you, where indeed he lieth on my master continually, as it were with tooth and nail, for a stranger, a scholar, born in Sicilia—they call him Roscus or Arsekiss, he hath a mad name, I can never hit upon it.

Cleander. And thou reckonest it as madly: is it not Erostrato?

Dulippo. That same, I should never have remembered it: and the villain speaketh all the evil of you that can be devised.

Cleander. To whom? 109

Dulippo. To my master, yea and to Polynesta herself sometimes.

Cleander. Is it possible? Ah, slave, and what saith he?

98 abuse] deceive. 99 lieth on] is urgent to.

Dulippo. More evil than I can imagine: that you are the miserablest and most niggardly man that ever was.

Cleander. Saith Pasiphilo so by me?

Dulippo. And that as often as he cometh to your house, he is like to die for hunger, you fare so well.

Cleander. That the devil take him else! 118

Dulippo. And that you are the testiest man, and most diverse to please in the whole world, so that he cannot please you unless he should even kill himself with continual pain.

Cleander. O devilish tongue!

Dulippo. Furthermore, that you cough continually and spit, so that a dog cannot abide it.

Cleander. I never spit nor cough more than thus, 'vho, vho', and that but since I caught this murr, but who is free from it?

Dulippo. You say true, sir; yet further he saith, your arm-holes stink, your feet worse than they, and your breath worst of all. 131

Cleander. If I quite him not for this gear!

Dulippo. And that you are bursten in the cods.

Cleander. O villain, he lieth, and if I were not in the street thou shouldest see them.

Dulippo. And he saith that you desire this young gentlewoman, as much for other men's pleasure as for your own.

Cleander. What meaneth he by that?

Dulippo. Peradventure that by her beauty you would entice many young men to your house. 141

Cleander. Young men? To what purpose?

Dulippo. Nay, guess you that.

Cleander. Is it possible that Pasiphilo speaketh thus of me?

Dulippo. Yea, and much more.

Cleander. And doth Damon believe him?

Dulippo. Yea, more than you would think: in such sort, that long ere this he would have given you a flat

120 diverse] uncertain. 127 murr] catarrh.

repulse, but Pasiphilo entreated him to continue you a suitor for his advantage. 151

Cleander. How for his advantage?

Dulippo. Marry, that during your suit he might still have some reward for his great pains.

Cleander. He shall have a rope, and yet that is more than he deserveth: I had thought to have given him these hose when I had worn them a little nearer, but he shall have a., &c.

Dulippo. In good faith, sir, they were but lost on him. Will you anything else with me, sir? 160

Cleander. Nay, I have heard too much of thee already.

Dulippo. Then I will take my leave of you.

Cleander. Farewell, but tell me, may I not know thy name?

Dulippo. Sir, they call me 'Foul fall you'.

Cleander. An ill-favoured name, by my troth: art thou this countryman?

Dulippo. No, sir, I was born by a castle men call 'Scab catch you'. Fare you well, sir! [*Exit*. 170

Cleander. Farewell! Oh God, how have I been abused? What a spokesman? What a messenger had I provided?

Carion. Why, sir, will you tarry for Pasiphilo till we die for hunger?

Cleander. Trouble me not, that the devil take you both.

Carion. These news, whatsoever they be, like him not.

Cleander. Art thou so hungry yet? I pray to God thou be never satisfied. 181

Carion. By the Mass, no more I shall as long as I am your servant.

Cleander. Go with mischance!

Carion. Yea, and a mischief to you, and to all such covetous wretches! [*Exeunt*.

ACT III

SCENE I

Enter Dalio, *the cook, and* Crapino, *the lackey*

Dalio. By that time we come to the house, I trust that of these twenty eggs in the basket we shall find but very few whole. But it is a folly to talk to him. What the devil, wilt thou never lay that stick out of thy hand? He fighteth with the dogs, beateth the bears, at everything in the street he findeth occasion to tarry: if he spy a slipstring by the way, such another as himself, a page, a lackey or a dwarf, the devil of hell cannot hold him in chains, but he will be doing with him. I cannot go two steps, but I must look back for my younker. Go to, halter-sick! if you break one egg, I may chance break, &c. 12

Crapino. What will you break? Your nose in mine, &c.?

Dalio. Ah, beast!

Crapino. If I be a beast, yet I am no horned beast.

Dalio. Is it even so? Is the wind in that door? If I were unladen I would tell you whether I be a horned beast or no.

Crapino. You are always laden either with wine or with ale. 21

Dalio. Ah, spiteful boy, shall I suffer him?

Crapino. Ah, cowardly beast, darest thou strike and say never a word?

Dalio. Well, my master shall know of this gear; either he shall redress it, or he shall lose one of us.

Crapino. Tell him the worst thou canst by me.

Enter hurriedly Erostrato *and* Dulippo

Erostrato. What noise, what a rule is this?

7 slipstring] truant. 11 halter-sick] determined to be hanged. 28 what a rule] what unruliness.

Crapino. Marry, sir, he striketh me because I tell him of his swearing. 30

Dalio. The villain lieth deadly, he reviles me because I bid him make haste.

Erostrato. Holla: no more of this! Dalio, do you make in a readiness those pigeons, stock doves, and also the breast of veal: and let your vessel be as clear as glass against I return, that I may tell you which I will have roasted, and which boiled. [*Exit* Dalio.

Crapino, lay down that basket and follow me. Oh, that I could tell where to find Pasiphilo! But look where he cometh that can tell me of him. 40

[Dulippo *is espied by* Erostrato.

Dulippo. What have you done with Philogano, your father?

Erostrato. I have left him within. I would fain speak with Pasiphilo; can you tell me where he is?

Dulippo. He dined this day with my master, but whither he went from thence I know not; what would you with him?

Erostrato. I would have him go tell Damon that Philogano, my father, is come and ready to make assurance of as much as he will require. Now shall I teach master doctor a school point: he travaileth to none other end but to catch *Cornua*, and he shall have them, for as old as he is, and as many subtleties as he hath learned in the law, he cannot go beyond me one ace.

Dulippo. O dear friend, go thy ways, seek Pasiphilo, find him out, and conclude somewhat to our contentation.

Erostrato. But where shall I find him? 59

Dulippo. At the feasts, if there be any, or else in the market with the poulterers or the fishmongers.

Erostrato. What should he do with them?

Dulippo. Marry, he watcheth whose caters buy the best meat. If any buy a fat capon, a good breast of veal, fresh salmon or any such good dish, he followeth to the house, and either with some news, or some stale jest he will be sure to make himself a guest.

Erostrato. In faith, and I will seek there for him.

Dulippo. Then must you needs find him, and when you have done, I will make you laugh. 70

Erostrato. Whereat?

Dulippo. At certain sport I made to-day with master doctor.

Erostrato. And why not now?

Dulippo. No, it asketh further leisure. I pray thee dispatch, and find out Pasiphilo that honest man.

[Dulippo *tarrieth.* Erostrato, *with* Crapino, *goeth out.*

SCENE II

Dulippo, *alone*

Dulippo. This amorous cause that hangeth in controversy between Domine doctor and me may be compared to them that play at primero. Of whom someone peradventure shall lose a great sum of money before he win one stake, and at last, half in anger, shall set up his rest; win it; and after that another, another, and another, till at last he draw the most part of the money to his heap: the other by little and little still diminishing his rest, till at last he become as near the brink as erst the other was; yet again peradventure fortune smiling on him, he shall, as it were, by piecemeal pull out the guts of his fellow's bags, and bring him barer than he himself was tofore: and so in play continue still (fortune favouring now this way, now that way,) till at last the one of them is left with as many crosses as God hath brethren. O how often have I thought myself sure of the upper hand herein! But I triumphed before the victory. And then how oft again have I thought the field lost! Thus have I

3 primero] a gambling card-game. 6 set up his rest] stake his all. 16 crosses] coins.

been tossed now over, now under, even as fortune list to whirl the wheel, neither sure to win nor certain to lose the wager. And this practice that now my servant hath devised, although hitherto it hath not succeeded amiss, yet can I not count myself assured of it; for I fear still that one mischance or other will come and turn it topsy-turvy. But look where my master cometh.

[Damon *coming in espieth* Dulippo *and calleth him.*

SCENE III

Damon *and* Dulippo.

Damon. Dulippo!

Dulippo. Here, sir.

Damon. Go in and bid Nevola and his fellows come hither that I may tell them what they shall go about, and go you into my study: there upon the shelf you shall find a roll of writings which John of the dean made to my father, when he sold him the Grange farm, endorsed with both their names: bring it hither to me.

Dulippo. It shall be done, sir. [*Exit.* 10

Damon. Go, I will prepare other manner of writings for you than you are aware of. O fools that trust any man but themselves nowadays! O spiteful fortune, thou doest me wrong; I think, that from the depth of hell pit thou hast sent me this servant to be the subversion of me and all mine! [*The servants come in.*] Come hither, sirs, and hear what I shall say unto you. Go into my study, where you shall find Dulippo, step to him all at once, take him and (with a cord that I have laid on the table for the nonce) bind him hand and foot, carry him into the dungeon under the stairs, make fast the door and bring me the key; it hangeth by upon a pin on the wall. Dispatch and do this gear

6 dean] vale.

as privily as you can: and thou, Nevola, come hither to me again with speed.

Nevola. Well I shall. [*Exit with servants.*

Damon. Alas, how shall I be revenged of this extreme despite? If I punish my servant according to his devilish deserts, I shall heap further cares upon mine own head; for to such detestable offences no punishment can seem sufficient, but only death, and in such cases it is not lawful for a man to be his own carver. The laws are ordained, and officers appointed to minister justice for the redress of wrongs: and if to the potestates I complain me, I shall publish mine own reproach to the world. Yea, what should it prevail me to use all the punishments that can be devised? The thing once done cannot be undone. My daughter is deflowered, and I utterly dishonested: how can I then wipe that blot off my brow? and on whom shall I seek revenge? Alas, alas, I myself have been the cause of all these cares, and have deserved to bear the punishment of all these mishaps. Alas, I should not have committed my dearest darling in custody to so careless a creature as this old nurse; for we see by common proof, that these old women be either peevish, or pitiful: either easily inclined to evil, or quickly corrupted with bribes and rewards. O wife, my good wife (that now liest cold in the grave) now may I well bewail the want of thee, and mourning now may I bemoan that I miss thee! If thou hadst lived (such was thy government of the least things) that thou wouldest prudently have provided for the preservation of this pearl. A costly jewel may I well account her, that hath been my chief comfort in youth, and is now become the corrosive of mine age. O Polynesta, full evil hast thou requited the clemency of thy careful father: and yet to excuse thee guiltless before God, and to condemn thee guilty before the world, I can count none other but my wretched self,

35 potestates] magistrates.

the caitiff and causer of all my cares. For of all the duties that are requisite in human life, only obedience is by the parents to be required of the child; where on the other side the parents are bound, first to beget them, then to bring them forth, after to nourish them, to preserve them from bodily perils in the cradle, from danger of soul by godly education, to match them in consort inclined to virtue, to banish them all idle and wanton company, to allow them sufficient for their sustentation, to cut off excess, the open gate of sin, seldom or never to smile on them unless it be to their encouragement in virtue, and finally, to provide them marriages in time convenient, lest (neglected of us) they learn to set either too much or too little by themselves. Five years are past since I might have married her, when by continual excuses I have prolonged it to my own perdition. Alas, I should have considered, she is a collop of my own flesh: what should I think to make her a princess? Alas, alas, a poor kingdom have I now caught to endow her with. It is too true that of all sorrows this is the head source and chief fountain of all furies: the goods of the world are uncertain, the gains little to be rejoiced at, and the loss not greatly to be lamented. Only the children cast away cutteth the parent's throat with the knife of inward care; which knife will kill me surely, I make none other account.

[Damon's *servants come to him again.*

SCENE IV

Damon. *Enter* Nevola

Nevola. Sir, we have done as you bade us, and here is the key.

Damon. Well, go then, Nevola, and seek Master Casteling, the jailer, he dwelleth by St. Anthony's gate,

78 collop] slice.

desire him to lend me a pair of the fetters he useth for his prisoners, and come again quickly.

Nevola. Well, sir.

Damon. Hear you, if he ask what I would do with them, say you cannot tell, and tell neither him nor any other what is become of Dulippo. 10

[Damon *goeth out.*

Nevola. I warrant you, sir. Fie upon the devil, it is a thing almost impossible for a man nowadays to handle money, but the metal will stick on his fingers. I marvelled always at this fellow of mine, Dulippo, that of the wages he received he could maintain himself so bravely apparelled; but now I perceive the cause, he had the disbursing and receipt of all my master's affairs, the keys of the granary, Dulippo here, Dulippo there, in favour with my master, in favour with his daughter, what would you more, he was *Magister factotum*: he was as fine as the crusado, and we silly wretches as coarse as canvas: well, behold what it is come to in the end; he had been better to have done less.

Another suppose.

Pasiphilo *enters suddenly and unexpectedly*

Pasiphilo. Thou sayest true, Nevola, he hath done too much indeed.

Nevola. From whence comest thou, in the devil's name?

Pasiphilo. Out of the same house thou camest from, but not out of the same door. 30

Nevola. We had thought thou hadst been gone long since.

Pasiphilo. When I arose from the table, I felt a rumbling in my belly, which made me run to the stable, and there I fell on sleep upon the straw, and have lain there ever since. And thou, whither goest thou?

22 crusado] a Portuguese gold coin, bearing the figure of a cross.

Nevola. My master hath sent me on an errand in great haste.

Pasiphilo. Whither, I pray thee? 40

Nevola. Nay, I may not tell. Farewell! [*Exit*.

Pasiphilo. As though I need any further instructions. O God, what news I heard even now, as I lay in the stable! O good Erostrato and poor Cleander, that have so earnestly striven for this damsel, happy is he that can get her, I promise you; he shall be sure of more than one at a clap that catcheth her, either Adam or Eve within her belly. O God, how men may be deceived in a woman! Who would have believed the contrary but that she had been a virgin? Ask the neighbours and you shall hear very good report of her: mark her behaviours and you would have judged her very maidenly: seldom seen abroad but in place of prayer, and there very devout, and no gazer at outward sights, no blazer of her beauty above in the windows, no stale at the door for the by-passers: you would have thought her a holy young woman. But much good do it *Domine doctor;* he shall be sure to lack no corn in a dear year, whatsoever he have with her else. I beshrew me if I let the marriage any way. But is not this the old scabbed quean that I heard disclosing all this gear to her master, as I stood in the stable ere now? It is she.

Another suppose.

[Pasiphilo *espieth* Psiteria *coming*.

SCENE V

Pasiphilo *and* Psiteria

Pasiphilo. Whither goeth Psiteria?

Psiteria. To a gossip of mine hereby.

Pasiphilo. What? To tattle of the goodly stir that thou keptst concerning Polynesta.

Psiteria. No, no: but how knew you of that gear?

56 stale] decoy. 60 let] hinder.

Pasiphilo. You told me.

Psiteria. I? When did I tell you?

Pasiphilo. Even now when you told it to Damon, I both saw you and heard you, though you saw not me: a good part I promise you, to accuse the poor wench, kill the old man with care, over and besides the danger you have brought Dulippo and the nurse unto, and many more, fie! fie! 13

Psiteria. Indeed, I was to blame, but not so much as you think.

Pasiphilo. And how not so much? Did I not hear you tell?

Psiteria. Yes, but I will tell you how it came to pass. I have known for a great while that this Dulippo and Polynesta have lain together, and all by the means of the nurse; yet I held my peace, and never told it. Now this other day the nurse fell on scolding with me, and twice or thrice called me drunken old whore, and such names that it was too bad: and I called her bawd, and told her that I knew well enough how often she had brought Dulippo to Polynesta's bed. Yet all this while I thought not that anybody had heard me, but it befell clean contrary, for my master was on the other side of the wall and heard all our talk, whereupon he sent for me and forced me to confess all that you heard. 30

Pasiphilo. And why wouldest thou tell him? I would not for, &c.

Psiteria. Well, if I had thought my master would have taken it so, he should rather have killed me.

Pasiphilo. Why? How could he take it?

Psiteria. Alas, it pitieth me to see the poor young woman how she weeps, wails, and tears her hair, not esteeming her own life half so dear as she doth poor Dulippo's: and her father, he weeps on the other side, that it would pierce an heart of stone with pity. But I must be gone. 41

Pasiphilo. Go, that the gunpowder consume thee, old trot! [*Exeunt.*

ACT IV

SCENE I

Feigned Erostrato *and* Crapino

Erostrato. What shall I do? Alas, what remedy shall I find for my rueful estate? What escape, or what excuse may I now devise to shift over our subtle supposes? For though to this day I have usurped the name of my master, and that without check or control of any man, now shall I be openly deciphered, and that in the sight of every man: now shall it openly be known, whether I be Erostrato the gentleman, or Dulippo the servant. We have hitherto played our parts in abusing others: but now cometh the man that will not be abused, the right Philogano, the right father of the right Erostrato. Going to seek Pasiphilo, and hearing that he was at the water gate, behold I espied my fellow Litio, and by and by my old master Philogano setting forth his first step on land. I to fuge and away hither as fast as I could to bring word to the right Erostrato, of his right father Philogano, that to so sudden a mishap some subtle shift might be upon the sudden devised. But what can be imagined to serve the turn, although we had month's respite to beat our brains about it, since we are commonly known, at the least supposed in this town, he for Dulippo, a slave and servant to Damon, and I for Erostrato, a gentleman and a student? [Erostrato *espieth* Psiteria *coming, and sendeth his lackey to her.*] But behold, run, Crapino, to yonder old woman before she get within the doors, and desire her to call out Dulippo: but hear you! If she ask who would speak with him, say thyself and none other. 29

5 control] rebuke. 10 abusing] deceiving.
15 to fuge] to flee.

SCENE II

Crapino, *feigned* Erostrato, *and* Psiteria

Crapino. Honest woman, you gossip, thou rotten whore, hearest thou not, old witch?

Psiteria. A rope stretch your young bones! Either you must live to be as old as I, or be hanged while you are young.

Crapino. I pray thee look if Dulippo be within.

Psiteria. Yes, that he is, I warrant him.

Crapino. Desire him then to come hither and speak a word with me, he shall not tarry.

Psiteria. Content yourself, he is otherwise occupied.

Crapino. Yet tell him so, gentle girl. 11

Psiteria. I tell you he is busy.

Crapino. Why is it such a matter to tell him so, thou crooked crone?

Psiteria. A rope stretch you, marry!

Crapino. A pox eat you, marry!

Psiteria. Thou wilt be hanged, I warrant thee, if thou live to it.

Crapino. And thou wilt be burnt, I warrant thee, if the canker consume thee not. 20

Psiteria. If I come near you, hempstring, I will teach you to sing sol fa.

Crapino. Come on, and if I get a stone I will scare crows with you.

Psiteria. Go, with a mischief! I think thou be some devil that would tempt me. [*Exit.*

Erostrato. Crapino: hear you! Come away, let her go with a vengeance, why come you not? [Erostrato *espieth* Philogano *coming, and runneth about to hide him.*] Alas, look where my master Philogano cometh: what shall I do? Where shall I hide me? He shall not see me in these clothes, nor before I have spoken with the right Erostrato. [*Exeunt.*

SCENE III

Enter Philogano, Ferrarese, *the innkeeper*, Litio, *a servant*

Philogano. Honest man, it is even so: be you sure there is no love to be compared like the love of the parents towards their children. It is not long since I thought that a very weighty matter should not have made me come out of Sicilia, and yet now I have taken this tedious toil and travail upon me, only to see my son, and to have him home with me.

Ferrarese. By my faith, sir, it hath been a great travail indeed, and too much for one of your age. 9

Philogano. Yea, be you sure! I came in company with certain gentlemen of my country, who had affairs to dispatch as far as to Ancona, from thence by water to Ravenna, and from Ravenna hither, continually against the tide.

Ferrarese. Yea, and I think that you had but homely lodging by the way.

Philogano. The worst that ever man had: but that was nothing to the stir that the searchers kept with me when I came aboard the ship. Jesus! How often they untrussed my male, and ransacked a little capcase that I had, tossed and turned all that was within it, searched my bosom, yea, my breeches, that I assure you I thought they would have flayed me to search between the fell and the flesh for farthings.

Ferrarese. Sure, I have heard no less, and that the merchants bob them sometimes, but they play the knaves still.

Philogano. Yea, be you well assured such an office is the inheritance of a knave, and an honest man will not meddle with it. 30

Ferrarese. Well, this passage shall seem pleasant unto you when you shall find your child in health and well. But I pray you, sir, why did you not rather send for

20 untrussed] unpacked. male] trunk. capcase] bag. 24 fell] skin. 26 bob] jeer at.

him into Sicilia, than to come yourself, especially since you had none other business? Peradventure you had rather endanger yourself by this noisome journey than hazard to draw him from his study.

Philogano. Nay, that was not the matter, for I had rather have him give over his study altogether and come home. 40

Ferrarese. Why? If you minded not to make him learned, to what end did you send him hither at the first?

Philogano. I will tell you—when he was at home he did as most young men do, he played many mad pranks and did many things that liked me not very well; and I thinking that by that time he had seen the world, he would learn to know himself better, exhorted him to study, and put in his election what place he would go to. At the last he came hither, and I think he was scarce here so soon as I felt the want of him, in such sort as from that day to this I have passed few nights without tears. I have written to him very often that he should come home, but continually he refused still, beseeching me to continue his study, wherein he doubted not (as he said) but to profit greatly.

Ferrarese. Indeed, he is very much commended of all men, and specially of the best reputed students. 58

Philogano. I am glad he hath not lost his time, but I care not greatly for so much knowledge. I would not be without the sight of him again so long for all the learning in the world. I am old now, and if God should call me in his absence, I promise you I think it would drive me into desperation.

Ferrarese. It is commendable in a man to love his children, but to be so tender over them is more womanlike!

Philogano. Well, I confess it is my fault: and yet I will tell you another cause of my coming hither, more weighty than this. Divers of my country have been here since he came hither, by whom I have sent unto him, and some of them have been thrice, some four or five times at his house, and yet could never speak with him. I fear he applies his study so that he will not lose the minute of an hour from his book. What, alas, he might yet talk with his countrymen for a while. He is a young man, tenderly brought up, and if he fare thus continually night and day at his book, it may be enough to drive him into a frenzy. 79

Ferrarese. Indeed, enough were as good as a feast. Lo! you, sir, here is your son Erostrato's house, I will knock.

Philogano. Yea, I pray you knock.

Ferrarese. They hear not.

Philogano. Knock again.

Ferrarese. I think they be asleep.

Litio. If this gate were your grandfather's soul, you could not knock more softly—let me come! Ho! ho! is there anybody within? 89

SCENE IV

The Ferrarese, Philogano, *and* Litio. Dalio *cometh to the window, and there maketh them answer*

Dalio. What devil of hell is there? I think he will break the gates in pieces.

Litio. Marry, sir, we had thought you had been asleep within, and therefore we thought best to wake you. What doth Erostrato?

Dalio. He is not within.

Philogano. Open the door, good fellow, I pray thee.

Dalio. If you think to lodge here, you are deceived, I tell you, for here are guests enough already. 9

Philogano. A good fellow, and much for thy master's honesty, by our Lady! And what guests, I pray thee?

Dalio. Here is Philogano, my master's father, lately come out of Sicilia.

Another suppose. *Philogano.* Thou speakest truer than thou art aware of; he will be, by that time thou hast opened the door. Open I pray thee heartily.

Dalio. It is a small matter for me to open the door, but here is no lodging for you; I tell you plain, the house is full.

Philogano. Of whom? 20

Dalio. I told you: here is Philogano, my master's father, come from Cathanea.

Philogano. And when came he?

Dalio. He came three hours since, or more; he alighted at the Angel, and left his horses there: afterward my master brought him hither.

Philogano. Good fellow, I think thou hast good sport to mock me.

Dalio. Nay, I think you have good sport to make me tarry here, as though I have nothing else to do: I am matched with an unruly mate in the kitchen. I will go look to him another while. 32

Philogano. I think he be drunken.

Ferrarese. Sure, he seems so: see you not how red he is about the gills?

Philogano. Abide, fellow, what Philogano is it whom thou talkest of?

Dalio. An honest gentleman, father to Erostrato, my master.

Philogano. And where is he? 40

Dalio. Here within.

Philogano. May we see him?

Dalio. I think you may, if you be not blind.

Philogano. Go to, go tell him here is one would speak with him.

Dalio. Marry, that I will willingly do.

Philogano. I cannot tell what I should say to this gear. Litio, what thinkest thou of it?

Litio. I cannot tell you what I should say, sir. The

world is large and long, there may be more Philoganos and more Erostratos than one, yea, and more Ferraras, more Sicilias, and more Cathaneas: peradventure this is not that Ferrara which you sent your son unto.

Another suppose.

Philogano. Peradventure thou art a fool, and he was another that answered us even now. But be you sure, honest man, that you mistake not the house?

Ferrarese. Nay then, God help, think you I know not Erostrato's house? Yes, and himself also: I saw him here no longer since than yesterday. But here comes one that will tell us tidings of him; I like his countenance better than the other's that answered at the window erewhile.

[Dalio *draweth his head in at the window; the* Siennese *cometh out.*

SCENE V

Philogano, Litio, Ferrarese, *and* Siennese

Siennese. Would you speak with me, sir?

Philogano. Yea, sir, I would fain know whence you are.

Siennese. Sir, I am a Sicilian, at your commandment.

Philogano. What part of Sicilia?

Siennese. Of Cathanea.

Philogano. What shall I call your name?

Siennese. My name is Philogano.

Philogano. What trade do you occupy? 10

Siennese. Merchandise.

Philogano. What merchandise brought you hither?

Siennese. None. I came only to see a son that I have here whom I saw not these two years.

Philogano. What call they your son?

Siennese. Erostrato.

Philogano. Is Erostrato your son?

Siennese. Yea, verily.

Philogano. And are you Philogano?

Siennese. The same. 20

Philogano. And a merchant of Cathanea?

Siennese. What need I tell you so often? I will not tell you a lie.

Philogano. Yes, you have told me a false lie, and thou art a villain and no better.

Siennese. Sir, you offer me great wrong with these injurious words.

Philogano. Nay, I will do more than I have yet proffered to do, for I will prove thee a liar and a knave to take upon thee that thou art not. 30

Siennese. Sir, I am Philogano of Cathanea, out of all doubt; if I were not, I would be loth to tell you so.

A stout suppose.

Philogano. Oh, see the boldness of this brute beast, what a brazen face he setteth on it!

Siennese. Well, you may believe me, if you list: what wonder you?

Philogano. I wonder at thy impudence, for thou, nor nature that framed thee, can ever counterfeit thee to be me, ribald villain and lying wretch that thou art [*coming to the door*]. 41

Dalio. Shall I suffer a knave to abuse my master's father thus? Hence, villain, hence, or I will sheath this good falchion in your paunch! If my master Erostrato find you prating here on this fashion to his father, I would not be in your coat for more cony skins than I got these twelve months. Come you in again, sir, and let this cur bark here till he burst. 49

A pleasant suppose.

[Dalio *pulleth the* Siennese *in at the doors.*

27 injurious] insulting. 47 cony] rabbit.

SCENE VI

Philogano, Litio, *and* Ferrarese

Philogano. Litio, how likest thou this gear?

Litio. Sir, I like it as evil as may be: but have you not often heard tell of the falsehood of Ferrara? And now may you see, it falleth out accordingly.

Ferrarese. Friend, you do not well to slander the city; these men are no Ferrarese, you may know by their tongue.

Litio. Well, there is never a barrel better herring between you both. But indeed your officers are most to blame, that suffer such faults to escape unpunished.

Ferrarese. What know the officers of this? Think you they know of every fault? 12

Litio. Nay, I think they will know as little as may be, specially when they have no gains by it; but they ought to have their ears as open to hear of such offences, as the inn gates be to receive guests.

Philogano. Hold thy peace, fool.

Litio. By the Mass, I am afeard that we shall be proved fools, both two.

Philogano. Well, what shall we do? 20

Litio. I would think best we should go seek Erostrato himself.

Ferrarese. I will wait upon you willingly, and either at the schools, or at the convocations, we shall find him.

Philogano. By our Lady, I am weary, I will run no longer about to seek him; I am sure hither he will come at the last.

A true suppose. *Litio.* Sure, my mind gives me that we shall find a new Erostrato ere it be long. 29

[Erostrato *is espied upon the stage running about.*

Ferrarese. Look, where he is! Whither runs he? Stay you awhile, I will go tell him that you are here. Erostrato, Erostrato, ho, Erostrato, I would speak with you!

8–9 never a barrel . . . you both] *a proverbial phrase for* nothing to choose between you.

SCENE VII

Feigned Erostrato, Ferrarese, Philogano, *and* Litio

Erostrato. Now can I hide me no longer. Alas, what shall I do? I will set a good face on, to bear out the matter.

Ferrarese. O Erostrato, Philogano, your father, is come out of Sicilia.

Erostrato. Tell me that I know not; I have been with him and seen him already.

Ferrarese. Is it possible? And it seemeth by him that you know not of his coming.

Erostrato. Why, have you spoken with him? When saw you him, I pray you? 11

Ferrarese. Look you where he stands, why go you not to him? Look you, Philogano, behold your dear son Erostrato.

Philogano. Erostrato! This is not Erostrato: this seemeth rather to be Dulippo, and it is Dulippo indeed.

Litio. Why, doubt you of that?

Erostrato. What saith this honest man?

Philogano. Marry, sir, indeed you are so honourably clad, it is no marvel if you look big. 20

Erostrato. To whom speaketh he?

Philogano. What, God help, do you not know me?

Erostrato. As far as I remember, sir, I never saw you before.

Philogano. Hark, Litio, here is good gear, this honest man will not know me.

Erostrato. Gentleman, you take your marks amiss.

Litio. Did I not tell you of the falsehood of Ferrara, master? Dulippo hath learned to play the knave indifferently well since he came hither.

A shameless suppose.

Philogano. Peace, I say! 31

Erostrato. Friend, my name is not Dulippo. Ask you throughout this town of great and small, they

27 take your marks amiss] take a wrong aim.

know me: ask this honest man that is with you, if you will not believe me.

Ferrarese. Indeed, I never knew him otherwise called than Erostrato: and so they call him, as many as know him.

Litio. Master, now you may see the falsehood of these fellows. This honest man, your host, is of counsel with him and would face us down that it is Erostrato: beware of these mates. 42

A needless suppose.

Ferrarese. Friend, thou doest me wrong to suspect me, for sure I never heard him otherwise called than Erostrato.

Erostrato. What name could you hear me called by, but by my right name? But I am wise enough to stand prating here with this old man. I think he be mad.

Philogano. Ah, runagate, ah, villain traitor, doest thou use thy master thus? What hast thou done with my son, villain? 51

Enter Dalio *and other servants*

Dalio. Doth this dog bark here still? And will you suffer him, master, thus to revile you?

Erostrato. Come in, come in, what wilt thou do with this pestel?

Dalio. I will rap the old cackabed on the costard.

Erostrato. Away with it! And you, sirrah, lay down these stones. Come in at door every one of you, bear with him for his age; I pass not of his evil words. 59

[Erostrato *taketh all his servants in at the doors.*

SCENE VIII

Philogano, Ferrarese, *and* Litio

Philogano. Alas, who shall relieve my miserable estate? To whom shall I complain? Since he whom

42 mates] fellows. 56 cackabed] a coarse term of abuse. costard] head. 59 pass not of] care not about.

I brought up of a child, yea, and cherished him as if he had been mine own, doth now utterly deny to know me: and you whom I took for an honest man, and he that should have brought me to the sight of my son, are compact with this false wretch, and would face me down that he is Erostrato. Alas, you might have some compassion of mine age, to the misery I am now in, and that I am a stranger desolate of all comfort in this country: or at the least, you should have feared the vengeance of God, the supreme judge, (which knoweth the secrets of all hearts) in bearing this false witness with him, whom heaven and earth do know to be Dulippo and not Erostrato.

Another suppose.

Litio. If there be many such witnesses in this country, men may go about to prove what they will in controversies here. 19

Ferrarese. Well, sir, you may judge of me as it pleaseth you: and how the matter cometh to pass, I know not, but truly, ever since he came first hither, I have known him by the name of Erostrato, the son of Philogano, a Cathanese. Now whether he be so indeed, or whether he be Dulippo (as you allege) let that be proved by them that knew him before he came hither. But I protest before God that which I have said is neither a matter compact with him nor any other, but even as I have heard him called and reputed of all men. 30

Philogano. Out and alas, he whom I sent hither with my son to be his servant, and to give attendance on him, hath either cut his throat, or by some evil means made him away: and hath not only taken his garments, his books, his money, and that which he brought out of Sicilia with him, but usurpeth his name also, and turneth to his own commodity the bills of exchange that I have always allowed for my son's expenses. O miserable Philogano, O unhappy old man! O eternal God, is there

A shrewd suppose.

no judge, no officer, no higher powers whom I may complain unto for redress of these wrongs? 42

Ferrarese. Yes, sir, we have potestates, we have judges, and above all we have a most just prince. Doubt you not but you shall have justice, if your cause be just.

Philogano. Bring me then to the judges, to the potestates, or to whom you think best; for I will disclose a pack of the greatest knavery, a fardel of the foulest falsehood that ever was heard of. 50

Litio. Sir, he that will go to the law must be sure of four things—first, a right and a just cause; then a righteous advocate to plead; next, favour *coram Judice*; and above all, a good purse to procure it.

Ferrarese. I have not heard that the law hath any respect to favour: what you mean by it I cannot tell.

Philogano. Have you no regard to his words, he is but a fool.

Ferrarese. I pray you, sir, let him tell me what is favour. 60

Litio. Favour call I, to have a friend near about the judge, who may so solicit thy cause as, if it be right, speedy sentence may ensue without any delays: if it be not good, then to prolong it till at the last thine adversary, being weary, shall be glad to compound with thee.

Ferrarese. Of thus much (although I never heard thus much in this country before) doubt you not, Philogano, I will bring you to an advocate that shall speed you accordingly. 70

Philogano. Then shall I give myself as it were a prey to the lawyers, whose insatiable jaws I am not able to feed, although I had here all the goods and lands which I possess in mine own country; much less being a stranger in this misery. I know their cautels of old. At the first time I come they will so extol my cause as

48 potestates] see III. iii. 35. 49 fardel] bundle.
75 cautels] artifices.

though it were already won; but within a sevennight or ten days, if I do not continually feed them as the crow doth her brats twenty times in an hour, they will begin to wax cold, and to find cavils in my cause, saying that at the first I did not well instruct them, till at the last they will not only draw the stuffing out of my purse but the marrow out of my bones.

Ferrarese. Yea, sir, but this man that I tell you of is half a saint.

Litio. And the other half a devil, I hold a penny.

Philogano. Well said, Litio; indeed I have but small confidence in their smooth looks. 88

Ferrarese. Well, sir, I think this whom I mean is no such manner of man; but, if he were, there is such hatred and evil will between him and this gentleman (whether he be Erostrato or Dulippo, whatsoever he be) that I warrant you he will do whatsoever he can do for you, were it but to spite him.

Another suppose.

Philogano. Why, what hatred is betwixt them?

Ferrarese. They are both in love and suitors to one gentlewoman, the daughter of a wealthy man in this city.

Philogano. Why, is the villain become of such estimation that he dare presume to be a suitor to any gentlewoman of a good family? 101

Ferrarese. Yea, sir, out of all doubt.

Philogano. How call you his adversary?

Ferrarese. Cleander, one of the excellentest doctors in our city.

Philogano. For God's love, let us go to him.

Ferrarese. Go we, then. [*Exeunt.*

ACT V

SCENE I

Feigned Erostrato

Erostrato. What a mishap was this, that before I could meet with Erostrato, I have light even full in the lap of Philogano, where I was constrained to deny my name, to deny my master, and to feign that I knew him not, to contend with him, and to revile him in such sort that, hap what hap can, I can never hap well in favour with him again. Therefore, if I could come to speak with the right Erostrato, I will renounce unto him both habit and credit, and away as fast as I can trudge into some strange country, where I may never see Philogano again. Alas, he that of a little child hath brought me up unto this day, and nourished me as if I had been his own: and indeed (to confess the truth) I have no father to trust unto but him. [Erostrato *espieth* Pasiphilo *coming towards him.*] But look where Pasiphilo cometh, the fittest man in the world to go on my message to Erostrato.

Another suppose.

SCENE II

Feigned Erostrato. *Enter* Pasiphilo

Pasiphilo. Two good news have I heard to-day already—one that Erostrato prepared a great feast this night, the other, that he seeketh for me. And I, to ease him of his travail, lest he should run up and down seeking me, and because no man loveth better than I to have an errand where good cheer is, come in post-haste even home to his own house. And look where he is!

Erostrato. Pasiphilo, thou must do one thing for me if thou love me. 10

Pasiphilo. If I love you not, who loves you? Command me.

Erostrato. Go then a little there, to Damon's house, ask for Dulippo, and tell him——

Pasiphilo. Wot you what? I cannot speak with him, he is in prison.

Erostrato. In prison? How cometh that to pass? Where is he in prison?

Pasiphilo. In a vile dungeon there within his master's house. 20

Erostrato. Canst thou tell wherefore?

Pasiphilo. Be you content to know he is in prison, I have told you too much.

Erostrato. If ever you will do anything for me, tell me.

Pasiphilo. I pray you, desire me not; what were you the better if you knew?

Erostrato. More than thou thinkest, Pasiphilo, by God.

Pasiphilo. Well, and yet it stands me upon more than you think to keep it secret. 31

Erostrato. Why, Pasiphilo, is this the trust I have had in you? Are these the fair promises you have always made me?

Pasiphilo. By the Mass, I would I had fasted this night with master doctor rather than have come hither.

Erostrato. Well, Pasiphilo, either tell me or, at few words, never think to be welcome to this house from henceforth. 40

Pasiphilo. Nay, yet I had rather lose all the gentlemen in this town. But if I tell you anything that displease you, blame nobody but yourself now.

Erostrato. There is nothing can grieve me more than Dulippo's mishap, no, not mine own: and therefore I am sure thou canst tell me no worse tidings.

Another plain and homely suppose.

Pasiphilo. Well, since you would needs have it, I will tell you—he was taken abed with your beloved Polynesta.

Erostrato. Alas, and doth Damon know it?

Pasiphilo. An old trot in the house disclosed it to him, whereupon he took both Dulippo and the nurse, which hath been the broker of all this bargain, and clapped them both in a cage, where I think they shall have sour sops to their sweetmeats.

Erostrato. Pasiphilo, go thy ways into the kitchen, command the cook to boil and roast what liketh thee best; I make thee supervisor of this supper. 58

Pasiphilo. By the Mass, if you should have studied this sevennight, you could not have appointed me an office to please me better. You shall see what dishes I will devise.

[Pasiphilo *goeth in*, Erostrato *tarrieth*.

SCENE III

Feigned Erostrato, *alone*

Erostrato. I was glad to rid him out of the way, lest he should see me burst of these swelling tears, which hitherto with great pain I have prisoned in my breast, and lest he should hear the echo of my doubled sighs, which bounce from the bottom of my heavy heart. O cursed I, O cruel fortune, that so many dispersed griefs as were sufficient to subvert a legion of lovers hast suddenly assembled within my careful carcase to fret this fearful heart in sunder with desperation. Thou that hast kept my master all his youth within the realm of Sicilia, reserving the wind and waves in a temperate calm (as it were at his command) now to convey his aged limbs hither, neither sooner nor later, but even in the worst time that may be. If at any time before thou hadst conducted him, this enterprise had been cut off without care in the beginning: and if never so little longer thou hadst lingered his journey, this happy day might then have fully finished our

11 reserving] maintaining. 17 lingered] deferred.

drifts and devices. But, alas, thou hast brought him even in the very worst time, to plunge us all in the pit of perdition. Neither art thou content to entangle me alone in thy ruinous ropes, but thou must also catch the right Erostrato in thy crooked claws, to reward us both with open shame and rebuke. Two years hast thou kept secret our subtle Supposes, even this day to decipher them with a sorrowful success. What shall I do? Alas, what shift shall I make? It is too late now to imagine any further deceit, for every minute seemeth an hour till I find some succour for the miserable captive Erostrato. Well, since there is no other remedy, I will go to my master Philogano, and to him will I tell the whole truth of the matter, that at the least he may provide in time, before his son feel the smart of some sharp revenge and punishment. This is the best, and thus will I do. Yet I know that, for mine own part, I shall do bitter penance for my faults forpassed: but such is the goodwill and duty that I bear to Erostrato as, even with the loss of my life, I must not stick to adventure anything which may turn to his commodity. But what shall I do? Shall I go seek my master about the town, or shall I tarry his return hither? If I meet him in the streets, he will cry out upon me, neither will he hearken to anything that I shall say, till he have gathered all the people wondering about me, as it were at an owl. Therefore I were better to abide here, and yet, if he tarry long, I will go seek him rather than prolong the time to Erostrato's peril. [Pasiphilo *returneth to* Erostrato.

SCENE IV

Feigned Erostrato *and* Pasiphilo

Pasiphilo. Yea, dress them, but lay them not to the fire till they will be ready to sit down. This gear goeth

26 success] result.

in order, but, if I had not gone in, there had fallen a foul fault.

Erostrato. And what fault, I pray thee?

Pasiphilo. Marry! Dalio would have laid the shoulder of mutton and the capon both to the fire at once like a fool; he did not consider that the one would have more roasting than the other. 9

Erostrato. Alas, I would this were the greatest fault!

Pasiphilo. Why, and either the one should have been burned before the other had been roasted, or else he must have drawn them off the spit, and they would have been served to the board either cold or raw.

Erostrato. Thou hast reason, Pasiphilo.

Pasiphilo. Now, sir, if it please you, I will go into the town and buy oranges, olives, and capers, for without such sauce the supper were more than half lost.

Erostrato. There are within already, doubt you not; there shall lack nothing that is necessary. 20

[Erostrato *exit into his house.*

Pasiphilo. Since I told him these news of Dulippo he is clean beside himself: he hath so many hammers in his head that his brains are ready to burst. And let them break, so I may sup with him to-night, what care I? [*Sees* Cleander *about to enter.*] But is not this *Dominus noster Cleandrus* that cometh before? Well said, by my troth, we will teach master Doctor to wear a cornered cap of a new fashion. By God, Polynesta shall be his; he shall have her out of doubt, for I have told Erostrato such news of her that he will none of her. 31

A knavish suppose.

SCENE V

Pasiphilo. Cleander *and* Philogano, *with* Litio, *come in, talking of the matter in controversy*

Cleander. Yea, but how will ye prove that he is not Erostrato, having such presumptions to the contrary?

Or how shall it be thought that you are Philogano, when another taketh upon him this same name, and for proof bringeth him for a witness which hath been ever reputed here for Erostrato?

Philogano. I will tell you, sir. Let me be kept here fast in prison, and at my charges let there be some man sent into Sicilia that may bring hither with him two or three of the honestest men in Cathanea, and by them let it be proved if I or this other be Philogano, and whether he be Erostrato or Dulippo my servant: and if you find me contrary, let me suffer death for it.

Pasiphilo. I will go salute master Doctor.

Cleander. It will ask great labour and great expenses to prove it this way, but it is the best remedy that I can see.

Pasiphilo. God save you, sir.

Cleander. And reward you as you have deserved.

Pasiphilo. Then shall he give me your favour continually. 21

Cleander. He shall give you a halter, knave and villain that thou art.

Pasiphilo. I know I am a knave, but no villain. I am your servant.

Cleander. I neither take thee for my servant nor for my friend.

Pasiphilo. Why, wherein have I offended you, sir?

Cleander. Hence to the gallows, knave.

Pasiphilo. What, soft and fair, sir, I pray you, *I prae, sequar*, you are mine elder. 31

Cleander. I will be even with you, be you sure, honest man.

Pasiphilo. Why, sir? I never offended you.

Cleander. Well, I will teach you: out of my sight, knave!

13 contrary] in the wrong. 24 a knave, but no villain] knave *is used in its earlier sense of* menial. 31 *I prae, sequar*] you go first, I will follow; *from* Terence, *Andria*, I. i. 171.

Pasiphilo. What? I am no dog, I would you wist.

Cleander. Pratest thou yet, villain? I will make thee—

Pasiphilo. What will you make me? I see well the more a man doth suffer you, the worse you are. 40

Cleander. Ah, villain, if it were not for this gentleman, I would tell you what I——

Pasiphilo. Villain! Nay, I am as honest a man as you.

Cleander. Thou liest in thy throat, knave.

Philogano. O sir, stay your wisdom.

Pasiphilo. What, will you fight? Marry, come on!

Cleander. Well, knave, I will meet with you another time. Go your way!

Pasiphilo. Even when you list, sir, I will be your man. 51

Cleander. And if I be not even with thee, call me cut.

Pasiphilo. Nay, by the Mass, all is one, I care not, for I have nothing: if I had either lands or goods, peradventure you would pull me into the law. [*Exit.*

Philogano. Sir, I perceive your patience is moved.

Cleander. This villain!—But let him go, I will see him punished as he hath deserved. Now to the matter, how said you? 59

Philogano. This fellow hath disquieted you, sir, peradventure you would be loth to be troubled any further.

Lawyers are never weary to get money.

Cleander. Not a whit, say on, and let him go with a vengeance!

Philogano. I say, let them send at my charge to Cathanea.

Cleander. Yea, I remember that well, and it is the surest way as this case requireth: but tell me, how is he your servant, and how come you by him? Inform me fully in the matter. 70

Philogano. I will tell you, sir. When the Turks won Otranto——

48 meet with you] be even with you. 52 call me cut] call me 'horse' (*a term of contempt*).

Cleander. Oh, you put me in remembrance of my mishaps.

Philogano. How, sir?

Cleander. For I was driven among the rest out of the town (it is my native country) and there I lost more than ever I shall recover again while I live.

Philogano. Alas, a pitiful case, by St. Anne!

Cleander. Well, proceed. 80

Philogano. At that time (as I said) there were certain of our country that scoured those coasts upon the seas with a good bark, well appointed for the purpose, and had espial of a Turkey vessel that came laden from thence with great abundance of riches.

Cleander. And peradventure most of mine.

Philogano. So they boarded them, and in the end overcame them, and brought the goods to Palermo, from whence they came; and amongst other things that they had was this villain my servant, a boy at that time, I think not past five years old. 92

A gentle suppose.

Cleander. Alas, I lost one of that same age there.

Philogano. And I being there, and liking the child's favour well, proffered them four and twenty ducats for him, and had him.

Cleander. What, was the child a Turk? Or had the Turks brought him from Otranto?

Philogano. They said he was a child of Otranto, but what is that to the matter? Once twenty-four ducats he cost me, that I wot well. 101

Cleander. Alas, I speak it not for that, sir; I would it were he whom I mean.

Philogano. Why, whom mean you, sir?

Litio. Beware, sir, be not too lavish.

Cleander. Was his name Dulippo then? Or had he not another name?

A crafty suppose.

Litio. Beware what you say, sir.

95 favour] appearance. 100 Once] Enough that.
105 lavish] effusive.

Philogano. What the devil hast thou to do? Dulippo? No, sir, his name was Carino. 110

Litio. Yea, well said, tell all and more too, do.

Cleander. O Lord, if it be as I think, how happy were I! And why did you change his name, then?

Philogano. We called him Dulippo, because when he cried as children do sometimes, he would always cry on that name, Dulippo.

Cleander. Well, then I see well it is my own only child whom I lost when I lost my country: he was named Carino after his grandfather, and this Dulippo whom he always remembered in his lamenting was his foster-father that nourished him and brought him up.

Litio. Sir, have I not told you enough of the falsehood of Ferrara? This gentleman will not only pick your purse, but beguile you of your servant also, and make you believe he is his son.

Cleander. Well, good fellow, I have not used to lie.

Litio. Sir, no, but everything hath a beginning.

Cleander. Fie, Philogano, have you not the least suspect that may be of me. 129

Litio. No, marry, but it were good he had the most suspect that may be.

Cleander. Well, hold thou thy peace a little, good fellow. I pray you tell me, Philogano, had the child any remembrance of his father's name, his mother's name, or the name of his family?

Philogano. He did remember them, and could name his mother also, but sure I have forgotten the name.

Litio. I remember it well enough.

Philogano. Tell it, then.

Litio. Nay, that I will not; marry, you have told him too much already. 141

Philogano. Tell it, I say, if thou can.

Litio. Can? Yes, by the Mass, I can well enough. But I will have my tongue pulled out rather than tell it, unless he tell it first. Do you not perceive, sir, what he goeth about?

Cleander. Well, I will tell you, then. My name you know already; my wife his mother's name was Sophronia; the house that I came of they call Spiagia.

Litio. I never heard him speak of Spiagia but indeed I have heard him say his mother's name was Sophronia. But what of that? A great matter, I promise you! It is like enough that you two have compact together to deceive my master.

Cleander. What needeth me more evident tokens? This is my son out of doubt whom I lost eighteen years since, and a thousand thousand times have I lamented for him: he should have also a mole on his left shoulder. 159

Litio. He hath a mole there indeed, and an hole in another place too; I would your nose were in it.

Cleander. Fair words, fellow Litio. Oh, I pray you, let us go talk with him. O fortune, how much am I bound to thee if I find my son!

Philogano. Yea, how little am I beholden to fortune, that know not where my son is become; and you, whom I chose to be mine advocate, will now (by the means of this Dulippo) become mine adversary?

Cleander. Sir, let us first go find mine; and, I warrant you, yours will be found also ere it be long.

A right suppose.

Philogano. God grant! Go we, then. 171

Cleander. Since the door is open, I will never knock nor call, but we will be bold to go in.

Litio. Sir, take you heed, lest he lead you to some mischief.

Philogano. Alas, Litio, if my son be lost, what care I what become of me?

Litio. Well, I have told you my mind, sir, do you as you please. 179

[*Exeunt into* Erostrato's *house*. Damon *and* Psiteria *come in*.

SCENE VI

Damon *and* Psiteria

Damon. Come hither, you old callet, you tattling huswife, that the devil cut out your tongue! Tell me, how could Pasiphilo know of this gear but by you?

Psiteria. Sir, he never knew it of me, he was the first that told me of it.

Damon. Thou liest, old drab, but I would advise you tell me the truth, or I will make those old bones rattle in your skin.

Psiteria. Sir, if you find me contrary, kill me.

Damon. Why, where should he talk with thee? 10

Psiteria. He talked with me of it here in the street.

Damon. What did you here?

Psiteria. I was going to the weaver's for a web of cloth you have there.

Damon. And what cause could Pasiphilo have to talk of it, unless thou began the matter first?

Psiteria. Nay, he began with me, sir, reviling me because I had told you of it: I asked him how he knew of it, and he said he was in the stable when you examined me erewhile. 20

Damon. Alas, alas, what shall I do then? In at doors, old whore! I will pluck that tongue of thine out by the roots one day. [*Exit* Psiteria.

Alas, it grieveth me more that Pasiphilo knoweth it than all the rest. He that will have a thing kept secret, let him tell it to Pasiphilo: the people shall know it, and as many as have ears and no more. By this time he hath told it in a hundred places. Cleander was the first, Erostrato the second, and so from one to another throughout the city. Alas, what dower, what marriage shall I now prepare for my daughter? O poor, dolorous Damon, more miserable than misery itself!

1 callet] drab.

The first suppose brought to conclusion.

Would God it were true that Polynesta told me erewhile that he who hath deflowered her, is of no servile estate (as hitherto he hath been supposed in my service) but that he is a gentleman born of a good parentage in Sicilia. Alas, small riches should content me, if he be but of an honest family: but I fear that he hath devised these toys to allure my daughter's love. Well, I will go examine her again; my mind giveth me that I shall perceive by her tale whether it be true or not. But is not this Pasiphilo that cometh out of my neighbour's house? What the devil aileth him to leap and laugh so like a fool in the highway? 45

[Pasiphilo *cometh out of the town laughing.*

SCENE VII

Pasiphilo *and* Damon

Pasiphilo. O God, that I might find Damon at home!

Damon. What the devil would he with me?

Pasiphilo. That I may be the first that shall bring him these news.

Damon. What will he tell me, in the name of God?

Pasiphilo. O Lord, how happy am I! Look where he is.

Damon. What news, Pasiphilo, that thou art so merry?

Pasiphilo. Sir, I am merry to make you glad: I bring you joyful news. 11

Damon. And that I have need of, Pasiphilo.

Pasiphilo. I know, sir, that you are a sorrowful man for this mishap that hath chanced in your house; peradventure you thought I had not known of it. But let it pass, pluck up your spirits, and rejoice; for he that hath done you this injury is so well born, and hath so

39 honest] honourable. 41 giveth] tells.

rich parents, that you may be glad to make him your son-in-law.

Damon. How knowest thou? 20

Pasiphilo. His father Philogano, one of the worthiest men in all Cathanea, is now come to the city and is here in your neighbour's house.

Damon. What, in Erostrato's house?

Pasiphilo. Nay, in Dulippo's house, for where you have always supposed this gentleman to be Erostrato, it is not so, but your servant whom you have imprisoned, hitherto supposed to be Dulippo, he is indeed Erostrato, and that other is Dulippo. And thus they have always, even since their first arrival in this city, exchanged names, to the end that Erostrato the master, under the name of Dulippo a servant, might be entertained in your house and so win the love of your daughter.

Damon. Well, then I perceive it is even as Polynesta told me.

Pasiphilo. Why, did she tell you so?

Damon. Yea, but I thought it but a tale.

Pasiphilo. Well, it is a true tale: and here they will be with you by and by, both Philogano, this worthy man, and master doctor Cleander. 41

Damon. Cleander? What to do?

Pasiphilo. Cleander? Why thereby lies another tale, the most fortunate adventure that ever you heard. Wot you what? This other Dulippo, whom all this while we supposed to be Erostrato, is found to be the son of Cleander, whom he lost at the loss of Otranto and was after sold in Sicilia to this Philogano. The strangest case that ever you heard: a man might make a comedy of it. They will come even straight, and tell you the whole circumstance of it themselves. 51

Damon. Nay, I will first go hear the story of this Dulippo, be it Dulippo or Erostrato that I have here within, before I speak with Philogano.

Pasiphilo. So shall you do well, sir. I will go, tell

them that they may stay awhile. But look where they come!

[Damon *goeth in*; Siennese, Cleander, *and* Philogano *come upon the stage*.

SCENE VIII

Pasiphilo, Siennese, Cleander, Philogano, *and feigned* Erostrato

Siennese. Sir, you shall not need to excuse the matter any further; since I have received no greater injury than by words, let them pass like wind, I take them well in worth, and am rather well pleased than offended; for it shall both be a good warning to me another time how to trust every man at the first sight; yea, and I shall have good game hereafter to tell this pleasant story another day in mine own country. 8

Cleander. Gentleman, you have reason, and be you sure that as many as hear it will take great pleasure in it. And you, Philogano, may think that God in heaven above hath ordained your coming hither at this present, to the end I might recover my lost son whom by no other means I could ever have found out.

Philogano. Surely, sir, I think no less, for I think that not so much as a leaf falleth from the tree without the ordinance of God. But let us go seek Damon, for methinketh every day a year, every hour a day, and every minute too much till I see my Erostrato. 19

Cleander. I cannot blame you; go we, then. Carino, take you that gentleman home in the meantime, the fewer the better to be present at such affairs.

[Pasiphilo *stayeth their going in*.

SCENE IX

Pasiphilo *and* Cleander *talk apart*

Pasiphilo. Master doctor, will you not show me this favour, to tell me the cause of your displeasure?

3–4 well in worth] in good part. 20 Carino] *feigned* Erostrato's real name. *See* v. v. 110.

Cleander. Gentle Pasiphilo, I must needs confess I have done thee wrong and that I believed tales of thee, which indeed I find now contrary.

Pasiphilo. I am glad then that it proceeded rather of ignorance than of malice.

Cleander. Yea, believe me, Pasiphilo.

Pasiphilo. O sir, but yet you should not have given me such foul words. 10

Cleander. Well, content thyself, Pasiphilo, I am thy friend as I have always been: for proof whereof, come sup with me to-night, and from day to day this seven-night be thou my guest. But behold, here cometh Damon out of his house!

[*Here they come all together.*

SCENE X

Cleander, Philogano, Pasiphilo, *and* Damon *with* Erostrato *and* Polynesta

Cleander (*to* Damon). We are come unto you, sir, to turn your sorrow into joy and gladness—the sorrow, we mean, that of force you have sustained since this mishap of late fallen in your house. But be you of good comfort, sir, and assure yourself that this young man, which youthfully and not maliciously hath committed this amorous offence, is very well able (with consent of this worthy man, his father) to make you sufficient amends; being born in Cathanea of Sicilia, of a noble house, no way inferior unto you, and of wealth (by the report of such as know it) far exceeding that of yours. 12

Philogano. And I here, in proper person, do present unto you, sir, not only my assured friendship and brotherhood, but do earnestly desire you to accept my poor child (though unworthy) as your son-in-law: and for recompense of the injury he hath done you, I

3 of force] necessarily.

proffer my whole lands in dower to your daughter, yea, and more would, if more I might. 19

Cleander. And I, sir, who have hitherto so earnestly desired your daughter in marriage, do now willingly yield up and quit claim to this young man, who both for his years and for the love he beareth her is most meetest to be her husband. For where I was desirous of a wife by whom I might have issue, to leave that little which God hath sent me, now have I little need, that (thanks be to God) have found my dearly beloved son whom I lost of a child at the siege of Otranto. 28

Damon. Worthy gentleman, your friendship, your alliance and the nobility of your birth are such as I have much more cause to desire them of you than you to request of me that which is already granted. Therefore I gladly and willingly receive the same, and think myself most happy now of all my life past, that I have got so toward a son-in-law to myself, and so worthy a father-in-law to my daughter: yea, and much the greater is my contentation, since this worthy gentleman, master Cleander, doth hold himself satisfied. [*bringing* Erostrato *forward*]. And now behold your son!

Erostrato. O father! 40

Pasiphilo. Behold the natural love of the child to the father! For inward joy he cannot pronounce one word; instead whereof he sendeth sobs and tears to tell the effect of his inward intention. But why do you abide here abroad? Will it please you to go into the house, sir?

Damon. Pasiphilo hath said well: will it please you to go in, sir? [*Enter* Nevola.

Nevola. Here I have brought you, sir, both fetters and bolts. 50

Damon. Away with them now!

Nevola. Yea, but what shall I do with them?

28 of a child] when he was a child. 45 abroad] out of doors.

Damon. Marry, I will tell thee, Nevola. To make a right end of our supposes, lay one of those bolts in the fire, and make thee a suppository as long as mine arm, God save the sample. Nobles and gentlemen, if you suppose that our Supposes have given you sufficient cause of delight, show some token, whereby we may suppose you are content.

Applause

FINIS

55 a suppository] a medical laxative.

NOTE I

The Four PP., ll. 29–50.

THE principal saints and shrines mentioned, so far as they can be identified, are as follows:

29 the Rhodes] the island of Rhodes, the home of the Knights Hospitallers, when driven out of Jerusalem. 30 Amias] ? Emmaus. 31 Saint Trunion] a saint held in devotion near Rouen. 32 Botolph] a Cornish saint, buried at Boston in Lincolnshire. Anne of Buxton] patron saint of a holy well at Buxton. 33 Armony] Armenia. 35 Waltham] site of a holy cross. Walsingham] in Norfolk, where there was a famous image of the Virgin. 37 Saint Cornelius] there was a fraternity in his honour at Westminster. James of Gales] Saint James of Compostella in Galicia. 38 Saint Winifred's Well] near Holywell, in Flintshire. 40 Saint Patrick's Purgatory] situated in a lake in South Donegal. 42 Redburne] near St. Albans, where the relics of St. Amphiball were kept. 41 The Blood of Hales] The miraculous blood shown at the abbey of Hales in Gloucestershire. 45 John Shorn] mentioned by Latimer, but otherwise unknown. 46 Catwade] in Suffolk, but the shrine is not known. King Henry] Henry VI. 49 Roke] Roche, a French saint, born in Montpellier, whose shrine was at Angleria in Lombardy. 50 Our Lady . . . oak] a wayside shrine to the Virgin over against an oak.

NOTE II

Ralph Roister Doister, Act III, Scene iii, ll. 53–96.

THIS mock requiem, introducing a number of Latin phrases, is a parody of the Ritual for the Dead in the services of the Roman Catholic Church. *Placebo domino* (Psalm cxvi. 9) begins the office for the dead at Vespers. *Dilexi quoniam* are the first words of the same Psalm. *Ne quando rapiat* (Psalm vii. 2) is from the Burial Service at Matins. *Dirige, Domine* begins an antiphon in the *Officium Defunctorum*. *Neque lux . . . neque* clink = without candle, cross, mourners, or bell.

A porta inferi, from the gate of hell, is from another antiphon. *Requiem aeternam* is a refrain in the Office for the Dead. *Audivi vocem de cælo* is from an antiphon in the *Officium Defunctorum*. *Qui Lazarum resuscitasti* is the beginning of another antiphon. *In Paradisum deducant te Angeli* is from the antiphon when the body was carried to the grave.

PRINTED IN GREAT BRITAIN
AT THE UNIVERSITY PRESS, OXFORD
BY VIVIAN RIDLER
PRINTER TO THE UNIVERSITY